Theory and Cases
in School-Based Consultation

Theory and Cases
in School-Based Consultation

A Resource for School Psychologists, School Counselors,
Special Educators, and Other Mental Health Professionals

LAURA M. CROTHERS, TAMMY L. HUGHES, KAREN A. MORINE

FOREWORD BY WILLIAM P. ERCHUL

Routledge
Taylor & Francis Group
New York   London

Routledge
Taylor & Francis Group
270 Madison Avenue
New York, NY 10016

Routledge
Taylor & Francis Group
2 Park Square
Milton Park, Abingdon
Oxon OX14 4RN

© 2008 by Taylor & Francis Group, LLC
Routledge is an imprint of Taylor & Francis Group, an Informa business

Printed in the United States of America on acid-free paper
10 9 8 7 6 5 4 3 2 1

International Standard Book Number-13: 978-0-415-96337-4 (Softcover)

Library of Congress Cataloging-in-Publication Data

Crothers, Laura.
    Theory and cases in school-based consultation : a resource for school psychologists, school counselors, special educators, and other mental health professionals / Laura Crothers, Tammy Hughes, Karen Morine.
        p. cm.
    Includes bibliographical references and index.
    ISBN 978-0-415-96337-4 (softcover)
    1. Educational counseling--Study and teaching. 2. School children--Mental health services. 3. School psychology. I. Hughes, Tammy L., 1977- II. Morine, Karen. III. Title.

LB1027.5.C695 2008
371.4071--dc22   2007045926

Visit the Taylor & Francis Web site at
http://www.taylorandfrancis.com

and the Routledge Web site at
http://www.routledge.com

This book is dedicated to those who inspire us and countless other dedicated educational professionals who positively impact the lives of children and their families.

John Lipinski III

Linda H. Metz

My girls—"M" & "G" —who have provided me with all of the knowledge and love that I have ever needed.

Mason Hughes Miller

Jeffrey A. Miller

My family and family of friends who nurture, support, and inspire me every day.

CONTENTS

FOREWORD

Human services consultation reflects a triadic problem-solving process in which a consultee (such as a teacher) provides an intervention to a client (such as a student) via assistance from a consultant, a professional with specialized expertise. Since the late 1940s, when psychiatrist Gerald Caplan launched the modern practice of mental health consultation, the consultant's major role has been to help consultees to help clients. Standard advantages attributed to consultation, compared to direct clinical services, include making more efficient use of a specialist's unique skills, enhancing consultees' skills, detecting clients' problems sooner, and, ideally, preventing these problems before they occur. Consultation occurring in K–12 schools is a more recent phenomenon, with a distinct literature traceable to the 1960s.

If you selected this book and were interested enough to open it to this page, I suspect you knew all of this already.

In casting about how to best introduce *Theory and Cases in School-Based Consultation: A Resource for School Psychologists, School Counselors, Special Educators, and Other Mental Health Professionals*, a couple of basic questions came to mind. What is known about how to consult effectively in schools? Despite its overall importance and centrality to school-based service delivery, consultation may be one of the least understood modes of contemporary practice. Whereas specialists in psychology, counseling, and special education can generally rely on an established assortment of tools to assist with matters of assessment, treatment, staff development, and so forth, school consultation is cloaked largely in mystery. I say this despite believing that consultation's extant knowledge base is informative and reasonably well developed; my main point is that consultation remains a complicated enterprise.

School consultation has been depicted as both art and science, with some elusive mixture of consultant technical expertise and interpersonal finesse seen as optimal. For instance, it is easy to fall prey to the misconception that a consultant is first and foremost an "expert," and consequently direct those who train consultants to emphasize the importance of technical knowledge over basic communication skills. A school consultant's understanding of curriculum design, progress monitoring methods, evidence-based practices, child development, and so on, certainly is important. However, mastery of these topics is insufficient to explain how and why, for example, within consultation a teacher may endorse an intervention, faithfully implement it, and successfully change a student's behavior—or never implement a planned intervention at all. A complex chain of events lies at the heart of school consultation and its inner workings are just beginning to be clearly understood. Among other things, it would seem that a consultant's use of strategic communication (including persuasion) is critical to the success of this process.

How does one learn how to consult effectively in schools? Providing high-quality educational and psychological services in today's schools via consultation is clearly challenging, and common failings of books purporting to teach one how to consult include a lack of detailed case studies and clear emphasis on skill development. In *Theory and Cases in School-Based Consultation*, Laura Crothers, Tammy Hughes, and Karen Morine directly confront these failings. In their presentation of six recognized models of consultation, the authors include numerous case studies with applied exercises to reinforce basic content and to aid in the acquisition of consulting skills. The inclusion of case study material is significant because it is a clear way to portray the richness of the blend of technical expertise and interpersonal finesse a consultant needs to operate effectively in schools. In addition, chapter 1 offers an incisive summary of the literature about how school consultation may best be taught, which directly benefits the instructors of consultation courses.

One of Gerald Caplan's enduring lessons is that because consultation involves a unique skill set, individuals must be specifically trained to be consultants. Along these lines, Laura Crothers and her coauthors are to be commended for sorting through the maze of alternatives present in the professional literature and providing a clear structure for beginning school consultants to follow. Consumers of *Theory and Cases in*

School-Based Consultation will find it to be highly readable, scholarly, and useful in practice.

William P. Erchul
Professor of Psychology
North Carolina State University

ACKNOWLEDGMENTS

Laura Crothers would like to extend her thanks to Conrad B. Metz and Dr. Ara J. Schmitt, who tirelessly reviewed chapters and made numerous valuable suggestions throughout the book. Laura Crothers and Tammy Hughes would like to acknowledge the assistance of Ph.D. candidates, Sarah O'Neill and Cindy L. Altman, for their excellent work in contributing to this book. Additionally, they would like to thank the school-based mental health personnel and teachers who have shared their experiences and concerns for the purpose of helping children.

Karen Morine would like to thank her professors at Duquesne University, who provide an academically challenging and motivating atmosphere while offering support, guidance, and encouragement. She would like to thank her fellow authors, Laura Crothers and Tammy Hughes, in particular, for serving as personal and professional mentors.

OVERVIEW AND OUTLINE

Consultation in schools, a service delivery model in which a clinician, serving as a consultant, uses problem-solving strategies (in order to alter an existing set of circumstances to become a desired set of circumstances) to address the needs of a consultee and a client, has become a necessary competency for school psychologists, school counselors, social workers, special educators, and other school-based educational and mental health professionals (Kratochwill & Bergan, 1990). An exciting innovation in the field of education, consultation is a time- and cost-efficient way to provide service to a large number of clients (e.g., children, families). In school systems, instead of providing direct service to all children and their families through counseling or intervention, consultants work with consultees, such as teachers and other educators, who then work with clients (children and their families) guided by consultative treatment plans. Consultants and consultees work collaboratively to share their knowledge bases to help solve academic, behavioral, and social/ emotional problems in children. Thus, consultation is an indirect vehicle through which school-based educational and mental health professionals can pool resources to positively impact children's development and functioning in several domains.

The standards-based education movement has been a focus of educational reform since the 1990s (Flinders, 2005). Likewise, the issue of providing services through consultation has become increasingly relevant as demands for educational accountability have surfaced. As the United States moved into the 21st century, concerns were expressed by the nation's citizens, educators, business and industry representatives, and political leaders regarding children's academic achievement, and whether they were being equipped by the public school system with the skills necessary to succeed in employment and/or postsecondary education settings. Thus, the *No Child Left Behind Act* (P.L.107–110) was enacted in 2001 to raise educational standards to ensure that all children, regardless of race, ethnicity, income, or disability status are able to read and calculate at grade level or above. P.L. 107–110 specifies that overall student achievement is the most important factor in determining a school district's effectiveness and that educational institutions must demonstrate adequate yearly progress in student learning.

In a time in which schools are expected to provide evidence of standards-based accountability, educational specialists and mental health professionals, acting as consultants, can be pivotal team members in ensuring that students are receiving evidence-based instruction, teachers are knowledgeable about students' developmental and instructional levels, and children's behavioral and emotional needs are addressed and do not impede the learning of themselves and other youngsters. Consultants can also be invaluable in advocating for objective measures of student improvement in behavior, emotional management, and academic functioning. Although important, teachers' subjective evaluations of student improvement are not wholly sufficient to document behavior change.

In following the consultative process, educational and mental health support personnel use persuasion, facilitated through the bond of relationships (e.g., referent power), to work collaboratively to meet the needs of children and their families. In doing so, consultants can encourage the use of empirically sound practices to help improve children's academic and behavioral functioning. For example, a pressing concern in education today is the failure to implement evidence-based practices (EBPs) in schools. One reason posited as to why EBPs are not sufficiently used in schools is a research-to-practice gap, in which research-driven, empirically based interventions have limited transportability to the school setting. Consultation can increase the use of EBPs by facilitating the transmission of information from consultants to other school-based professionals, as well as reducing barriers to EBP implementation, such as intervention complexity, because consultants can provide training, guidance, and supervision to consultees to improve intervention integrity (Auster, Feeney-Kettler, & Kratochwill, 2006).

In teaching school-based mental health and educational professionals to use the consultative process in school systems, college and university professors must teach the various theories that underpin consultation, but also must present and model the skills necessary for effective consultation. Currently there is a paucity of modeling examples and exercises in which students who are training to become school-based mental health and educational professionals can practice their consultative skills. Thus, the purpose of this book is to familiarize practitioners, students, and trainers with various models of consultation, each presented with varying levels of empirical evidence, and more importantly, to provide information to enable such individuals to select the most appropriate consultative theory and model based upon the referral issue, age, gender, and characteristics of students, attributes of teachers, and the qualities of the school, educational, and community systems.

This text provides an applied perspective on a wide variety of school-based consultative approaches, including an overview of mental health consultation, behavioral consultation, social cognitive theory consultation, Adlerian consultation, ecological/organizational consultation, and instructional consultation. Since consultation can, in the short term, improve the academic, behavioral, and social functioning of specific students, and in the long term, increase consultees' competence to positively impact upon a greater number of children and adolescents, thereby assisting districts in meeting multiple goals, including the demonstration of improvement in students' annual progress, it is a practice that school-based mental health and educational support personnel should support. Finally, although there is evidence that administrators feel comfortable with the traditional service delivery of school psychologists and other educational and mental health support personnel (Bramlett & Murphy, 1998), consultation is a time- and cost-effective means of providing service to large numbers of students, a compelling argument that is difficult to refute.

OUTLINE OF THE BOOK

Theory and Cases in School-Based Consultation: A Resource for School Psychologists, School Counselors, Special Educators, and Other Mental Health Professionals was developed as a companion or case study book to be used in teaching consultation in educational systems to students in college and university settings. The design of the book includes an exploration of the theory and practice of six consultative theories as well as case studies and applied exercises that can be used to role-play newly learned consultative skills. Because the book was not designed as an accompaniment to a specific text, this work may be used alongside any current text in a consultative course or as a professional resource for those practitioners wishing to practice or enhance their skills in consultation.

Each chapter of this text has been structured to provide a thorough review of a specific consultative model, beginning with its theoretical underpinnings, followed by the underlying assumptions of each consultative approach, and continuing with the knowledge that must be acquired in order to successfully use that particular consultative theory. The progression of topics varies somewhat from chapter to chapter, but typically includes the communication patterns and processes required in each consultative model, the stages of consultation, information regarding the roles and responsibilities of the consultant and consultee, and a summary of the research exploring the effectiveness of each consultative theory. After each consultative approach has been presented, 12 case studies are provided specifically relating to each consultative theory. The case studies include problems or issues that involve children, families, educators, and school systems, and each is followed by a series of discussion questions. In the following paragraphs, each chapter is briefly summarized.

In the first chapter, an overview of school-based consultation is provided. A brief discussion of consultation stages and processes, procedures for establishing a consultative relationship, roles, skills, and characteristics of the consultant, issues for consideration when working with parents, multicultural factors and consultative processes, and ethical and legal considerations follow. Additionally, the topic of teaching consultation in higher education settings is explored, along with recommendations that may be used in teaching from this text.

Mental health consultation (MHC) is reviewed in chapter 2, and includes a definition of MHC, followed by information supporting the importance of increasing knowledge of how interpersonal psychodynamics and environmental factors affect children, teachers, and systems in schools. The underlying assumptions of MHC are reviewed, along with influences on communication patterns and processes of MHC. The stages of MHC, including relationship building, conducting assessment procedures, selecting interventions, and the follow-up evaluation of such interventions are all considered from both psychodynamic and environmental vantage points. Information regarding the roles and responsibilities of the consultant and consultee in MHC, and the specifics of school-based practice are reviewed. Finally, studies exploring the effectiveness of and obstacles to the implementation of MHC are presented, and examples are offered of child-based/level problems, family-based/level problems, educator-based/level problems, and systems-based/level problems, which can be viewed through the lens of mental health consultative practices. At the end of each case study, a list of discussion questions is offered.

Chapter 3 includes a discussion of behavioral consultation (BC), including conjoint behavioral consultation (CBC). Information is provided regarding the importance of verbal communication in the BC process. The general stages of consultation are then reviewed, including formal entry, establishing an effective relationship, assessment, problem definition and goal-setting, intervention or strategy selection, intervention implementation, intervention evaluation, and termination. Additionally, BC processes are summarized, along with consultant roles and consultee characteristics, a summary of the effectiveness of BC, and examples of behavioral consultative child-based/level problems, family-based/level problems, educator-based/level problems, and systems-based/level problems, and a list of discussion questions are provided.

In chapter 4, the social cognitive theory model of consultation (SCTC) is reviewed. Information is provided regarding the assumptions of social cognitive theory (SCT) and the role of motivation in the consultation process. The SCTC process is then described, including its characteristics and the nature of the consultative relationship, the assessment process, the statement of the problem and identification of goals, the selection and implementation of interventions, and the monitoring and evaluation of interventions. Additionally, the role of the consultant in SCTC is discussed, with the chapter then providing a summary of the effectiveness of SCTC. To conclude, this chapter offers related examples of child-based/level problems, family-based/level problems, educator-based/level problems, and systems-based/level problems, along with a list of discussion questions.

Chapter 5 focuses on Adlerian consultation (AC), including a definition of AC, followed by information underscoring the importance of the social environment in this consultative approach. According to Adler, inadequate environments characterized by hostility, rejection and/or neglect lead children to choose attitudes and behaviors reflective of maladjustment and psychological disturbances. The underlying assumptions of AC are subsequently presented. The stages of AC, including initiation of the relationship, assessing the problem, setting goals and interventions, and analyzing the results are all considered from both individual and environmental vantage points. Information regarding the roles and responsibilities of the consultant and consultee in AC, and the specifics of school-based practice are reviewed. Finally, the effectiveness of AC is explored, and cases are provided in which AC can be used (examples of child-based/level problems, family-based/level problems, educator-based/level problems, and systems-based/level problems). At the end of each case study, a list of discussion questions is provided.

Similarly, in chapter 6, organizational and systems consultation (OSC) is introduced, including the history of and rationale for the use of this model. The issues of organizational development and organizational change are discussed, including the stages of organizational readiness, implementation support, and diffusion. Two general models of OSC are presented: organizational development consultation (ODC) and intervention assistance consultation (IAC). The processes of ODC are reviewed, including problem definition, assessment, and diagnosis, development of implementation standards, and measurement and evaluation of implementation standards. Regarding IAC, several issues are discussed, such as the individual vs. team approach, training in consultation and data-based interventions, leadership and team membership, record keeping, permission to intervene, diagnostic interventions, process interventions, techno-structural interventions, individual interventions, and program evaluation and accountability. Finally, the evidence supporting the effectiveness of OSC methods is presented. This chapter also contains cases that may be approached from OSC, including examples of child-based/level problems, family-based/level problems, educator-based/level problems, and systems-based/level problems, as well as a list of discussion questions.

In chapter 7, instructional consultation (IC) is presented, including its use in helping teachers solve students' academic problems. In this chapter, information is presented regarding the use of instructional consultation (IC) in school systems. First, IC is defined, followed by information supporting the importance of increasing quality instruction in schools. Then, the underlying assumptions of IC are reviewed, along with the communication patterns and the process of IC. The stages of IC, including entry and contracting, problem identification and analysis (including the use of curriculum-based measurement [CBM] and curriculum-based assessment [CBA]), intervention implementation, termination, and development of a written record are also presented. Information regarding Instructional Consultation Teams (ICT), the role of the consultee in IC, IC and response to intervention (RTI) models, and multicultural issues relating to IC are reviewed. Finally, obstacles to the implementation of IC are explored. This chapter similarly includes cases that can be solved from an IC approach, including examples of child-based/level problems, family-based/level problems, educator-based/level problems, and systems-based/level problems, and a list of discussion questions.

Finally, in chapter 8, arguments for the effectiveness of consultation are presented. Data regarding the efficacy of each consultative theory and practice are compared and contrasted.

CHAPTER 1

Introduction

OVERVIEW OF THE NEED FOR CONSULTATION IN SCHOOLS

Working as a consultant is among the more exciting and gratifying roles in which mental health and educational specialist professionals can engage. At a time in which schools are expected to provide evidence of standards-based accountability, such individuals can be influential team members in ensuring that students are benefiting from evidence-based practices (EBPs), that teachers are knowledgeable about children's developmental and instructional levels, and that children's behavioral and emotional needs are addressed and not impeding their own learning and that of other youngsters. In their article in which the future of the profession of school psychology was discussed, Meyers, Meyers, and Grogg (2004) report that the problem of shortages of such professionals are expected to increase in the coming years; therefore, service delivery models that influence the greatest number of children with limited resources are needed. Moreover, models that focus on prevention and early remediation of student academic, behavioral, and emotional problems, such as consultation, provide an answer to such systemic problems as shortages of professionals, budget constraints, and an increasingly needy student population.

Working as a school-based consultant may also assist educational specialists, such as school psychologists and curriculum experts, in implementing reform efforts, such as inclusive pedagogical practices. In striving to take a proactive role in promoting inclusion, school-based professionals can use consultation to inform other educators regarding the methods in which inclusive practices can be advanced, as well as the benefits of implementing such procedures (Farrell, 2006). Consultation is also an intuitive fit for educational support personnel such as school psychologists and school counselors, as they advocate for moving away from within-child attributions for poor student progress and behavior and moving toward an analysis of systemic, environmental, or instructional factors in explaining the causality of such problems. Further, consultation can interrupt the prevalent cycle of referral-test-place into special education endemic in school systems, can assist educators in successfully providing services to students in Tiers I and II of response-to-intervention (RTI) models, as well as in promoting the likelihood that children receive educational programming in the least restrictive environment that meets their needs.

Bramlett and Murphy (1998) describe the contributions of various professions to school-based consultation, first discussing the literature in special education focusing on consultation issues relevant to collaboration and school-based teaming (Idol, Paolucci-Whitcomb, & Nevin, 1993), and then reviewing the research in community psychology in organizational or systems-level change and prevention efforts to avoid the development of problems (Juras, Mackin, Curtis, & Foster-Fishman, 1997). Similarly, instructional consultation stemmed from the merging of the knowledge domain of instructional psychology in the field of school psychology with the process of collaborative consultation from the discipline of special education (Rosenfield, 1995). In both the disciplines of special education and school psychology, collaborative problem solving has been advocated as a process in which parents and teachers "engage actively in the process and share power in decision making" (Allen & Graden, 1995, p. 669), which will be discussed later in the chapter.

Additionally, there is research suggesting that consultation is one of the roles that some educational and mental health support personnel, such as school psychologists, are satisfied with or very much enjoy in their role functioning. In a study of 97 school psychologists, most reported that they desired to spend more time engaging in direct and indirect intervention, such as consultation, professional development, and networking, and less time in assessment, multidisciplinary meetings, and administrative duties (Brown, Holcombe, Bolen, & Thompson, 2006). Despite their desire to engage in consultative practices, however, school psychologists do not spend most of their time engaging in consultation, with estimates varying from about 11% to 20% of role functioning devoted to consultative activities (Agresta, 2004; Bramlett, Murphy, Johnson, Wallingsford, & Hall, 2002).

However, evidence is mixed regarding the pleasure experienced associated with engaging in consultative activities by other educational and mental health professionals, such as school counselors and social workers. For example, Protulipac (2004) found that school counselors, similar to the findings associated with school psychologists, reported a desire to increase consultation time with teachers, administrators, and parents, with the highest percentage of respondents indicating that they would like to increase their frequency of consultation with counselors in community agencies. In another study undertaken regarding the roles of school psychologists, counselors, and social workers, however, social workers and school counselors indicated a desire to spend more time in individual and group counseling, and less time in consultative activities (Agresta, 2004).

There are a number of impediments that diminish the likelihood of school-based educational and mental health practitioners engaging in consultation, which will be discussed shortly. Additionally, it may be that consultative activities would be more desirable, and thus used to a greater degree, if school-based educational and mental health professionals utilized a style of consultation consistent with their training and role definitions in school settings. For example, social workers who are interested in providing consultation to special educators may benefit from using a model emphasizing the description of student skills, while enhancing teachers' empathy for and understanding of students. Such an approach may assist teachers in adopting a psychosocial perspective of student functioning, as well as learning new skills in assessment and self-awareness (Drisko, 1993). School counselors could provide consultation to regular and special educators in using preventative mental health approaches, such as a comprehensive developmental guidance program curriculum, and could also engage in advocacy for children's and families' civil rights and due process in education.

Meyers and Nastasi (1999) have identified a prevention framework that can be delineated into the categories of primary prevention, risk reduction, early intervention, and treatment, all of which are areas in which school social workers and counselors, as well as professionals such as school psychologists, can target for intervention. Further, school psychologists can use their knowledge of children's development and quality instruction to provide consultation in curricular choices and adaptation and EBPs in children's behavior and emotional problems.

Additionally, there are, perhaps, several reasons that explain why educational and mental health support personnel do not work as consultants to a greater extent: (1) Assessment in determining student eligibility for special education services continues to drive much of the functioning of educational and mental health support personnel, thus limiting the amount of time available for consultative activities (Gilman & Gabriel, 2004); (2) many administrators appear be satisfied with the status quo functioning of educational and mental health specialists such as school psychologists, thus providing no incentive for role definitions to be changed (Gilman & Gabriel, 2004); and (3) consultation may not be carried out authentically or with integrity in the school setting. Bramlett and colleagues (2002) explain, "Although behavioral consultation has received the most research support in the school psychology literature (Bramlett & Murphy, 1998; Sheridan, Welch, & Orme, 1996), it seems that many practicing school psychologists are not implementing this model as it was originally defined (Bergan & Kratochwill, 1990). Most respondents in our survey revealed that they did not adhere to the four-stage problem-solving model delineated in the behavioral consultation literature (i.e., problem identification, problem analysis, plan implementation, and plan evaluation). In a majority of cases, evaluations of consultation or the intervention are not being conducted" (p. 331).

There also appear to be systemic, organizational barriers affecting time spent in consultation. First, constraints exist that diminish the implementation of consultation in schools, including lack of time (due to enormous testing caseloads), and the inability of schools to support or be amenable to a change in service delivery, such as unfavorable organizational climate and building administrators' attitudes, classroom structures, and funding issues (Bramlett & Murphy, 1998; Forman, 1995; Gutkin & Bossard, 1984; Martens & Witt, 1988). Second, there are consultant variables, including expertise, motivation, and interpersonal skills, among others, and consultee variables, such as problem-solving skills, status in the school, classroom management skills, concern about looking bad, self-confidence, communication skills, and a sense of control that can influence the success of consultation (Bramlett & Murphy, 1998; Gutkin & Hickman, 1990). Third, the availability of consultation to school staff influences its use in schools, such as whether school psychologists are based in the consultee's building (Bramlett & Murphy, 1998; Stenger, Tollefson, & Fine, 1992). Finally, administrative factors (e.g., principals who are resistant to consultation due to traditional views of the role of the school psychologist—primarily testing and placing) can diminish the likelihood that consultation will be accepted and implemented (Bramlett & Murphy, 1998). Thus, this book may be helpful in facilitating school-based mental health and educational specialists' learning of the requisite skills to engage in multiple kinds of consultation, helping them to circumvent the barriers just mentioned, and thereby preventing many of the student problems that would otherwise result in a referral for determining eligibility for special education services.

BASIC TERMINOLOGY

Before proceeding further, it may be helpful to first define the terminology used in this book. The three main individuals involved in the consultative process are as follows: consultant, consultee, and client. Typically, the consultant collaborates with a consultee to provide indirect services to the client (Brown, Pryzwansky, & Schulte, 2001). In the practice of school-based consultation, the educational or mental health professional (the consultant) works directly with the classroom teacher or principal, for example (the consultee), to improve the teacher's or principal's skills in working with the student, school, or family (the client). In summary, the consultant indirectly provides services to the client via his or her consultative relationship with the consultee. Although consultative models vary, research has isolated several key elements that supersede the particular contribution of any one theory. Therefore, the next sections of the chapter will include a general definition of consultation, power bases used in consultation, characteristics of school-based consultation, issues that should be considered in working with teachers, and a brief review of intervention acceptability.

Consultation is generally defined as a nonhierarchical problem-solving relationship between consultee and consultant in which the goal of the consultative relationship is to improve the consultee's functioning with clients (e.g., students, schools, caregivers) and to improve the skills of the consultee (e.g., classroom teacher, principal) so that he or she will be able to independently provide services to the client in the future (Caplan, 1970; Zins & Erchul, 2002). Thus, consultation is conceptualized as an indirect service because the educational specialist or mental health professional consults with a consultee (e.g., classroom teacher, principal) in order to improve the functioning of the client (e.g., student, school, caregiver). Frequently, in schools, educational support personnel such as school psychologists, school counselors, and social workers work in a consultative relationship with a consultee, the classroom teacher, in order to improve the academic, behavioral, or emotional functioning of the student.

Researchers have emphasized the importance of consultation as a preventative approach in meeting the needs of children, families, and schools (Meyers et al., 2004; Zins & Erchul, 2002). Although professions such as school psychology might traditionally be viewed as an individualized, referral-based service, there is an impetus to enhance the practice of school psychology, as well as other educational support professions, to include the delivery of indirect services, such as consultation (Graden, 2004; Meyers et al., 2004). The issue of consultation was addressed at the 2002 International Futures Conference of School Psychology, and was highlighted as an important, yet often underemphasized role of school psychologists (Cummings et al., 2004). Similarly, in a survey of 370 school psychologists, assessment was named as the primary responsibility of those surveyed, with consultation identified at a distant second (Bramlett et al., 2002). It should be noted that while consultation is an indirect service, it may be used in conjunction with direct services, such as determining postintervention outcomes or efficacy, for example (Zins & Erchul, 2002).

In their often-cited work, Zins and Erchul (2002) define school consultation as "a method of providing preventively oriented psychological and educational services in which consultants and consultees form cooperative partnerships and engage in reciprocal, systematic problem-solving processes guided by ecobehavioral principles. The goal is to enhance and empower consultee systems, thereby promoting students' well-being and performance" (p. 626). In this definition of school consultation, collaborative problem-solving between the consultant and consultee is emphasized, in contrast to other definitions of consultation that underscore the consultant's power in the relationship (Caplan, 1970). In the next section, a review of the literature on power bases used in consultation will be provided.

French and Raven (1959) first defined social influence as the tendency of an authoritative agent to impart changes in beliefs, attitudes, and/or behavior in a target. In addition, they described social power as the ability of an influencing agent to promote change by using any available resources. French and Raven identified 14 social power bases in their model of social influence (see Table 1.1). An example of social power bases includes a *positive expert,* in which the target does what the agent says because the agent is perceived as an expert in a certain field, or a *negative expert*, in which the target does the exact opposite of what the agent says because of the belief that the agent is thinking of his/her own best interests (Erchul, Raven, & Wilson, 2004), with further research indicating the existence of a two-factor model of power differentiating between hard and soft power bases (Koslowsky, Schwarzwald, & Ashuri, 2001). Hard power bases are those that reflect typical

Table 1.1 Definition of Raven's Social Power Bases

SOCIAL POWER BASE	DEFINITION
Positive Expert[b]	Target does what the agent says because the agent is perceived as an expert in a certain field.
Negative Expert[a]	Target does the exact opposite of what the agent says because s/he assumes that the agent is thinking of his/her own best interests.
Positive Referent[b]	Target does what the agent says because s/he wants to be associated with or be similar to the agent.
Negative Referent[a]	Target does opposite of what the agent says because s/he does not want to be associated with or be similar to the agent.
Impersonal Reward[c]	Target complies because s/he perceives that the agent can give a tangible reward of some sort for complying.
Personal Reward[b]	Target complies because s/he believes the agent will approve of or like him/her for complying.
Impersonal Coercion[c]	Target complies because s/he perceives that the agent has the power to tangibly punish him/her for noncompliance.
Personal Coercion[c]	Target complies because s/he believes that the agent will disapprove of or dislike him/her for noncompliance.
Direct Information[b]	Target complies because information given by the agent makes logical sense to him/her.
Indirect Information[a]	Target complies because s/he overhears from a third party how well a particular course of action worked in a similar situation.
Formal Legitimate/Position[c]	Target feels obligated to comply because the agent occupies a position of authority.
Legitimacy of Reciprocity[c]	Target feels obligated to comply with a request because the agent has done something positive for the target in the past.
Legitimacy of Equity[c]	Target feels obligated to comply as a way of compensating for the agent's prior hard work.
Legitimacy of Dependence[b]	Target feels obligated to comply because the agent is unable to accomplish a certain action without the target's help.

[a] This power base is not included on the Interpersonal Power Inventory (IPI).
[b] Denotes a soft power base.
[c] Denotes a hard power base.

Source: (From "The Relationship between Gender of Consultant and Social Power Perceptions within School Consultation," by W. P. Erchul, B. H. Raven, & K. E. Wilson, 2004, *School Psychology Review, 33,* p. 584.) Copyright 2004 by the National Association of School Psychologists, Bethesda, MD, www.nasponline.org. Reprinted by permission of the publisher.

perceptions of power, such as the use of coercion and being direct, while soft power bases tend to involve more subtle, nondirective means of influence (Erchul et al., 2004).

Erchul et al. (2004) examined the relationship between school psychologists' gender and perceptions of social power during consultation using Raven's (1993) model of social power. Using a sample of 134 nationally certified school psychologists, the researchers found that female school psychologists perceived soft power bases as more effective in influencing teachers than did male school psychologists. These results may indicate that females use a different communication style than males when interacting with others. Further, female school psychologists also rated hard power bases as more effective than male school psychologists. Although these findings suggest that female school psychologists tend to see both kinds of power bases as effective in consultation, it may be that, taken together, the research suggests that males and females perceive soft power bases as more influential in consultation with teachers.

These results emphasize the importance for both novice and seasoned consultants to consider the power of social influence in the consultation relationship, as well as the influence of communication style (i.e., soft versus hard power bases) during consultation. Erchul and Chewning (1990) argue that while establishing a cooperative partnership between consultant and consultee is important (Zins & Erchul, 2002), it is helpful when the consultant provides leadership in the process (Bramlett & Murphy, 1998). The researchers suggest that consultants can be both directive and collaborative by establishing an atmosphere of respect and trust, as well as using effective interview techniques during the consultative process. Now that issues of power in consultation have been reviewed, the process of school consultation will be described.

As referenced in its definition, school consultation is characterized by a problem-solving process that is primarily guided by the consultant but continually adjusts according to the needs of the consultee. Thus, the consultative process systematically moves through a series of stages with continual input from all participants. Specific to school consultation, the concept of empowerment is emphasized. In this framework, the consultant recognizes and acknowledges that the consultee and other participants possess or may develop skills to improve their current situation when provided with support (Rappaport, 1981). More specifically, the consultee possesses competence, but may not have sufficient technical expertise to solve the problem independently. The consultant's role in this case, then, is to support or empower the consultee in improving his or her skills so that he or she is prepared to solve problems independently in the future (Zins & Erchul, 2002). Although the consultant works with the consultee to improve his or her skills, the consultant is also concerned about the student's welfare and functioning. Thus, the central goal of school consultation is to enhance the functioning and welfare of students (Zins & Erchul, 2002).

The consultative problem-solving process is similar to other consultation paradigms and includes the following steps: (1) establishment of a cooperative partnership, (2) problem identification and analysis, (3) intervention development and selection, and (4) intervention implementation, evaluation, and follow-up. For the problem identification stage, there are several detailed steps to follow when interviewing a consultee, such as a teacher. The interview covers five areas, including the definition of a problem, identifying the antecedent determinants of the identified problem behavior, identifying the consequences that may maintain the behavior, assessing relevant variables within the environment, and identifying the available resources. During the problem definition step, the problem behavior is operationally defined so that the behavior is easier to measure. In addition, the frequency and duration of the problem as well as the intensity and severity of the behavior is assessed. When identifying antecedents of the target behavior, temporal and situational antecedents are considered. The consultant and consultee then explore possible positive consequences that could improve the target behavior, as well as possible inappropriate negative consequences that may maintain the behavior. After consequences are explored, other environmental variables are assessed, such as instruction, school routines, and behavior and attitudes on the part of the child. Finally, the student's strengths and potential resources, such as peer tutors, are identified to ensure the most success (Peterson, 1968). The subsequent steps are explained in further detail in upcoming sections.

Before engaging in school consultation, it is important for consultants to be aware of issues specific to teachers and teachers' perceptions of student problems and the consultative process. In an investigation of teachers' perceptions of the cause of student problems, Ysseldyke, Christenson, Algozzine, and Thurlow (1983) found that the vast majority of difficulties were attributed by teachers to intra-child variables, some were attributed to home factors, while a small percentage of student difficulties were believed to be the result of teacher or school variables (Athanasiou, Geil, Hazel, & Copeland, 2002). Similarly, Athanasiou et al. (2002) noted that teachers in their study were likely to attribute difficulties in the classroom to within-child characteristics. Correspondingly, teachers were more likely to endorse treatments directed at the student, such as therapy and the student taking responsibility for the problem and its solution, in comparison to school psychologists (Athanasiou et al., 2002). In summary, research suggests that teachers often perceive students' academic achievement as being more influenced by factors they perceive as outside of their (the teachers') control.

In conducting consultation with classroom teachers, it may be valuable for school-based consultants to pay attention to the communication patterns used by educators. O'Brien and Miller (2005) found that while teachers were motivated to portray their explanations of student behavior as objective, factual, and non-self-interested, consultants can actually identify certain kinds of consultee behaviors as maintaining a "within-child" attribution for problem behavior and acknowledge these ascriptions while advocating for a systems or environmental attributional set.

Historically, teachers have been equivocal regarding consultation. Alderman and Gimpel (1996) concluded that teachers do not rate consultation as being their preferred method of service, and find consultation as being only moderately effective in changing clients' behavior. However, other factors mediate this relationship: (1) increased teaching experience is predictive of less interest in engaging in consultation, (2) teachers with high problem-solving skills are more likely to seek out consultative services (Stenger, Tollefson, & Fine, 1992), and (3) when teachers choose consultation as an intervention, they still want consultants to provide direct services to a student with problem behavior if the educators perceive the consultation as unsuccessful (Tanner-Jones, 1997).

Athanasiou and colleagues (2002) investigated teachers' beliefs and perceptions related to the consultative process with school psychologists. Teachers indicated that one of the most important factors impacting their perceptions of the consultative process was the amount of time the consultant devoted to them, and further valued the emotional and concrete, action-based support related to the intervention plan provided by school psychologists. Teachers perceived school psychologists who allowed them time to express their concerns, share ideas, and meet during a structured time period as more credible than those who allocated less time to such activities. Despite the lack of intervention effectiveness in some cases, teachers still perceived the consultative process as positive. Interestingly, the support provided to the teachers by the school psychologist was the foremost reason that these educators would choose to engage in consultation in the future (Athanasiou et al., 2002).

In investigating the sources of teacher resistance to school-based consultation, Gonzalez, Nelson, Gutkin, and Shwery (2004) found that factors such as the characteristics of the school psychologist, the school principal's support for consultation, personal teaching efficacy, teacher–school psychologist similarity, classroom management/discipline efficacy, adequacy of time available for consulting, opportunity for reciprocation, and teacher consultation insight were not statistically significant sources of impediments to successful consultation. However, the researchers did find that school psychologists who spend an appreciable amount of time in the school building are perceived by teachers as accessible, thus encouraging the greater use of consultative services (Gonzalez et al., 2004). These findings further emphasize the importance of the consultative relationship as an integral component of the consultative process. Specifically, time devoted to understanding the presenting problem, as well as the availability of the school psychologist, are important factors to consider when initiating or maintaining a consultative relationship. Intervention effectiveness may be less important to teachers overall than the formation of a collaborative professional relationship between educational and mental health support personnel such as school psychologists and teachers.

Additionally, there is research that indicates that consumers' acceptance of interventions is an issue that school-based consultants should consider because success in collaborative school-based consultation is partly dependent upon whether teachers implement interventions suggested by consultants (Truscott, Richardson, Cohen, Frank, & Palmeri, 2003). Jones and Lungaro (2000) investigated whether teachers found an intervention linked to a functional assessment more acceptable in comparison to treatments based on arbitrarily selected reinforcers, and found significantly higher pretreatment acceptability ratings, as well as likelihood of use for a treatment linked to functional assessment of behavior. These researchers posit that such data highlight the importance of using assessment information in school-based consultation, since teachers may rate interventions based on such data more favorably.

Traditionally it has been found that educators tend to prefer cognitive and cooperative interventions instead of behavioral ones. However, in a study comparing the acceptability of mathematics interventions, both teacher candidates and students rated cognitive and behavioral interventions as equally acceptable, suggesting that educators in training may be more open to different kinds of interventions than teachers already in practice (Arra & Bahr, 2005). This is an important finding to recognize, and may actually encourage school-based consultants to be more adventurous and diverse in their suggestion of interventions.

Truscott and colleagues (2003) used rational persuasion (RP), a technique presented in the business literature, to influence consultee perceptions regarding proposed interventions. Rational persuasion includes intervention information, reasons why it is important to decide to use the intervention, and potential objections to the intervention along with arguments designed to refute such objections. Researchers found that the influence of RP upon intervention acceptability, perceived effectiveness, and commitment-to-implement ratings was inconsistent, with the favorable results of RP dependent upon the intervention. Based upon these findings, the researchers conclude that school-based consultants should not spend more time in RP than is helpful, nor should they use the technique if the time costs seem extensive. Although intervention acceptability is an important predictor of consultation success, there is still much to be understood about the relationships among intervention acceptability, integrity, and effectiveness.

THE CONSULTATIVE PROCESS

Most models of consultation characterize the stages of consultation in a problem-solving framework that outlines very specific steps involved in the process. The stages of consultation may follow a linear order, but do not always occur in such a rigid fashion. Instead, the consultant and consultee may revisit one stage at a later time without damaging the integrity of the relationship or intervention outcomes (Brown et al., 2001). The following stages, described in "Behavioral Consultation" (chapter 3), are used in many of the consultative models and will provide the reader with a foundation for the information presented in the subsequent chapters.

The first stage of consultation involves formal entry into the organization (Brown et al., 2001), followed by the important step of establishing a relationship with the consultee. The nature of the consultation relationship can be characterized as a "cooperative partnership" according to Zins and Erchul (2002, p. 627). The consulting educational or mental health professional and teacher then work together, cooperatively, in a nonhierarchical relationship characterized by equality rather than a power differential. Thus, both the consultant and consultee bring unique perspectives regarding the presenting problem.

Rosenfield (2003) has identified the importance of communication, particularly in interpersonal dialogue, in both the process and outcome of consultation. However, impediments to effective consultation often exist in language barriers, including professional jargon and slang. In one study, multidisciplinary team professionals were found to use language that was discipline specific, including such terms as *positive regard* and *fluid intelligence,* with members failing to acknowledge and reconcile the assumptions unique to their professional languages. Further, team members also evidenced personal forms of slang, social language in which individuals use informal and pseudoprofessional terms. The author of this study, Knotek (2003), then used consultee-centered consultation strategies to raise team members' awareness of their use of jargon and slang in the consultative process, thereby facilitating the collaborative problem-solving ability of the team. Such barriers can be addressed through the strategies identified in Table 1.2 (Knotek, 2003).

During the assessment stage of the consultative process, consultee characteristics, the immediate and larger environment, and characteristics of the client are examined in regard to the presenting problem. These three domains influence the definition and analysis of the problem behavior (Brown et al., 2001). After assessing client, consultee, and environmental characteristics, the nature of the presenting problem becomes more apparent. Research suggests that the problem definition stage is the most important in the consultative process and the most predictive of outcomes (Bergan & Tombari, 1976). In order to accurately define the problem, the consultant and consultee should spend time assessing the factors (environmental characteristics, consultee characteristics, client characteristics) that may be related to the presenting problem. After a thorough assessment of the problem, it is defined in specific behavioral terms with accompanying objectives (Brown et al., 2001; Zins & Erchul, 2002). During this time, baseline data may be collected regarding the frequency, duration, and intensity of the problem. In addition, antecedents of the behavior and consequences that maintain the behavior are identified.

When selecting interventions, it is important to keep in mind that there are several avenues through which a problem may be solved (Katz & Kahn, 1978). Consequently, the consultant should consider the skills of the consultee, as well as the ease with which he or she is able to implement intervention strategies (Brown et al., 2001). Similarly, strategy acceptability is the extent to which the consultee believes that the intervention strategy is viable. Research suggests that acceptability of an intervention is associated with whether the intervention is actually

Table 1.2 Examples of Discourse Associated with Consultee-Centered Consultation Strategies

CONSULTATION STRATEGIES	DISCOURSE EXAMPLES
Building coordinate process Foster independence	We have plenty of time to work on this. Tell me more about what you're thinking about Jose.
Match consultees needs through clarifying questions and perception checking	You came to SST telling us that you were most upset with Tracy's behavior. However, most of your presentation of the problem has focused on her lack of success with reading. What is it that is so frustrating about Tracy's progress in reading?
One-downmanship	I do not have a ready answer for that. You are the expert on the student. What do you think? How would the rest of you describe this issue?
Summary statements	We have been saying that Juan is well-behaved most days. However, we've noted that he seems to have difficulties on Mondays.
Addressing lack of knowledge Insufficient understanding	Leroy's attention problem may not be ADHD (attention deficit hyperactivity disorder). There are other explanations for students having difficulties attending to a task or paying attention.
Addressing lack of skill Joint exploration of problem through "we" questions	We know that Mark struggles during transitions. At what other times do we see similar behaviors?
Addressing lack of self-confidence Fostering hope	How have others of you worked through this kind of situation before?
Addressing a lack of objectivity Unlinking through verbal focus on the client	Marsha, you have said that Chris is illiterate, but you've also described some wonderful picture story books he has made. Tell us more about these picture books.
Exploring alternative views of case through clarifying questions	What are some other possible explanations for Sammi's behavior during SSS (sustained silent reading)?

Source: (Making Sense of Jargon during Consultation: Understanding Consultees' Social Language to Effect Change in Student Study Teams, by S. E. Knotek, 2003, *Journal of Educational and Psychological Consultation, 14*, p. 188.)

implemented (Reimers, Wacker, & Koeppl, 1987). Further, consultees such as teachers tend to prefer interventions that are easy to implement, time efficient, nonintrusive, and effective (Elliot, 1988; Witt, 1986; Witt, Elliott, & Martens, 1984).

During the implementation stage of the consultative process, it is helpful to review the roles and responsibilities of the participants in implementing the intervention. Other issues to be addressed during this stage include identifying potential reinforcers, determining the time and day the intervention should be implemented, and producing a written outline delineating each person's responsibilities (Brown et al., 2001; Zins & Erchul, 2002). After the implementation of the intervention(s), the effectiveness of the intervention must be evaluated. Further, issues of generalization, fading, and follow-up must be explored. The termination of the consultation relationship should be discussed at the outset of the consultative process. Termination typically occurs when the consultant and consultee agree that the established goals have been attained by the consultee or client. However, researchers have identified specific reasons for an early termination of the consultation relationship. Early termination may be necessary when consultation has not advanced as expected (Gallessich, 1982), or when a serious issue arises that requires an immediate intervention (Caplan, 1970).

Each step in the consultative process, from entry to termination, is integral to successful outcomes, treatment integrity, and consultee satisfaction. The relationship between consultant and consultee is emphasized throughout the process, and is one of the most important aspects of the entire process. Although successful outcomes may not consistently occur within a good relationship, if one exists, the consultee will be more likely to seek the consultant for assistance in the future. In the next section, the roles and characteristics of consultants will be presented, followed by a discussion of the role of technology in the consultative process.

Although many professionals, including school psychologists, counselors, and social workers, may engage in consultation, little research fully explicates the practitioner characteristics that allow consultants to be successful. However, some researchers have identified key attributes associated with effective consultants, including self and other awareness (Caplan, 1970), multicultural sensitivity (Arrendondo et al., 1996), and good interpersonal skills. Richardson and Molinaro (1996) discuss how consultants with a traditional Eurocentric value system may unassumingly impose their values on consultees. Thus, it is imperative that consultants appreciate how their understanding of their own cultural biases, race, and communication style impacts their consultative effectiveness.

In addition to a multicultural awareness and understanding, effective consultants possess particular skills that impact the consultation relationship. In the pre-entry and entry phase of the consultative process, consultants must, again, have adequate self-understanding. In particular, consultants must be able to accurately analyze their own strengths, weaknesses, and consultative skills. The ability of the consultant to utilize his or her skills is helpful in assuring the consultee that the consultant will be able to benefit the client. Lastly, consultants, both internal and external, should possess marketing skills or the ability to persuade others that they may benefit from their service (Kurpius & Fuqua, 1993; Kurpius, Fuqua, & Rozecki, 1993).

Rogers (2000) enumerated six cross-cultural competencies necessary in effective consultation, including: (1) understanding one's own and others' culture, (2) developing cross-cultural communication and interpersonal skills, (3) examining the cultural embeddedness of consultation, (4) using qualitative methodologies, (5) acquiring culture-specific knowledge, and (6) understanding of and skill in working with interpreters. School-based consultants need to be cognizant of the specific issues related to English-language learners (ELL), including the common programmatic options available, research regarding bilingual education programs, and guidelines and recommendations for consultation practices related to culturally and linguistically diverse consultees and clients.

Wizda (2004) argues that one of the most important roles for consultants is to help build schools' capacity to meet the needs of an increasingly diverse population. Ochoa and Rhodes (2005) provide an excellent source of information on this topic, emphasizing that school-based consultants addressing the issue of bilingual education should be familiar with school-specific issues and resources. In particular, consultants should have an understanding of student-specific skills and needs, including knowledge about students' educational history, language history, current language proficiency and second-language acquisition process, and parental desires and needs, such as culture-specific communication styles, expected parental roles, expected roles for school personnel, families' level of acculturation, and roadblocks to equitable parental participation (e.g., parents' English language skills). Additionally, consultants need to be aware of the specific skills and needs of school personnel (consultees' role-specific skills and needs, bilingual education issues, court rulings, and federal law), and student-specific skills and needs, programs of choice, potential barriers to program participation, and student-specific program adaptations (Ochoa & Rhodes, 2005).

Of note to consultants may be a common problem plaguing culturally diverse students, the mismatch between the values and expectations of home and school. LaRoche and Shriberg (2004) emphasize that it is important for consultants to examine the interrelationships between the home and school setting, as well as to educate school personnel about common cultural values of students from diverse backgrounds. For example, it is helpful for educators to recognize that in addition to the difficulties Latino children and their families face when acculturating to the American school system, such individuals also frequently struggle with issues of poverty, discrimination, poor housing, and limited English fluency. It is especially necessary for consultants to review the literature that documents the variables and processes that allow children from diverse backgrounds to succeed, as well as to work to develop and implement culturally sensitive parent involvement initiatives. When parents have been invited to be partners in the education of their children and are supported in doing so, children from diverse backgrounds are thereby better supported in the multiple contexts of their lives (LaRoche & Shriberg, 2004).

Another skill of effective consultants is the ability to form a relationship with the consultee through the use of strong interpersonal skills. Brown et al. (2001) delineate the specific interpersonal skills necessary to establish a good consultant–consultee relationship. These skills include active listening skills and the ability to adapt to the racial/ethnic background of the consultee, the ability to determine resistance on the part of the consultee or whether the consultee is displaying appropriate behavior related to his or her cultural background, the ability to understand how cultural background may contribute to perceptions of power within the relationship, and the skill of maintaining a clear focus on the client during the consultation relationship, rather than discussing personal difficulties on the part of the consultee.

Srebalus and Brown (2001) propose several guidelines to encourage relationship building when working with different cultural groups. They discuss the cultural differences in maintaining eye contact, and suggest that consultants be respectful of individuals who avoid or minimize eye contact. In particular, Asian Americans and Native Americans typically find direct, prolonged eye contact offensive. When working with individuals from these cultural backgrounds, then, it is important to consider the degree of eye contact to be used. In addition to eye contact, there are cultural differences relating to interpersonal space. Srebalus and Brown (2001) suggest that if consultees move away or toward you in order to adjust the personal space to their comfort, then consultants should remain as previously seated rather than adjusting their own personal space. Different cultural groups vary in their use of nonverbal communication. Thus, consultants should be aware of the effect of their nonverbal communication (e.g., head nods and smiles) when consulting, and adjust their nonverbal style as needed. Finally, consultants should use active listening techniques with all cultural groups in order to provide feedback regarding what has been communicated (both verbally and nonverbally) and to demonstrate understanding.

Meyers et al. (2004) discuss the role of electronic tools that facilitate communication, collaboration, and dissemination of resources, as well as assist the process of consultation and promotion of preventative goals. Although budgetary limitations continue to be a problem in school systems, many continue to invest in computing and network technologies, potentially allowing for videoconferencing with experts in the field in consultation (O'Neill, 2001). Technology can also facilitate consultation through online communities, such as e-forums in which individuals can post questions and comments and communicate with professionals both nationally and internationally. Further, computers and networks may be helpful for recordkeeping, shared calendars for initiating consultative appointments, analysis of data regarding educational epidemiologica! issues, and exchange of information for ongoing client-centered, consultee-centered, or system-centered consultation (Meyers et al., 2004). One of the issues associated with using technology in consultation, however, is the importance of considering possible ethical violations, particularly those related to confidentiality. Thus, a brief discussion of ethical issues will subsequently be presented.

ETHICAL CONSIDERATIONS IN THE CONSULTATIVE PROCESS

For various reasons, it is important to discuss the ethical considerations that must be taken into account during the consultative process. Fuqua and Newman (2006) discuss the role of ethics and morality in organizations, proposing that consultants as well as the consultative process morally influence organizations either negatively by ignoring moral issues, or positively by acknowledging or promoting discussions of potential moral issues. Moral issues can ultimately affect an organization's functioning if not properly addressed in the context of consultation. Although each profession has its own ethical standards, those native to the discipline of psychology will be reviewed to provide a foundation for consideration of such issues for all educational and mental health professionals.

The American Psychological Association Ethical Principles of Psychologists and Code of Conduct (APA, 2002) provides psychologists with ethical and legal guidelines regarding the practice of psychology, including consultation services. This guiding document assists psychologists in using the ethical principles in their role functioning, including consultation. Thus, ethical guidelines are important to consider in the consultation relationship.

General Principles

The general principles of the APA's ethical code that apply to consultation include beneficence and nonmaleficence, fidelity and responsibility, integrity, justice, and respect for people's rights and dignity. The first principle, *Principle A: Beneficence and Nonmaleficence*, asserts that psychologists first do no harm, ensuring the protection and welfare of clients. *Principle B: Fidelity and Responsibility* states that psychologists practice faithfulness in keeping promises, in discharging and accepting legal responsibilities, and maintaining appropriate relationships. This principle also asserts that psychologists maintain competence in their work, as well as seek assistance from other professionals as necessary. The third principle, *Principle C: Integrity*, states that psychologists maintain integrity in psychological activities including communicating in an honest manner, keeping promises, and refraining from stealing, cheating, or engaging in fraud. *Principle D: Justice* calls for psychologists to maintain fair and equitable access to treatment. In terms of consultation, consultants must select techniques or approaches that will meet the needs of the consultee. Finally, the last principle, *Principle E: Respect for People's Rights and Dignity*, states that psychologists maintain privacy and confidentiality, as well as a respect for cultural and individual differences, including race, gender, age, ethnicity, and culture. These principles are important to the consultation relationship in that the consultant must remain cognizant of the consultee's and client's welfare.

Competence. The ethical standard, *Competence*, states that psychologists provide services that are within their boundaries of competence. Psychologists must first do no harm. As such, consultants should only provide services that are within their boundaries of competence. A consultant who has limited or no training in school consultation may not be adequately equipped to acknowledge but redirect teachers' intra-child attributions for academic difficulties, for example. Consultants, then, must not provide consultation services that are outside their education or training experience.

Confidentiality. The ethical standard, *Privacy and Confidentiality*, states that psychologists are obligated to protect confidential information. Consultants must explain confidentiality and its limits at the outset of the consultation relationship. This ensures that the information shared between the consultant and consultee remains confidential, and also that the consultee is aware that confidentiality may be broken under certain circumstances, such as if the client is in imminent danger. Meyers et al. (2004) also caution professionals to be cognizant of the risks to confidentiality in the consultative process as a result of the use of e-mail and the storage of electronic files, and to use strategies to increase protection of confidential information, including file encryption and firewalls.

Informed Consent. An issue raised by Scholten, Pettifor, Norrie, and Cole (1993) is that of informed consent in consultation conducted in response to addressing students' problems prior to a referral for special education evaluation (Zins, Curtis, Graden, & Ponti, 1988). Depending upon the amount of contact with the student client, informed consent may or may not be needed. Scholten et al. (1993) argue that prohibiting any form of student involvement without parental consent may inhibit informal problem solving and may not be in the best interest of student clients. For example, requiring parental consent for observing a child in class or holding a problem-solving discussion about a student may not seem necessary, since there is no direct contact between the consultant and the child. However, the authors also argue that the training of educational and mental health consultants needs to include systematic review of potential ethical dilemmas and how such issues can be avoided or remedied (Scholten et al., 1993).

The ethical standards presented here, including beneficence and nonmaleficence, fidelity and responsibility, integrity, justice, respect for people's rights and dignity, competence, and confidentiality generally apply to consulting psychologists. The present 2002 APA ethical code does not directly contain specific guidelines for consultation services. However, the ethical code provides a set of principles and standards for appropriate ethical behavior in the work-related activities of psychologists, which includes consultation. Consulting, as a psychological service, should follow ethical guidelines to ensure the protection of clients, as well as the maintenance of confidentiality, respect, and dignity. Overall, the ethical code provides a set of procedures to follow, while protecting the individuals who receive services from consultants.

TRAINING COLLEGE AND UNIVERSITY STUDENTS IN CONSULTATIVE PRACTICES

University and college training programs with educational and human-service orientations, such as in school psychology, school counseling, school social work, and special education, are increasingly teaching consultation to their students in recognition of the need for such individuals to assume consultative roles in facilitating the implementation of legal mandates in school systems (e.g., least restrictive environment; Individuals with Disabilities Education Improvement Act [IDEIA], 2004), and in meeting the needs of an ever-diverse school-age population in the most typical classroom possible (Riley-Tillman & Chafouleas, 2003). Serving the educational needs of all students may require expertise that is not available within the school system. Further, even if such knowledge is available, service providers in related disciplines (e.g., school psychology, school counseling, school social work, etc.) may have difficulty communicating and collaborating due in part to demanding schedules, use of inconsistent terminology, and different training experiences and backgrounds associated with various professional fields. Nevertheless, because consultation is an effective means of helping to modify educational practices and programs in order to meet children's needs, it is seen as a valuable activity in school systems (Bramlett & Murphy, 1998).

In other disciplines, such as medicine, consultation has been used for many years. Physicians have long provided external consultation to school systems (e.g., Caplan, 1970). Today, in responding to the need identified in the previous paragraph, most school-based educational and mental health support personnel (e.g., school psychologists, school counselors, and school social workers) have added consultation to their professional role responsibilities (Shullman, 2002). There appears to be general agreement that consultation (both external and internal) is an important skill for professionals who practice in and with schools (Conoley & Conoley, 1991). Although there is documented support for the need for consultation services in the schools (Meyers et al., 2004), there is limited consensus regarding who should be trained in consultative skills, which models should be included in educational curricula used to teach consultation, or how those skills should taught to and modeled for students. In this section, an examination of the teaching of consultation is provided, as well as guidance in how to use this text in teaching school-based consultation.

CONSULTATIVE TEACHING PRACTICES

Within the last 20 to 25 years, school psychology has been one of the disciplines that have widely adopted the perspective of a need for consultation training for college and university students preparing to work as educational and mental health specialist practitioners in school settings. Consequently, the research subsequently presented will focus on training in consultative practices for school psychologists, although the conclusions are certainly applicable for students in other educational specialist and mental health professions.

In 2004, Anton-LaHart and Rosenfield surveyed 104 school psychology training programs, based on a list obtained from the National Association of School Psychologists (NASP), requesting that the programs identify all of the consultative models taught in their programs. More than half of survey respondents (63%) reported providing instruction in more than two consultation models, with most programs teaching skills in behavioral (91%) consultation, and more than half teaching skills in mental health (59%), instructional (53%), and organizational (52%) consultation. Most often a stage-based model was presented (96%) to students in order to guide their decision making during consultation. In the college or university classroom, instructional time was devoted to discussions of consultative theory, content in consultation, and intervention development.

In programs with a second consultation course, expanded intervention development, progress monitoring, and process maintenance skills were highlighted. In consultation coursework, skills that received the least amount of instructional time were communication (0% to 20%) and multicultural competencies (0% to 10%; Anton-LaHart & Rosenfield, 2004). Although this research does not capture the total sample of school psychology training programs, approximately 65% of programs are NASP-affiliated, and identify consultation as a necessary competency for students preparing to become school psychologists. Thus, these data reveal the manner in which training programs are likely to teach consultative skills.

The number and type of consultation models taught to those students training to become school psychologists has long been an area of contention in the field (Anton-LaHart & Rosenfield, 2004). Some instructors believe that it is best for students to study a single model, thereby concentrating on depth of understanding in that one consultative theory. However, others argue that training in multiple consultation approaches is beneficial to students, as it better matches the diversity of real-life practice (Anton-LaHart & Rosenfield, 2004; Meyers, 2002; Tindal, Parker & Hasbrouk, 1992). However, even when students receive instruction in multiple models of consultation, trainers must select which ones, among the many available, to offer to students in their consultative coursework.

Suggestions for Teaching Consultation

When preparing to teach consultation, college and university instructors must consider the knowledge that should be acquired by students, as well as the dispositions that students need to demonstrate in order to successfully engage in consultation. For example, students need to demonstrate knowledge and application of systematic problem solving, and be able to link problems with evidence-based interventions (Alpert & Taufique, 2002; Bramlett & Murphy, 1998; Davis, 2003; Meyers, 2002). Dispositions that should be demonstrated by students in training to become educational and mental health specialists in school settings include the ability to engage in self-reflection, self-evaluation (Bramlett & Murphy, 1998; Davis, 2003; Meyers, 2002; Sandoval & Davis, 1984; Tindal et al., 1992), and satisfactory social and communication skills. Often, role playing is a central teaching technique used in the classroom, while supervised practice cases are used in the field in order to provide students with opportunities to engage in supervised demonstrations of consultative skills.

Beyond these broad premises, the orientation to teaching consultation is varied. Meyers (2002) focused on early skill development in consultation, describing coursework essential to preparing the novice. First, prospective consultants should understand the scope of indirect service delivery; specifically, that the process of consultation has the potential to develop services that range from preventative to primary, secondary, and tertiary intervention programs (Meyers, 2002). Second, consultants-in-training need to be aware of the level of consultation (e.g., child-centered, consultee-centered) provided. Finally, Meyers (2002) emphasizes that problem-solving strategies should be implemented systematically so that important steps are not skipped.

Teaching a systematic stage-based consultation process is often seen as a hallmark of best practice consultation. However, there have been at least two studies documenting that the consultative processes demonstrated in applied school settings are not consistent with stage-based practice (Doll et al., 2005; Tindal, et al., 1992). Thus, the viability of this recommendation is still being investigated. Along with the knowledge and dispositions discussed previously, it is important for students to make the connection between theories and practice (Meyers, 2002). In fact, most researchers and trainers advocate for direct instruction paired with practice activities (Bramlett & Murphy, 1998; Davis, 2003; Gutkin, 2002; Meyers, 2002; Sandoval & Davis, 1984; Shullman, 2002; Tindal, et al., 1992). Practice experience should include modeling of appropriate skills by the instructor, student role playing of consultative scenarios, followed by the opportunity to practice in a field-based setting.

In addition to these recommendations, Davis (2003) argues that leadership skills are the critical skill set that can influence a student's success in consultation. Students should begin by familiarizing themselves with the school environment, including the organizational structure and communication and reporting hierarchies. Then, course activities should facilitate the development of leadership skills (Davis, 2003). For example, instructors can randomly assign articles to students that detail an aspect of consultation. Then, each student is required to facilitate a 30-minute class discussion on the article. The goal of the interaction is not merely to summarize the content of the article; rather, it is to encourage discourse with peers. This activity requires that students initiate and sustain a collaborative effort among members of the class, mirroring skills required of consultants. Davis (2003) also recommends using videotaped interactions to provide feedback to student consultants. This assignment can be dynamic, in which the instructor pauses the tape to provide feedback or observers practice giving written feedback to peers, with comments compiled into constructive commentaries. Although Davis (2003) writes from the perspective of a trainer of school counselors, he reports that his recommendations would apply to a variety of school-based professionals (e.g., school psychologists, school social workers, etc.).

Finally, Sandoval and Davis (1984) highlight the importance of teaching students to address ethical issues. For example, the authors suggest that instructors teach students how to address difficulties between the consultant and the consultee. That is, how does one develop and maintain a consultative relationship for the purpose of serving the client when interpersonal conflicts may arise? Using mental health consultation, discussed in detail in chapter 2, students may be asked to consider why the consultative outcome resulted from the actions undertaken. By practicing reflective feedback, consultants will improve decision making regarding potentially difficult situations, including those involving ethical dilemmas (Sandoval & Davis, 1984).

Contextual Considerations in Teaching Consultation

There has been some research that calls for understanding the contextual issues of the consultative process, considering both the reality of the broad social milieu as well as the details of addressing positive social change for children. This line of work reveals the complexity of delivering consultative services that seemingly fall at the individual level, but yet are necessarily influenced by the system (e.g., school, federal mandates). Riley-Tillman and Chafouleas (2003) discuss the need to consider social influences when engaged in intervention development during the consultative process. These authors argue that only in the context of the social milieu can effective interventions be developed. Specifically, they caution that dramatic changes to the current classroom system are likely to be rejected or poorly implemented. Thus, training programs should provide instruction to college and university students in building a knowledge base of interventions that are evidence based while weighing the social influences that can impact intervention efficacy.

Kress, Norris, Schoenholz, Elias, and Seigle (2004) consider the importance of child-centered social and emotional learning, explaining that current educational standards (e.g., No Child Left Behind [NCLB]) focus exclusively on academic issues and are not conducive to providing instruction in the areas of social and emotional development. These authors propose that consultants illustrate, through curricular mapping, the overlap between academic learning and social/emotional learning. The purpose of showing teachers the overlapping of skills is to maximize the impact of the curriculum upon academic achievement *and* social and emotional development (Kress et al., 2004). Curricular mapping examples are provided in Table 1.3. A blank form that can be used with teachers is provided in Table 1.4.

Gutkin (2002) and Klein and Harris (2004) emphasize that training should go beyond teaching consultants to work with individuals (e.g., teachers), to include a focus on working with groups (e.g., teaching teams, families, community agencies). This would allow for itinerant consultation focusing on classroom and community needs (Kelley, 2004; Klein & Harris, 2004), but would also require consultants to be trained in facilitating group processes and to understand the dynamics of group decision making (Gutkin, 2002; Shullman, 2002). Those who support a focus in group dynamics in consultation assert that group consultation is especially important to address the family's role in solving problems for children at school, since it is the social context of the family that can influence children's school success, particularly during early childhood (Kelley, 2004; Klein & Harris, 2004). Other researchers have cautioned that because group consultation is not routinely taught in training programs, students should not be encouraged to engage in such practices, since inadequate training can lead to poor outcomes (Wilson, Gutkin, Hagen, & Oats, 1998).

Expand Training to the Consultee

Kelley (2004) argues that consultees (e.g., teachers) should receive increased training in the process of consultation. That is, rather than focusing solely on the development of the consultant's skills, training

Table 1.3 Curricular Mapping Planning Form

DOMAIN	GRADE (LEVEL)	EDUCATIONAL STANDARD (USE STATE STANDARDS)	SKILL (SHOWS STANDARD IS MET)	SOCIAL EMOTIONAL SKILL (TAILORED TO MEET CHILD'S NEED)
English Language Arts	K-4	Learn to follow instructions in large and small group settings that are formal and informal	Questioning Responding Listening	Assertiveness Creativity Reciprocal communication skills
Math	6-8	Understand numbers, ways of representing numbers, relationships among numbers, and number systems	Understand and use ratios and proportions to represent quantitative relationships	Compare and contrast personal values and interests to total interest Compare and contrast others values and interests to total interest Notice similarities and differences among groups
Writing	8-11	Persuasive Writing	Include convincing, elaborated and properly cited evidence Include a clearly stated position or opinion Develop reader interest Anticipate and counter reader concerns and arguments	Explain your feelings/ experiences Understand how personal narratives are derived from life experiences Get to know others Show respect for others Demonstrate perspective taking and empathy skills

Note: This does not require special curricula. Social emotional skills emphasized can be tailored to the child's need.

Source: Information in this table has been adapted from Kress, Norns, Schoenholz, Elias, and Siegle (2004).

Table 1.4 Curricular Mapping Planning Form

DOMAIN	GRADE (LEVEL)	EDUCATIONAL STANDARD (USE STATE STANDARDS)	SKILL (SHOWS STANDARD IS MET)	SOCIAL EMOTIONAL SKILL (TAILORED TO MEET CHILD'S NEED)

efforts should seek to improve consultees' ability to request and receive help in the service of children. Kelley (2004) states that this could be accomplished through collaboration between consultant and consultee training programs in which joint training sessions would be available to teachers and other school personnel.

Welch et al. (1992) discuss the benefits of an interdisciplinary consultation course taught by a team of professors from educational administration, educational studies, special education, school counseling, and school psychology. In this study, Welch et al. (1992) developed a course that merged the collective knowledge of university personnel from multiple disciplines to highlight the competing challenges faced by school personnel serving in various roles. The objectives of the course were to increase functional problem solving across roles in the system. Team problem solving, change theory, role theory, and conflict resolution were addressed in coursework. The authors of this study concluded that the realities of implementing interdisciplinary programs (such as the one described) in higher education are more complex and cost intensive than may be feasible for most programs. Further, the roles and their associated schemas adopted by the preservice students (e.g., general education teachers, administrators, etc.) were difficult to modify (Welch et al., 1992).

Similarly, Harris and Zetlin (1993) offered university coursework to a small group of practicing teachers in an effort to increase consultative collaboration among school personnel in an urban school with a diverse student body. The practicing teachers faced numerous administrative and personnel changes in their schools, and there was little funding available for external consultants. The course content included general information about assessment, identification of gifted and special education students, teaching strategies, facilitating student empowerment (especially for language-minority youth), and how to build discipline in a manner that supports social skill development and self-esteem. Instructors required teachers to journal how course content applied to their daily practice in the classroom. They also designed, implemented, and monitored an intervention under the supervision of the instructor. The authors of this study concluded that the authentic experience of this endeavor was essential to the positive outcomes reported by teachers (Harris & Zetlin, 1993). Specifically, teachers' ability to define the scope and pace of activities in the course improved feelings of ownership in the outcome. This result is important, as it provides support for using such training as a method of achieving one of the primary goals of consultation—having the consultee retain responsibility for implementation of the intervention.

When comparing the Welch et al. (1992) and Harris and Zetlin (1993) findings, it is possible that more experienced teachers, who were faced with real-world problems, were better able to benefit from training in the consultative process, thereby facilitating more favorable outcomes. While there is not enough evidence for any strong conclusions, these studies highlight the complexity of the effective teaching of consultation.

Field-Based Supervision
While there is general agreement that fieldwork experiences are superior to role play experiences for students, there is limited research detailing the pragmatics of selecting an appropriate consultation placement, the criteria for selecting a supervisor, and how to evaluate the skills demonstrated by consultants (Alpert & Taufique, 2002). Cramer and Rosenfield

(2003) have identified the dearth of research examining the process of supervising the development of consultation skills, and recommend a developmental framework to teach the types of skills that require supervision, including how to provide supervisor support and how to use a scaffold to provide competency-based feedback. Essentially, novice consultants require structured supervision sessions, concrete strategies suggested for increasing skills, and specific details offered regarding consultative process. As consultants become more competent, they then can become more responsible for identifying their supervision needs. Finally, advanced students will be able to self-monitor their areas of expertise and those areas not yet in their repertoire of skills.

Cultural Considerations

There is also consensus that multicultural knowledge and skill development should be taught and encouraged in training programs, despite the limited instructional time reported in the survey described earlier (Anton-LaHart & Rosenfield, 2004). Ingraham (2000) has detailed the type of awareness required in multicultural and cross-cultural school consultation. These domains include: (1) understanding one's own culture and the impact of one's culture on others, (2) respecting and valuing other cultures, (3) understanding individual differences within cultural groups and the multiple cultural identities prevalent in many individuals, (4) cross-cultural communication, including the approaches for developing and maintaining rapport throughout consultation, (5) understanding cultural saliency and how to build bridges across salient differences, and (6) understanding the cultural context for engaging in consultation and the appropriateness of interventions. Ingraham (2000) concludes that successful learning about multicultural issues is obtained through ongoing professional development, provided in both formal and informal formats. Further, in-depth learning occurs when individuals seek feedback and cultural guides. Table 1.5 summarizes Ingraham's (2000) recommended readings for increasing multicultural awareness in consultants.

HOW TO USE THIS TEXT

The review provided above establishes that training paired with experiential opportunities and supervision is needed to develop professional practice skills in consultation. This book was developed to facilitate this learning in the next generation of school-based educational and mental health consultants. Case examples are provided and framed within specific theoretical orientations in order to provide students with a

Table 1.5 Eight Domains for Consultant Learning and Development in MSC and Supporting Literature

Ingraham, C. L. (2000). Consultation through a multicultural lens: Multicultural and cross-cultural consultation in schools. *School Psychology Review, 29*, 320-343.

Copyright 2000 by the National Association of School Psychologists, Bethesda, MD. www. nasponline.org. Reprinted by permission of the publisher.

1.	*Understanding one's own culture (race, ethnicity, socioeconomic context, acculturation, etc.).* Arredondo et al., 1996, Brown, 1997, Gibbs, 1980; Harris, 1996; Ingraham & Tarver Behring, 1998; Lynch & Hanson, 1998; Parsons, 1996; Pinto, 1981; Ponterotto et al., 1995; Ramirez et al., 1998, Sue & Sue, 1999; Tarver Behring & Ingraham, 1998
2.	*Understanding the impact(s) of one's own culture on others.* Arredondo et al., 1996; Gibbs, 1980, Ingraham & Tarver Behring, 1998; Lynch & Hanson, 1998; Ramirez et al., 1998, Sue & Sue, 1999; Tarver Behring & Ingraham, 1998
3.	*Respecting and valuing other cultures (with some knowledge of the history, values and beliefs of others cultural groups and models of racial/ethnic/cultural identity).* Arredondo et al., 1996, Harris, 1996; Henning-Stout & Brown-Cheatham, 1999; Ingraham & Tarver Behring, 1998; Lynch & Hanson, 1998; Pinto, 1981; Ponterotto et al., 1995; Ramirez et al., 1998; Soo-Hoo, 1998; Sue & Sue, 1999; Tarver Behring & Ingraham, 1998
4.	*Understanding individual differences within cultural groups and the multiple cultural identities prevalent in many individuals.* Ingraham & Tarver Behring, 1998; Leong, 1996; Pedersen, 1994; Sue et al.,1996; Sue & Sue, 1999; Tarver Behring & Ingraham, 1998
5. (a)	*Cross-cultural communication.* and Arredondo et al., 1996; Brislin & Yoshida, 1994; Cushner & Brislin, 1997; Lynch & Hanson, 1998
5. (b)	*Multicultural consultation approaches for developing and maintaining rapport throughout consultation.* Gibbs, 1980, Harris, 1996, Ingraham & Tarver Behring, 1998, Ramirez et al., 1998; Tarver Behring & Ingraham, 1998
6.	*Understanding cultural saliency and how to build bridges across salient differences*
7.	*Understanding the cultural context for consultation (dominant culture, culture of the school or community).* See text for MSC adaptation of Leong, 1996; Soo-Hoo, 1998; Sue et al., 1996. See text for MSC adaptations of Parsons, 1996; Pinto, 1981
8.	*Multicultural consultation and interventions appropriate for the consultee(s) and client(s).* Barnett et al., 1995; Ingraham & Tarver Behring, 1998; Lynch & Hanson, 1998; Ramirez et al., 1998; Soo-Hoo, 1998; Tarver Behring & Ingraham, 1998

Source: (Consultation through a multicultural lens: Multicultural and crosscultural consultations by C. L. Ingraham, 2000, *School Psychology Review*, 29, 320–343.) Copyright 2000 by the National Association of School Psychologists, Bethesda, MD. www.hasponline.org. Reprinted by permission of the publisher.

theory-into-practice skill set (Dinkmeyer & Carlson, 2006; Meyers, 2002). We believe that case studies allow the consultants-in-training time to conceptualize and process information at a rate that matches their abilities, prior to actual field experiences. This in turn empowers students to recognize their supervision needs, and actively participate in the development of a framework for ongoing professional development with the support of their supervisors.

The cases provided in this book were selected to highlight examples that apply to the theoretical model presented in the corresponding chapter. *Answers* are not provided, as the authors of this text recognize that theoretical frames can only guide the fluid dynamics found in real-life situations. Rather, authors provide questions that match the theoretical structures presented as a means of highlighting the salient features of the case. Creativity and active discussion among college and university trainers and students are encouraged. It is anticipated that course instructors will provide their scientific and clinical expertise and offer insight into the cases related to each theoretical orientation. We hope that the cases in this book help to provide an authentic, problem-based learning activity. All cases presented are based in whole or in part on real children. Confidentiality of all children and families has been maintained.

SUMMARY

In this chapter, the contributions made by numerous disciplines to the study and practice of consultation were briefly reviewed. Further, information was presented regarding educational and mental health support personnel's preferences for consultative practices, as well as suggestions for increasing such individuals' desire for performing consultation. Barriers to engaging in consultative activities were identified, a general definition of consultation was provided, and the practice of school consultation was reviewed, including information regarding power bases, characteristics of school consultation, issues associated with working with teachers, and intervention acceptability. Additionally, the consultative process was briefly described, with information provided regarding formal entry, techniques to be used in establishing an effective relationship, assessment, defining the problem and setting goals, selecting interventions or strategies, implementation of these interventions or strategies, evaluating the success of these interventions and strategies, and termination of the consultative relationship. A discussion of the roles of consultants was presented, along with consultant characteristics, such as self-other awareness, multicultural sensitivity, and interpersonal skills. The issues of technology in consultation were briefly explored, and a review of ethical considerations in the consultative process was provided. Additionally, the topic of teaching consultation in higher education settings was raised, along with recommendations that may be used in teaching from this text. The terminology and key concepts in consultation, including the process and roles for consultants and consultees presented in this chapter will provide a framework that can be applied to specific models of consultation depicted in the subsequent chapters. Moreover, the readers now be exposed to several different consultative models and applied exercises relating to these theoretical approaches.

CHAPTER 2

Mental Health Consultation

OVERVIEW

The psychiatrist Gerald Caplan is credited with being one of the first mental heath professionals to write about the importance of consultation (Brown, Pryzwansky, & Schulte, 2001; 2006). In his work at a child guidance center in Israel after World War II, he noted that by providing support to those providing child care, rather than delivering traditional therapy directly to immigrant children, the caregivers were able to serve a great number of children and manage a broader range of the children's difficulties (Caplan, 1970; Caplan & Caplan, 1993). Caplan's work has been termed mental health consultation (MHC), and is used in a variety of contexts, including school systems.*

MHC provides technical expertise with respect to mental health symptoms and disorders to help caregivers address such difficulties. Since personal needs can interfere with daily functioning, by responding to such needs, consultation services can *preventatively* address issues related to mental health. In fact, Caplan was attentive to how the personal needs of both child and caregiver can impact the child's functioning (Caplan 1970, 1974). He notes that adults comprise an important part of a child's environment. In view of this, ineffective or disturbed adults can negatively impact children. Thus, in Caplan's model the social environment and interpersonal psychodynamic perspectives are important to consider when planning interventions (Caplan, 1970).

---

* Authors Brown et al. (2001, 2006) have been leaders in the field of school psychology in describing and advocating for the use of MHC. Some portions of this chapter have been adapted from these authors' work, and readers are encouraged to consult their original writings for greater detail.

The social environment of children is influenced by a variety of caregivers. Caplan (1970) noted that caregiving groups need to find ways to work together to provide an effective social environment to prevent difficulties and improve children's mental health. That is, when there is an adequately supportive social environment, children will demonstrate increased coping effectiveness and, in turn, more adaptive behaviors and less psychological disturbance.

Highlighting the fact that the caregiver's individual psychology impacts children distinguishes MHC from other types of consultation. Caplan (1974) noted that the personalities of caregivers can interfere with their professional functioning, and at times can decrease their effectiveness when working with children. Specifically, he found that caregivers tended to report high numbers of referrals in domains in which they had less skill and experienced frustration, often narrowly focusing on these deficits to the exclusion of areas of strength.

When confronted with behaviors with which they experienced management difficulties, caregivers consistently requested help with the same types of problems (e.g., learning problems or aggression). Caplan (1974) was able to increase the functioning of caregivers by: (1) training them to understand and cope with the problem sets they tended to refer for intervention, (2) lending a sympathetic ear to their struggles while providing an objective broadening of their perspective on the difficulties children were facing, and (3) providing support to consultees in their own environmental contexts, rather than bringing children to medical offices for assistance (Caplan, Caplan, & Erchul, 1994). By addressing both the interpersonal psychodynamic issues and the social contexts of the caregivers, these individuals were able to demonstrate better communication and functioning. These findings support the modern use of consultation with teachers and children in school systems, rather than only serving children by providing treatment in clinical settings (Conoley & Conoley, 1991). Recent research shows that school teams that do not benefit from the components found in the MHC model tend to produce poor consultative practices and negative outcomes for children (Doll et al., 2005).

Definition of MHC

Caplan (1970) defined consultation as a voluntary, nonhierarchical relationship between two people, each of whom has an area of expertise, and in MHC, one of them is a mental health professional. In this relationship, the consultee defines the problem and that problem must fall in the area of mental health requiring specialized knowledge from an outside source. MHC is used to promote the mental health functioning of a client; that client may have a formal mental disorder or idiosyncratic personality characteristics, or it may be that the interpersonal aspects of the work situation need to be addressed. Recommendations provided are tailored to the identified difficulty and can be accepted or rejected by the consultee who is responsible for the administration of the support to the client.

For Caplan (1970), an important purpose of consultation is to improve the functioning of the consultee so that they may be more effective with similar problems in the future. Caplan is clear that the recommendations given to the consultee are aimed at improving the consultee's job performance. Through improved job performance, the consultee's well-being may be enhanced and the consultation may well become a therapeutic experience. He does not advocate for direct therapeutic intervention with the consultee; however, Caplan does acknowledge that the consultee's emotions can interfere with his or her functioning, a common problem called *theme interference*. Theme interference is essentially a lack of objectivity, one of four main sources of problems detailed in a later section, in which the consultee's feelings about the current client are patterned after his or her previous experiences with someone he or she perceives as similar. In this situation, the preset theme operating at the unconscious level interferes with the consultee's ability to objectively view the client, negatively impacting the consultee's effectiveness. In order to address a consultee's theme interference, Caplan focuses on the actual functioning of the client. It is in this indirect way that the interpersonal psychology of the consultee is addressed by the consultant, who addresses psychodynamic issues as they relate to the social environment of the consultee.

Assumptions of MHC

As stated, the primary assumption of MHC is that the interplay of individual psychodynamic and social environmental factors is influenced to change a client's functioning. The strength of this assumption is that it offers opportunities for multiple explanations of a client's behavior and for multimodal interventions.

MHC assumes that a partnership between an external professional (consultant) and internal professional (consultee) is essential for implementing effective interventions. While technical expertise is important, it is only the consultee who can translate knowledge into effective interventions consistent with his or her environment. In MHC, new skills are to be learned by the consultee because he or she is active in the implementation of the interventions. Accordingly, the consultant is responsible for facilitating this learning in the consultee. New learning carries the message that the consultee is competent and can manage work problems independently. Of course, skills alone do not ensure the use of newly learned information. As noted previously, maladaptive interpersonal functioning of the consultee (e.g., theme interference) may prevent the use of known or acquired skills. In this instance, the consultant facilitates new learning by addressing interpersonal barriers to an effective application of the consultee's skills.

Assumed Sources of Difficulty

Consultees' difficulties are assumed to originate from four possible vectors: (1) lack of knowledge, (2) lack of skill, (3) lack of confidence, and (4) lack of objectivity (Caplan, 1963). When consultees lack knowledge, this is typically attributable to their limited understanding about the role mental health issues play in directing or contributing to the difficulty. Providing educational information for the purpose of increasing knowledge is an essential piece of MHC and has been used, for instance, to help consultees work with clients from cultural groups that are outside their range of experience (Ingraham, 2000, 2004).

Lack of skill is found when the consultee understands the problem, but the solutions applied are not satisfactory in addressing the problem. Lack of skill is difficult to address in consultation, as it is likely that the skill needed is not native to the consultee's professional role. If the skill is appropriate for the consultee to develop, consultation can be used to help consultees acquire the necessary expertise. This is best accomplished by mentors who work in the same field as does the consultee.

Lack of confidence occurs when the consultee is faced with a problem that falls within his or her skill set, but he or she is unsure that the appropriate skill can be successfully applied. Here again, confidence should be developed through the consultee's own professional field. In MHC the consultant would provide support for the here and now experience, and also help find a mentor within the consultee's field to further build confidence.

Lack of objectivity was referenced in the previous example of theme interference. One example of theme interference exists when the consultee's feelings about the current client are patterned after the consultee's previous experiences, which unconsciously influence his or her expectations for this person or situation. When this type of theme interference occurs, the consultee's expectations derived from a previous negative experience, for example, are predetermined; thus, feelings of hopelessness may interfere with problem solving in the context of the current situation, and a self-fulfilling prophecy cycle is enacted. The need to address such theme interference has been a central aspect of Caplan's writings over the years.

Caplan (1970) describes a total of five types of objectivity problems; all include the loss of professional distance. The remaining four examples of losing professional distance occur when: (1) the consultee feels a direct personal involvement with the client, (2) the consultee identifies with the client or the situation to the point of losing perspective, (3) the consultee's feelings and expectations are unconsciously displaced onto the client as if the consultee were having the client's experience, and (4) when there is a characterological distortion.

These first three of the examples above have found their way into the common lexicon of work-related problems, in which too much empathy can lead to enmeshed relationships. Characterological distortions occur when a personality factor, such as the consultee's need for perfection, interferes with his or her ability to work with a client who shows disdain or disregard for order. Caplan (1970) describes loss of objectivity as the most common reason for consultation. Although each case will vary, the consultant's questions, observations, and behavior are aimed at bringing distance and objectivity to the situation, while providing support to the consultee in an attempt to relieve his or her interpersonal needs.

Consultation Process

Caplan (1970) considers both the environment (institution or individual), and interpersonal psychodynamic needs of the client and/or consultee throughout the consultation process. Building relationships, conducting assessment procedures, selecting interventions, and engaging in the follow-up evaluation of results all have psychodynamic and environmental influences. Although Caplan (1970) does differentiate among different types of consultation cases, the process is essentially the same, and continues to be used in adapted MHC models.

Relationship Building

Building a relationship may require a series of interactions in order to build rapport and establish oneself as a credible contact (Caplan, 1970). Consultant interactions should be characterized by: (1) empathy, (2) tolerance of the feelings in oneself and others, and (3) a recognition of the premise that by gathering information in a systematic and objective manner one can understand the behavior of others. With respect to procedure, Caplan (1970) reports that consultants should begin by meeting with a member of the highest level of administration at the institution. Meeting with administrators provides the opportunity to clarify support structures, such as how decisions are made, formal and functional lines of communication, and how funds or resources are distributed. Agreements made with the administration are typically formal (written), as they define explicit roles and responsibilities (Caplan & Caplan, 1993).

The relationship with the consultee is likely the single most important element in the MHC process. Without a good relationship in which the consultee is open about the problem that he or she is experiencing and is active in the consultative process, the consultation will not progress.

Further, Caplan (1970) considers all communication between the consultant and the consultee confidential. The need for maintaining confidentiality should be stated explicitly in preparatory discussions with the consultee, as well as in prerequisite communications with administrators. Additionally, interactions should be nonjudgmental, and consultants must work to maintain equality in the relationship, correcting any movement toward a superior/subordinate role.

Assessment

In MHC the consultant independently, often privately (Brown, et al., 2006) assesses both the consultee and the organizational factors contributing to the client's difficulty, thus influencing the course of consultation. Through gentle probing questions, the consultant can broaden his or her understanding of how the consultee conceptualizes the problem. Then the consultant and consultee jointly determine what data need to be collected to inform the decision making necessary in the consultative process.

Interventions

The consultee then formulates and selects interventions, and carries the responsibility for administering them. The only role the consultant may play in intervention is addressing any interpersonal consultee difficulties.

Follow-Up and Evaluation

In MHC the consultant not only seeks feedback on the outcome of the intervention, but also seeks feedback about the consultation experience for the purpose of improving consultation service delivery. Although Caplan (1970) notes the difficulties in measuring indirect services, he does recommend evaluating change in the consultee's perception of the problem, the generalizability of skills, and the achievement of the desired outcome in the client.

MHC in Schools

Over the years, Caplan has focused on formalizing and promoting the importance of consultation from a mental health perspective. So successful are his efforts that the American Academy of Child and Adolescent Psychiatry (AACAP, 2005) has established practice parameters for psychiatric consultation to schools that cite his original work as foundational. Many technical terms in Caplan's early work (e.g., Caplan, 1970; 1974) have been updated to better fit the language used today, and two of these changes are substantive for the work conducted in schools.

First, the concept of *collaboration* has been added to facilitate the functional implementation of consultation in schools. In mental health collaboration, there is joint responsibility for all aspects of the consultation process (Pryzwansky, 1974). Consider, for example, the reality that school teams may not be free to accept or reject consultative advice that is provided by an expert within their system. In response, Caplan, Caplan, and Erchul (1995) agree that mental health collaboration expands the concept of consultation, viewing collaboration as complementary to consultation and acknowledging that collaboration may replace MHC in schools. Today, schools work with both external (e.g., psychiatrists, law enforcement, clergy) and internal (e.g., counselors, social workers, school psychologists) consultants; therefore, both MHC and mental health collaboration models remain active in practice (Conoley & Conoley 1991). In Table 2.1, the differences between MHC and mental health collaboration models are explored.

Second, Meyers, Brent, Faherty and Modafferi (1993) argue that consultee variables should be addressed directly as well as indirectly. Direct questions, confrontations, and support for expressing the teacher's own authority conflicts, dependency, anger and hostility, or identification with the student or situation are recommended (Meyers et al., 1993). To address this indirectly has the potential to be manipulative because the consultee may not be aware of the need to deal with his or her role in the client's difficulty. Caplan et al. (1995) agreed that when collaboration is the method used, then it may be appropriate to be more direct in addressing consultee needs. They clarified that manipulation for the purpose of coercion did not have a place in MHC, but indirect manipulation was ethically appropriate for supporting others who may not yet be ready to become aware of their interpersonal issues (Caplan et al., 1995).

In their 1995 review, Caplan et al. highlighted nine useful aspects of MHC that had endured over a 30-year period and are applicable to schools. The authors argue that consultants should continue to: (1) focus on the interconnection between individual and environment, (2) use formal contracts to define roles and responsibilities, (3) engage in

Table 2.1   Mental Health Consultation and Mental Health Collaboration Contrasted on Key Dimensions

DIMENSION	MENTAL HEALTH CONSULTATION	MENTAL HEALTH COLLABORATION
Location of consultant's home base	External to the organization	Internal to the organization
Type of psychological service	Generally indirect, with little or no client contact	Combines indirect and direct services, and includes client contact
Consultant–consultee relationship	Assumes a coordinate and non-hierarchical relationship	Acknowledges status and role differences within the organization and thus the likelihood of a hierarchical relationship
Consultee participation	Assumes voluntary participation	Assumes voluntary participation, but acknowledges the possibility of forced participation
Interpersonal working arrangement	Often dyadic, involving consultant and consultee	Generally team based, involving several collaborators
Confidentiality of communications within relationship	Assumes confidentiality to exist, with limits of confidentiality (if any) specified during initial contracting	Does not automatically assume confidentiality, given organization realities and pragmatic need to share relevant information among team members
Consultee freedom to accept or reject consultant advice	Yes	Not assumed to be true, as a collaborator's expertise in his or her specialty area is generally deferred to by team
Consultant responsibility for case/program outcome	No	Shares equal responsibility for overall outcome, and primary responsibility for mental health aspects of case or program

Source: (From "Caplanian Mental Health Consultation: Historical Background and Current Status," by G. R. Caplan, R. B. Caplan, and W. P. Erchul, 1994, *Consulting Psychology Journal, 46*, p. 7.) Copyright 2007 American Psychological Association. Reprinted with permission of the author.

Table 2.2 Caplan and Caplan's Consultation Classification in Terms of Level, Target, and Goal

	CLIENT-CENTERED CASE	CONSULTEE-CENTERED CASE	PROGRAM CENTERED ADMINISTRATIVE	CONSULTEE-CENTERED ADMINISTRATIVE
Level	Case	Case	Administrative	Administrative
Target	Client	Consultee	Program	Consultee
Goal	Behavioral change in client	Enhanced consultee performance in delivering services to clients	More effective delivery of program	Enhanced consultee performance in programming

Source: (From *Psychological Consultation and Collaboration in Schools and Community Settings* (3rd ed.), by A. M. Dougherty, 2000, Belmont, CA: Wadsworth, (p. 238).) Copyright 2000 by Wadsworth, a division of Thomson Learning. Reprinted with permission. www.thomsonrights.com.

a nonhierarchical relationship, (4) address consultee difficulties such as theme interference, (5) refrain from highlighting the original source of a consultee's difficulty (e.g., insight therapy), (6) maintain an indirect approach to address the consultee's difficulties, (7) systematically reflect on the consultation process to increase the consultee's awareness, (8) continue to focus on the broad interrelationships among the client, teachers, and schools, and (9) teach consultation skills directly.

Types of MHC in the Schools

Caplan's (1970) original work differentiated two broad divisions of consultation: *case consultation*, addressing problems of the client or mental health needs of the client and *consultee-centered consultation*, focusing on the needs of the consultee. In Table 2.2, Caplan and Caplan's consultation classification system in terms of level, target, and goal is summarized. Within case consultation, consultants use their expertise to plan problem-solving strategies about a particular case (e.g., child) or administrative difficulty (e.g., program the child attends). Similarly, in consultee-centered consultation, the consultant works to improve the consultee's problem-solving skills in a particular case (e.g., addressing theme interference) or administrative difficulty (e.g., problems in a system).

Caplan's work was expanded upon by Alpert (1976), Meyers (1973, 1995), and Meyers, Parsons, and Martin (1979) to develop school-based models that differentiated child-, system-, and teacher-oriented consultation. These concepts fit into Caplan's original work, and are often helpful organizational tools for school teams to consider (Meyers, 1995). This is due to the ever-present need to provide services to the child, as well as the increasing need to serve all children through the school systems and communities in which children function.

Child-centered (case) consultation is the original form of MHC, in which consultants and consultees focus upon specific academic or behavioral problems of a single child or identified group. These tend to be high-risk children or groups that already require accommodations due to special education requirements or disability status. In fact, the legal requirement to serve children who qualify for special education in the least restrictive environment tends to keep children with mental health needs in general education classes, resulting in the need for MHC services to assist teachers and school and community systems that provide such services. The needs of these children are often complex, leading some researchers to advocate for combining MHC with behavioral consultation to promote effective school and clinic-based services (Conoley & Conoley, 1991).

System-centered (administrative) consultation focuses on school improvement, organizational change, and prevention programming designed to benefit all students (Kerr, 2001). Schools may work with outside community agencies to accomplish large-scale improvements (AACAP, 2005), with examples including home-school collaboration initiatives (Bramlet & Murphy, 1998), violence-prevention programming (Astor, Pitner & Duncan, 1996) and crisis response teams (Kerr, 2001). Programming can be available for students as young as preschool, and through higher education (Knotek, 2006). More recently, this type of consultation is being adjusted to extend to public health concerns, integrating mental and physical health intervention (Nastasi, 2004).

Teacher-centered consultation is the most prevalent type of consultation used in schools today. The focus of this type of consultation is on the teacher's (consultee's) difficulties in dealing with a student. Consistent with Caplan's (1970) original model, researchers show that teachers who are supported in broadening their understanding of student needs provide more versatile support to students, and foster a better social environment at school (Achinstein & Barrett, 2004), resulting in increased resiliency in children (Benard, 2004). In striving to improve student outcomes, school systems should focus on improving the interpersonal psychodynamics and social environment that affect teachers (consultees).

While MHC has been used in schools, researchers note that the most common consultation request is for children's academic concerns, without consideration of interpersonal needs, even when these needs are evident (Hanko, 2002). Further, this narrow academic focus is even found in schools where interpersonal issues may be the most salient problems that children experience, such as specialized behavioral programs (Jacobson, 2005) and military schools (Horton, 2006). Farouk (2004) argues that the interpersonal psychodynamic needs of teachers are influenced by the school culture and subgroups within that culture, in turn impacting children's learning (Farouk, 2004). The effect of interpersonal needs is largely underestimated (Hargreaves, 1994), and consultation taking into account the interaction of interpersonal and environmental needs is underused (Farouk, 2004; Hanko, 2002).

Effectiveness of MHC

There is limited research examining the outcomes of consultative processes. Of the studies available, most do not focus on MHC. Researchers conducting a meta-analysis of the use of MHC found that this approach had a positive effect on both consultees and clients (Medway & Updyke, 1985). However, others have argued that the studies examined were not pure examples of MHC (Gutkin & Kurtis, 1990). Sheridan, Welch and Orme (1996) examined efficacy studies published after the Medway and Updyke (1985) investigation, and again found positive effects of MHC. However, Sheridan et al. (1996) were also unable to document that the consultations provided in these later studies were indeed only MHC. At present, there is little supporting empirical evidence for the effectiveness of MHC (Brown, Pryzwansky & Schulte, 2006; Gutkin & Kurtis, 1999).

Supporters of MHC argue that measurement of the changes in interpersonal variables proves to be just as difficult for consultation models as for counseling models. That is, interpersonal issues are subjective and are difficult to measure without inference. For the empiricist, the necessity of relying upon influence to measure behavioral change identified as the result of the consultants' influence is problematic. Exhortations to implement studies using randomized clinical trials to increase clarity in the measurement and interpretation of findings are countered by the inapplicability of such findings to practice. These researchers highlight the importance of interpersonal and social context, concluding that the objective comparison of sanitized samples hinders accurate interpretations applicable to diverse groups (Henning-Stout & Meyers, 2000). Others argue that it is the quality of the consultant–consultee relationship that should be measured, rather than the indirect effects. For example, a quality interpersonal relationship with a consultant is often reported to improve teacher functioning (Bostic & Rauch, 1999).

Complicating the search for empirical support is the need to make modifications to MHC. Researchers who consider the role of culture and diversity, as they relate to the consultation experience, found that MHC and other consultative models required substantial modification when being used with diverse groups (Behring, Cabello, Kushida, & Murguia, 2000).

Barriers to MHC
Although addressing interpersonal psychodynamics may be a strength of MHC, it is also a barrier to being taught at the university level (Larney, 2003). Many training programs do not teach psychodynamically oriented skills (Hanko, 2002) and further, psychodynamic skills may not be valued by school psychologists (e.g., Watkins, 2000). In summary, helping teachers to understand the impact of their own as well as student interpersonal needs remains a challenge (Hanko, 2002).

CASES IN MENTAL HEALTH CONSULTATION
MHC/Student Example 1
Danny is a 12-year-old boy who attends seventh grade at Any Middle School. He lives with his twin sister Linda and mother Lydia. His parents are estranged, and the mother reports that she and her husband quietly argue over the pending divorce. Danny's father, Greg, has regular weekly visitations, and at times he brings his new girlfriend, Candy.

Danny and his sister were originally members of a set of triplets, but as the result of delivery complications, one of the infants did not survive. Born prematurely at 27 weeks gestational age, Danny was hospitalized due to a loss in his birth weight and some breathing difficulties. As an infant, he was described as irritable, reportedly due to an underdeveloped nervous system. However, by age 2 he was described as less irritable, although still exhibiting excessive motor movement. His medical history is also remarkable for inguinal hernias, which were successfully treated at 2 months.

Danny's educational history began in a private kindergarten, at which time test results placed his skills within normal limits, where they remain today. In the first grade, Danny moved to a public school, where he enrolled in the Any School District. Danny's mother reports that both Danny and his twin showed some separation concerns during this period, which seemed to resolve in a timely manner.

Although Danny is not gregarious, he does establish and maintain friendships. Danny often shares his friends with his twin sister, who is a popular school cheerleader. Danny's mother describes him as sensitive and, at times, overly emotional and tearful when compared to his sister and other children his age; she hypothesizes that the separation and impending divorce are having a more negative impact on Danny than upon Linda or herself. Danny's mother confides, "We are disappointed but adjusting." However, she adds that almost any topic can result in tearful displays both at home and school. Danny's father agrees and reports the same concerns regarding his son's increased sensitivity. When the timeline of events was examined, it became evident that Danny's tearfulness began over a year ago, well before the marital separation.

Discussion Questions

1. What makes this case suitable for MHC?
2. State explicitly the interpersonal and environmental issues. Is there an interaction, and if so, what does that mean?
3. What issues need to be addressed with the mother, father, and school?
4. What communication style would be important?

MHC/Student Example 2

Jamal is a 10-year-old boy who suffers from sickle-cell anemia; he attends the fourth grade at Next Elementary School. Captain Michael Warner (a captain in the military) is a single father of two children—Jamal and his sister Tonika, who attends Next High School. The children's mother died in an automobile accident 3 years ago, before the captain was transferred to the area. Enjoying frequent promotions, Captain Warner and his family have moved four times since Jamal started kindergarten. The family lives on the military base, which is rumored to be closing, so it is likely that the family will move sometime later this year. Consistent child care has been a problem, and the captain believes that he may be relying on Tonika more than he should to provide care for Jamal.

Although sickle-cell anemia is an inherited blood disorder that can be identified through genetic screenings, the Warners did not participate in such screenings. Shortly after Jamal's birth, however, they were provided details of the diagnosis. Sickle-cell anemia is a disorder that affects hemoglobin, the protein found in red blood cells that helps carry oxygen throughout the body, and results in abnormally shaped cells that can clog blood vessels, depriving the body of oxygen. In areas where blood flow is blocked, sufferers experience severe pain. Anemia is the rapid breakdown of red blood cells, resulting in a cell count that falls below normal levels. Having too few blood cells is associated with feeling tired and having trouble fighting infections. In teens with sickle-cell anemia, growth may occur more slowly, and puberty is reached later than in unaffected individuals. Further, sickle-cell crises have been correlated with emotional distress and may be induced by strenuous exercise.

This school year, Jamal has had a series of episodes that have resulted in extended absences from school. During those times, the teachers providing homebound schooling including coordinated and monitored instruction, both at the hospital and when Jamal was recovering at home. At school, Jamal works with the school nurse to manage his pain. However, both the nurse and his teachers are concerned about Jamal's peer relationships. Not only is Jamal new to the school, but he also has limited opportunities for contact with peers due to restrictions on his physical activity, and as a result of hospitalizations and extended absences. His father notices that Jamal does not have any close friends and is open to discussing this concern with the school.

Discussion Questions

1. What makes this case suitable for MHC?
2. Whom will the teacher and nurse work with?
3. What communication style would be important?
4. How will you measure success?

MHC/Student Example 3

Jaqill is a 15-year-old female who attends the Alternative Education School. Contact with her parents has not been established this year, yet Jaqill regularly attends school and maintains "Bs" and "Cs" with accommodations. Both parents have a history of drug use, and both have been in and out of jail. Her father is alleged to deal crack cocaine. Although Jaqill's school records are incomplete, it is known that she carries a diagnosis of ADHD (attention deficit hyperactivity disorder), ODD (oppositional defiant disorder), and bipolar disorder, and has a corresponding educational classification of emotional disturbance. Currently, she has been prescribed with Trazodone (a sedative/antidepressant), Zyprexa (an atypical antipsychotic reported to treat bipolar disorder), and Depakote (a mood stabilizer). It is unknown if she is compliant with this treatment protocol.

Recently, Jaqill's teachers report that her emotional state has declined. She reports profound and pervasive episodes of negative emotions and feelings of inadequacy. The social worker reports a rumor that her parents have been picked up by the police for drug use and both are awaiting trial and are expected to receive extended jail sentences. Her grandmother is declining to have Jaqill stay at her home, and it is likely that Jaqill will have to be placed in a crisis stabilization unit for homeless youth.

Discussion Questions

1. What type of consultation would be used according to Caplan?
2. State explicitly the interpersonal and environmental issues. Is there an interaction and if so what does that mean?
3. Are there any consultee issues to consider? Anticipate how the teacher, social worker, and school administrator may experience this mother and father. Is this a problem? How will you know?
4. Why is it important that the consultee retain responsibility for implementing the interventions?

MHC/Family Example 1
Regina is a 12-year-old female student whose behavior has recently become strange. Specifically, she is repeatedly late to class and has begun to report fantastic stories to explain her tardiness. For example, she recently reported that the door of the girl's bathroom was welded shut, requiring her to escape to get to class. In recent weeks she has complained that people have followed her home. Regina's teachers have been unable to contact her mother; however, they did note that the answering machine had a strange religious message saying that Jesus had willed the caller to contact the family at this time.

After interviewing Regina, you discover that her mother has a long history of schizophrenia and has recently gone off her medications, becoming "sick." Regina describes her mother's sickness as pale pasty skin, loss of hair, and increased suspicions of men following her. Regina reports that she adores her mother, and that at times she thinks her mother may be correct about men following them. In fact, there has been an unknown vehicle in the neighborhood that is only moved late at night. Sympathetic to her mother's distress, Regina reports that she prides herself on being the only person that her mother trusts. Upon questioning Regina regarding other family members involved with her and her mother, you find out that Regina's grandmother lives nearby. You schedule a meeting with Regina's grandmother, who confirms Regina's report. The grandmother confides that she worries about Regina staying alone in the home with her mother, not because of any danger, but because Regina seems to imitate her mother's behaviors.

Discussion Questions

1. Is this a good case for collaboration case, and if so, why?
2. Whom would the consultant work with?
3. Whom will the teacher work with?
4. Are there any consultee issues to consider? Anticipate how the mother may experience the school system. Is this a problem? How will you know?

MHC/Family Example 2

Danielle is a 17-year-old high school senior who attends Caring High School. She has been living alone in an apartment since her mother moved out of state for a job. Her mother originally planned for Danielle to stay with a trusted neighbor, but a shoplifting charge and curfew violations resulted in her removal from the home. The neighbor does continue to check on Danielle's well-being from time to time, but is unsure of her role given Danielle's need for a legal guardian in court appearances.

Danielle is in close contact with a female music teacher at her school whom she trusts; this teacher is the mother of one of her classmates. The teacher has helped Danielle find the community service opportunity required by her probation, and has provided a few dinners when Danielle did not get food from the restaurant where she works as a hostess. Although Danielle has always been thin, the teacher notices that she has lost a significant amount of body weight. Also, the apartment seems to have morphed into a 24-hour party spot for restaurant workers. On more than one occasion, the neighbor has found Danielle engaged in sexual behaviors at her apartment. Fearing that Danielle is spinning out of control, the neighbor and the music teacher contact her mother and all approach you to find out who can help Danielle.

Discussion Questions

1. What makes this case suitable for MHC?
2. What type of consultation would be used according to Caplan?
3. Explicitly state the interpersonal and environmental issues. Is there an interaction and if so, what does that mean?
4. Are there any consultee issues to consider? Anticipate how Danielle's mother may experience the music teacher and the neighbor. Is this a problem? How will you know?

MHC/Family Example 3

Mrs. Patterson has contacted the principal of the school her son Dave attends, reporting that her son suffers from asthma. She explains that Dave has a rare form of asthma that is exacerbated by a negative emotional tone in others. Mrs. Patterson has presented a letter to the bus coordinator from a neurologist requesting that the bus driver use a friendly tone at all times when transporting Dave back and forth to school. Mrs. Patterson feels that the bus driver is ill-tempered and uses language that is tinged with complaint and negative emotion, and she is becoming increasingly concerned.

Meanwhile, the principal is unable to locate any medical documentation in Dave's school records. When he talks with the special education faculty members, they report that Dave is not being served in special education. After being consulted, the school social workers report that Mrs. Patterson has a history of reporting medical difficulties for Dave along with documentation from numerous doctors, but none of the paperwork has been found to be credible.

Discussion Questions

1. Whom would the consultant work with?
2. Whom will the principal work with?
3. Are there any consultee issues to consider? Anticipate how the mother may experience the principal, and whether this will be a problem. How will you know?
4. What communication styles are important?

MHC/Educator Example 1

Randy is a 7-year-old first grader who attends the Concerned Elementary School. His teacher reports that he has difficulty controlling his behavior and shows poor sustained attention. Specifically, his teacher reports attention-seeking behaviors, loud outbursts, and argumentative, oppositional behaviors when redirected.

Randy's mother reports that he has always enjoyed school and had relatively no behavior difficulties until this year. However, she says that schools are "places of punishment" and everyone is looking to "bother me at home when there is nothing wrong."

Record reviews indicate that during her pregnancy, Randy's mother was diagnosed with placenta previa, with documented hemorrhaging resulting in an emergency C-section at 37 weeks gestation. Due to his mother's loss of blood and his low birth weight of 4 lb 2 oz, Randy was transported to Special Hospital for treatment. Subsequent to his stabilization, Randy was described as hyperactive and fidgety. Between the ages of 2 and 3, he was prescribed Ritalin, reportedly for hyperactivity. However, this treatment was discontinued by his mother after his hyperactivity was reported to have increased while on the medication.

In school, Randy has had a behavior modification plan over the last 2 years in both kindergarten and first grade, but with limited improvement. In the past, Randy has received supplemental general education instruction including one-on-one instruction with a teacher; with these supports he has adequately progressed through the curriculum. He does enjoy positive feedback; however, he needs "so much attention" that the teacher feels that she does not have enough time to interact with the other children.

Randy's mother describes him as socially typical. She admits that he can be "hyper" at school, but is firm that he is not hyper at home. She explains this discrepancy by the "fact that he is provoked by other children." Teachers describe Randy as somewhat immature and demanding of one-on-one attention in both adult and peer interactions. He has difficulty sharing and cooperating with others, and tends to be persistent with demands, showing difficulty discontinuing a (positive or negative) behavior that he desires.

Discussion Questions

1. What type of consultation would be used according to Caplan?
2. State explicitly the interpersonal and environmental issues. Is there an interaction and if so what does that mean?

3. Are there any consultee issues to consider? Anticipate how the teacher may experience the mother. Is this a problem? How will you know?
4. What issues need to be addressed with mother, teacher, and school?

MHC/Educator Example 2

Nick is a 16-year-old male diagnosed with high-functioning autism (HFA). His cognitive abilities are in the average range, and his language skills are relatively intact. He does show some pragmatics of speech difficulties, in which his reasoning is overly concrete. Moreover, his primary difficulties are in social interactions.

In school, Nick, who has an instructional aide to help with his social development, relies on his aide to initiate social interactions. He has made some progress in monitoring the facial expressions of his peers, trying to figure out their tone of voice and body language in an effort to clarify their intentions. However, almost all skills in this area are facilitated through support by the teacher and aide; he has made only limited progress toward independent functioning in this area.

Nick now lives with his maternal grandparents, Tom and Clair, after the recent death of his mother. Although he attends the same Local Affluent High school, he reports that he is dissatisfied with the new bus stop. Under stress, Nick tends to repeat movie phrases, and in the past has engaged in stereotypic hand flapping, a behavior that he has learned to suppress. Recently, however, his hand flapping has returned. He shows awareness of this stereotypic movement, acknowledges that it has increased, yet reports no dissatisfaction with its return.

Nick's grandparents report that his motor and verbal repetitions seem to be increasing in intensity, to the point of disrupting his sleep. They are concerned that they are not dealing with their own grief, and feel out of control. Nick's aide and teacher are not certain how to proceed with Nick. All of Nick's communication is exclusively related to the repetition of movie phrases; beyond that he will not talk with them. Specifically, they want to know whether they should address the symptoms of autism or address the loss and grief in order to facilitate a return to his social development in school.

Discussion Questions

1. What type of consultation would be used according to Caplan?
2. Whom would the consultant work with?
3. Are there any consultee or systems issues to consider? Anticipate how the teacher and aide may differ in their views regarding who holds the responsibility for helping Nick. How does this affect the nature of the consultative relationship?
4. What issues need to be addressed with teachers and Nick's grandparents?

MHC/Educator Example 3

Max is a 5-year-old who has attended the Young Kid Institute since age 3 after an evaluation that indicated Max exhibited some delays in personal, social, and adaptive development. His treatment plan indicates that Max is in need of behavior management and independent self-help skills. Over the course of treatment, Max has benefited from occupational, speech and language, and behavioral interventions. Specifically, Max is now able to dress himself, toilet independently, and better utilize language to express his needs. He continues to evidence deficits in communication, peer relationships, and negotiation skills, following multi-step directions, and using appropriate language rather than physical or verbal aggression to express himself.

Max is now approaching school age and requires transition services to maintain gains and clarify needs, so that he can benefit from the educational environment. His current teacher indicates Max has improved from his initial presentation as a boy who screamed and frequently used physical aggression to express himself, to a boy who is only occasionally physically aggressive, and is relying more on verbal aggression for expression. His teacher adds that Max is now more responsive to verbal praise, although he is quickly satiated by reinforcers. She reports that Max's academic progress is adequate, with learning at expected levels, and that he shows no difficulty in mastering concepts, despite difficulties with behavior and attention. A record review indicates that Max's hearing and vision is reported to be within normal limits.

Max's mother reports that her pregnancy was without complications. She continued using her Klonopin (.5 mg) prescription for a sleep disorder on the advice of her physician. She indicates that during delivery the umbilical cord was wrapped around Max's shoulder, resulting in a decreased fetal heart rate. Although the birth was completed without intervention, Max's mother is concerned that Max suffered a lack of oxygen during the delivery. Nevertheless, developmental milestones were within normal parameters until age one. At about age 1, Max was difficult to calm. At age 2 his parents noticed delays in language skill development, including the use of gesturing to express needs. Max's aggression toward others (e.g., hitting, biting, spitting, kicking) increased, and he became self-abusive and overly sensitive to loud noises and touch. Max's mother reports that he was diagnosed with sensory integration dysfunction at that time. These symptoms continued and worsened as he moved into his 3rd year of life.

He also began exhibiting behaviors of revenge and retribution for perceived inappropriate restraints on his behaviors by his parents, became actively defiant toward all adults, and began to blame inanimate objects (blanket) for his behavior. When Max was 3 years of age, his brother Ryan was born, an event that was reported to have exacerbated his symptomatology. For example, Max's behaviors became predatory in nature, such that he would wait for opportunities to: (1) Attack others, such as smothering his new brother with a pillow, pouring shampoo in Ryan's eyes and nose while he was in his crib, or hitting and pinching him, and trying to hang/strangle a 2-year-old niece, and (2) act cruelly toward animals, such as throwing a neighbor's guinea pig onto the floor and on another occasion down the stairs, as well as on separate occasions when he pulled his own cat's hair, poked it in the eye, and placed it in a bathtub of water.

At this time, Max was prescribed the medication Adderall for attention-related problems, but his parents report the medication "made him worse," whereby tantrums became full-blown rages, characterized by flailing arms and legs, pinching, and biting, and so forth. Max threatened to run away, burn or "break down" his house, not go to school, or to call his mother stupid and state that he hated her. Occasionally, Max would state that he was sorry and that he could not control himself. His parents report his apologies seemed qualitatively different than his earlier blaming of monsters and blankets for his destructive behavior.

Due to his extreme behavioral outbursts, sensitivity to touch and loud sounds, failure to progress adequately in speech and language skills, and toileting delays, Max was taken for several psychological and neurological evaluations. Currently, he has been diagnosed with attention deficit hyperactivity disorder (ADHD), hyperactive type, oppositional defiant disorder (ODD), and expressive language disorder.

The transition-to-kindergarten team met to discuss Max's educational needs. They have asked for your opinion on how to set up a successful classroom experience for Max, the other students, and the teacher. Max's parents remain supportive and work diligently to meet his needs.

Discussion Questions

1. What makes this case suitable for MHC?
2. State explicitly the interpersonal and environmental issues. Is there an interaction, and if so, what does that mean?
3. What type of consultation would be used according to Caplan?
4. How will you measure success?

MHC/Systems Example 1

Ms. Maria is a veteran science teacher at City High School. This year the faculty and staff have seen an increase in gang activity around the building. In October, a neighborhood youth, who did not attend the school, was reportedly shot in a gang-related incident. Tensions between rival gang members who attend the school have not seemed to cool and dissipate. Most concerning is the number of students who have brought weapons to school. In the last month, school custodians have located two weapons hidden just off school property. As a longtime employee, Ms. Maria heard from the building staff a detailed account of the incident, which did not match the official report given to the teachers.

Working with the principal, Ms. Maria, along with other teachers, requested an evaluation of the school's safety procedures. Administrators reported that they have followed all of the district requirements, and have judged the school as secure. Fearing for their safety, the teachers have requested that the district pay for stress management training. Additionally, a small group of teachers have asked that you help them in dealing with the stress.

Discussion Questions

1. What makes this case suitable for MHC?
2. Whom will Ms. Maria work with? How will the consultant consider her role?
3. Are there any consultee or systems issues to consider? Anticipate how the administrative need to convey the satisfactory implementation of safety requirements may exacerbate the

teachers' fears. How does this affect the nature of the consultative relationship?

4. Why is it important that the consultee retain responsibility for
implementing the interventions?

MHC/Systems Example 2

Cecelia is a 16-year-old female athlete who attends the 10th grade at
Conservative High School. Quiet in demeanor, she has a few close friends
who compete with her on the track team. Grades are important for her
to be eligible to participate in competitive races, so she studies often and
does not participate in many social activities. A group of girls have concerns that Cecelia may be a homosexual, and they find her disinterest in
dating evidence of her sexual orientation. Initial discussions about their
impressions of Cecelia have ballooned into obsessive gossiping and following of Cecelia to gather evidence to prove their suspicions.

A rumor is quickly spread and the male track coach begins to receive
phone calls from "concerned parents" about Cecelia being allowed to
change clothes in the locker room, where he cannot observe her behavior. Although teammates want to rally around Cecelia, they fear that
their sexuality will also be questioned, so the team remains silent. Cecelia's parents advise her to "weather the storm," thinking that this is a
high school prank and it will pass. Feeling unsupported, Cecelia begins
to worry excessively that people are talking about her. She starts to lose
weight and reports symptoms of distress to her coach and parents. Fearing that she will cry when she speaks, she withdraws from schoolmates.
Her close friends approach the coach for help. He approaches you.

Discussion Questions

1. What makes this case suitable for MHC?
2. What type of consultation would be used according to Caplan?
3. What communication styles would be important?
4. Why is it important that the consultee retain responsibility for
implementing the interventions?

MHC/Systems Example 3

Fredrick is a 12-year-old boy who has just transferred to the sixth grade
at Highly Competitive School from a small private school out of state.
Fredrick is diagnosed with a language-based learning disability. He has
received early intervention services for a speech delay, starting at age

4 and reading support was added to his speech services at the end of second grade due to his poor progress in reading. Although he continues to make adequate progress in his reading skills, Fredrick is very negative in his self-evaluation. He lists his inadequacies aloud, and emphasizes his continued articulation problem where his "r," "t," and "l" sounds make his speech difficult to understand. Frequently he refers to himself as "stupid," and his frustration is increasingly leading to anger outbursts. Concerned about his low self-esteem and possible symptoms of depression, because it runs in his family, his parents have approached the principal about addressing his social and emotional development.

After consulting with Frederick's speech and reading teachers, the principal reports that he is concerned that Fredrick won't get anything beneficial from meeting with the counselor or working with the emotional-support teacher. He notes that the counselor is only in the building 1 day a week and the emotional-support teacher wouldn't know what to do with Frederick. Also, although Fredrick struggles, the struggle ultimately pays off for him and he is learning. The principal is afraid if Frederick is coddled, there will be no expectations of Frederick at school.

Discussion Questions

1. What makes this case suitable for MHC, or is this a collaboration case?
2. Are there any consultee issues to consider? Anticipate how the parents may experience the principal. Is this a problem? How will you know? Anticipate how the teachers experience the principal. Is this a problem? How will you know?
3. How will responsibility be divided for implementing the interventions?
4. How will you measure success?

SUMMARY

In this chapter, information was presented regarding the use of MHC in school systems. First, MHC was defined, followed by information supporting the importance of increasing knowledge of how interpersonal psychodynamics and environmental factors affect children, teachers, and systems in schools. The underlying assumptions of MHC were reviewed, along with influences on communication patterns and processes of MHC. The stages of MHC, including relationship building, conducting assessment procedures, selecting interventions, and the follow-up evaluation of such interventions were all considered from both psycho-dynamic and environmental vantage points. Information regarding the roles and responsibilities of the consultant and consultee in MHC, and the specifics of school-based practice were reviewed. Finally, obstacles to the implementation of MHC were explored. In the next chapter, behavioral consultation will be reviewed, along with the presentation of case studies in which this approach may be practiced.

CHAPTER 3

Behavioral Consultation

INTRODUCTION

Educational and mental health support personnel typically use behavioral consultation (BC) to collaboratively work with a consultee (the classroom teacher), as a means to improve the functioning of individual students, who are the clients. Behavioral consultation is derived from the theory of behaviorism, in which psychological theorists such as Watson (1930) studied only what could be directly observed and measured—behavior—and in doing so discounting constructs such as mental states and cognitions, since they can only be inferred. More recently, Bandura (1977b, 1978), a neobehaviorist, developed a social cognitive theory model that has also been used in the development of BC techniques. Because the contribution of social cognitive theory is so extensive, however, a separate chapter (chapter 4) is devoted to the discussion of this theory in reference to social cognitive theory consultation.

Using the tenets of behaviorism, some of the first and most notable examples of BC were a behavior-operant model developed by Bergan (1977) and an updated model proposed by Bergan and Kratochwill (1990). In following a BC model, consultants use a structured and systematic problem-solving method that enables the consultant (the educational or mental health professional) and teacher (the consultee) to collectively identify, define, and analyze the problem, and evaluate the effectiveness of the intervention. Akin-Little, Little, and Delligatti (2004) propose that the behavioral method of consultation can be preventative in nature when mental health or educational specialists assist teachers in learning strategies to manage future behavior problems. However, BC is principally used to help a teacher cope with the immediate behavior problem of a child or adolescent.

Although there are several models of BC (Brown, Pryzwansky, & Schulte, 2001), Sheridan and Kratochwill's (1992) conjoint behavioral consultation (CBC) and Bergan and Kratochwill's (1990) behavioral-operant model are among the most recognized and empirically supported models of BC. Other models of BC include Tharp and Wetzel's (1969) model of consultation utilizing aspects of behavioral modification, Piersel's (1985), Russell's (1978), and Keller's (1981) consultative models based on operant theories of psychology, and Bandura's (1977b) social learning theory model.* Because there are similarities between CBC and BC, a brief explanation of CBC will be provided, after which the remainder of the chapter will be devoted to a review of the BC process.

Conjoint Behavioral Consultation

Conjoint behavioral consultation (CBC; Sheridan & Kratochwill, 1992) is a type of consultation that relies on both parents and teachers, as consultees, to address concerns related to a student, such as in the domains of academic, social, and behavioral functioning. Research indicates that CBC is an effective indirect treatment service for a variety of childhood and adolescent disorders, including anxiety disorders (Auster, Feeney-Kettler, & Kratochwill, 2006), academic problems (Galloway & Sheridan, 1994), social skills deficits (Colton & Sheridan, 1998), social withdrawal (Sheridan, Kratochwill, & Elliot, 1990), and irrational fears (Sheridan & Colton, 1994). The four main goals of CBC include: (1) sharing responsibility for solving the presenting problem, (2) improving communication between the child, family, and school, (3) obtaining broad, practical information that is related to the presenting problem, and (4) improving the skills of the child, family, and school personnel (Sheridan & Colton, 1994). Thus, the use of CBC in the school setting can positively impact students as they function in both classroom and home environments.

The problem-solving stages used in CBC are analogous to those used in BC. The first step in the consultative process is *conjoint problem identification*. During this step, the consultant and the consultee (e.g., parent[s], teacher) identify their concerns for the child, determine the environmental factors that contribute to the child's presenting problem, and define a goal. During this stage, progress-monitoring procedures

---

* This chapter is not meant to represent an exhaustive review of BC models. Readers are encouraged to consult the original writings of this topic for further understanding and more complete information.

are also identified. The second stage of the consultative process, *conjoint problem analysis*, typically occurs several weeks after the initial meeting. During this stage, baseline data on the presenting problem is collected and analyzed. A functional analysis of the child's behavior can also be conducted at this stage in order to better understand the factors that are contributing to or maintaining the behavior. The consultant and consultee revisit the previously identified goal during this time and make adjustments as needed, based on additional information collected during the functional behavioral analysis, observations, and so forth. Finally, an intervention plan is developed that includes specific procedures for implementation. The third stage, *conjoint treatment implementation*, is characterized by the implementation and monitoring of the intervention. The consultant can provide training to the consultee as needed. In the last stage of CBC, *conjoint treatment evaluation*, the consultant and consultee evaluate the effectiveness of the interventions, including whether the treatment goals have been attained (Gortmaker, Warnes, & Sheridan, 2004; Sheridan & Colton, 1994).

Behavioral Consultation

In 1977, Bergan initially presented his model of BC, which incorporated the use of operant learning theory. Then, in 1990, Bergan and Kratochwill broadened the scope of Bergan's original model of consultation to one that has become one of the most well known and empirically supported. This model is grounded in behavioral psychological principles, such as systematic problem solving and the use of behavioral techniques in the consultative process, with the behavioral consultant using such techniques throughout the consultative process.

Bergan and Kratochwill (1990) define consultation as an indirect problem-solving process between consultant and consultee. In this model, the consultant uses psychological principles relevant to the presenting problem in his or her communication, while employing verbal structuring techniques that increase the possibility of the consultee accepting intervention recommendations proposed by the consultant. The consultant's role is structured and directive in nature, while the consultee is expected to take an active role in describing the problem and ultimately implementing the intervention to encourage behavior change in the client(s). This aspect of the model is somewhat controversial in nature because the consultant uses verbal structuring techniques to guide and reinforce the consultee in accepting the consultant's suggestions and interventions. Although the consultant's techniques may be viewed as manipulative, from the outset of the consultative relationship the consultant's intent to influence the consultee's compliance is made very clear (Brown et al., 2001).

Bergan and Kratochwill (1990) emphasize the importance of communication in the consultative relationship. The consultant's main goal in the consultative process is to elicit pertinent information regarding the presenting problem. Further, the consultant is attentive to the consultee's expression of the problem, guiding the process as necessary. The consultant obtains historical information from the consultee by structuring questions related to seven subcategories including: (1) background environment, (2) setting in which the behavior occurs, (3) parameters of the behavior, (4) special characteristics of the client, (5) nature of the observations made, (6) previous intervention plans, and (7) types of additional data that may be needed to solve the problem. This information is used to better understand the client's current functioning, as well as the interplay between the problem and environmental variables.

The first subcategory, *background environment*, emphasizes distant or remote variables that may affect the presenting problem of the client, such as a question directed to a teacher about a student's attendance record from 2 years ago. In contrast, the *setting in which the behavior occurs* subcategory taps into the immediate environmental variables that affect the problem behavior. During this stage the consultant analyzes the possible antecedents and consequences of the problem behavior by asking the consultee about the events that lead to the problem and the resulting effects (Bergan & Kratochwill (1990).

The *parameters of the behavior* subcategory expands the description of the presenting problem by defining the behavior in descriptive terms. This includes a discussion of the incidence of the behavior, the duration of the behavior, the intensity of the behavior, and when the behavior occurs. The consultant may also gather information regarding the antecedents and consequences of the behavior during this time. Additionally, the consultant asks questions of the consultee regarding the pattern of the behavior, such as "When was the problem first noticed?" The *special characteristics of the client* subcategory includes the consultant asking the consultee specific questions regarding the client's functioning, such as history of learning disabilities, medical concerns, or emotional/ behavior disorders, for example (Bergan & Kratochwill (1990).

Another aspect of consultant–consultee verbal communication includes the subcategory of the *nature of the observations made*. The consultee's observations assist the consultant in identifying the problem. Consultees such as teachers can conduct structured or unstructured observations of the student (client) in the classroom, lunchroom, or playground, in addition to other relevant settings, which will increase the ability of the consultee to identify and describe the presenting problem. During the *previous intervention plans* subcategory, the consultant finds out what the consultee has tried up to that point in time, suggesting other interventions that might work, and eliciting answers regarding intervention plans the consultee has not yet attempted. At the end of this process, the consultant and consultee must agree on a specific intervention plan. In order to accomplish this, the consultant typically uses a plan validation elicitor such as, "Can we agree that the best approach to dealing with this concern is a behavioral contract?" The final subcategory of verbalizations is *types of additional data that may be needed to solve the problem.* During this final step, the consultant garners any supplementary information related to the problem (Bergan & Kratochwill (1990).

The BC process is characterized by structured interactions between the consultant and the consultee. In addition to the aforementioned consultant–consultee verbal interactions, Bergan and Kratochwill (1990) discuss the consultant's verbal processes of specification, evaluation, inferences, summarization, and validation during the consultative process. These verbal processes are used within each of the seven subcategories presented previously. The process of *specification* includes the consultee offering increasingly specific information regarding the client's problem behavior. Initially, the consultant uses a line of general questioning and then switches to very specific questions. The verbal process of specification aims to determine the distant and immediate environmental variables that contribute to the problem, define the problem in objective terms, and to gain agreement between the consultant and consultee on an intervention plan.

During the *evaluation process*, the consultant determines the consultee's beliefs, opinions, and feelings toward the client. For example, this may include whether a teacher enjoys having the student in the classroom despite his or her difficulties in maintaining attention. In addition, the consultant is able to give positive and negative feedback to the consultee regarding his or her implementation of the intervention during this time (Bergan & Kratochwill (1990).

The *inferences process* involves generalizing from the data. According to Bergan and Kratochwill (1990), the consultant and consultee use particular phrases when making inferences, including "I assume," "I believe," and "I feel." These statements amalgamate data while offering relevant information about the client's functioning. The verbal process of *summarization* allows the consultant or consultee to summarize all of the information gathered through the verbal exchanges between them. Finally, the verbal process of *validation* occurs when the consultant and consultee agree on the nature of the problem. The consultant and consultee must reach a consensus regarding the nature of the presenting problem, the goals, and the intervention strategies that will be used.

Bergan and Kratochwill (1990) discuss the use of consultant leads during the consultative process. The consultant leads the consultative process by using elicitors and emitters. *Elicitors* draw information from the consultee using open-ended or close-ended statements or questions. For example, the consultant may phrase statements or questions beginning with, "Tell me more about" or ask "What is the . . ." *Emitters*, commonly used in psychotherapy, are used to summarize content or affirm the consultee's feelings. Elicitors and emitters are used in conjunction with the verbal processes in order to effectively gather and organize the data, as well as structure an appropriate intervention plan. It should be noted that research indicates that educational specialists or mental health support personnel who use controlling verbalizations with teachers are less likely to be favorably perceived than consultants who use emitters, elicitors, and support (Hughes & DeForest, 1993). Thus, the consultant must maintain a balance of assertiveness and supportiveness in a BC model.

General Consultation Processes

Most behavioral models of consultation characterize the stages of consultation in a problem-solving framework that outlines very specific steps involved in the process. The stages of consultation are followed in a linear order, but may not occur in such a rigid fashion. Instead, the consultant and consultee may revisit one stage at a later time without damaging the integrity of the relationship or intervention outcomes (Brown et al., 2001).

Formal Entry

The first stage of consultation involves formal entry into the organization. For most school-based educational or mental health specialists employed by a school district, entering a classroom or school building occurs without difficulty because they are internal to the organization. External consultants, who are unfamiliar to the organization, may go through specific steps of formal entry before beginning the consultative process. Although consultees informally accept internal consultants, such as school counselors, school psychologists, and social workers, researchers suggest that consultants nonetheless strive to explain the details of the consultative process in a formal meeting. Suggested areas of discussion include the goals of consultation, confidentiality and its limits, suggested timeframes for service, times the consultant will be available, and how to request consultative services, among others (Brown et al., 2001).

Establishing an Effective Relationship

One of the most important steps in the consultative process is establishing a relationship with the consultee. The nature of the consultative relationship can be characterized as a "cooperative partnership," according to Zins and Erchul (2002, p. 627), in which both parties understand the roles and responsibilities within the relationship, and are actively pursuing a common goal for the student to achieve. The consulting mental health or educational professional and teacher then work together in a nonhierarchical relationship that is characterized by equality rather than a power differential. Thus, both the consultant and consultee offer unique perspectives regarding the presenting problem. Educational or mental health specialists may draw on expertise in psychological theory and research-based academic interventions, while the teacher might offer information regarding his or her teaching style, behavior management techniques, and classroom observations that assist in determining and defining the presenting problem.

In order for a successful partnership to occur between consultant and consultee, as well as for successful outcomes, the consultee must have a positive perception of his or her role in the consultative process. In an attempt to foster such a perception, the consultant takes an active lead in establishing a nonhierarchical relationship with the consultee, so that the consultee feels comfortable in expressing his or her concerns without the fear of judgment. When the consultee perceives himself or herself as being an active participant in the consultative process, then he or she will be more effective in implementing the proposed interventions and feel a sense of ownership in the process (Brown et al., 2001). The consultant can assist in forming the relationship by being nonjudgmental in his or her reactions to the consultee's statements or actions.

The responsibilities of the consultees include providing contextual information about the presenting problem and assisting in determining appropriate interventions (Zins & Erchul, 2002). Consultants, on the other hand, guide the problem-solving process, while the consultee provides the content or relevant information. The consultant and consultee engage in a cooperative relationship that is characterized by common goals, such as improving a student's reading comprehension. However, Zins and Erchul (2002) caution against denying or rejecting the unique expertise of each individual in the consultative relationship. Although the consultative relationship is cooperative, these researchers argue that educational specialists or mental health professionals must recognize and use their own specialized knowledge in the consultative process, while also recognizing the consultee's own skills and special contribution to the relationship and course of action. Similarly, researchers have argued that consultants must maintain control over the process, taking the lead when necessary (Busse, Kratochwill, & Elliott, 1999; Zins & Erchul, 2002). Thus, consultants must appropriately use both collaborative and directive techniques when working with consultees.

In a study of school counselors' consultative behaviors, it was found that during the initial stage of contact, certain response modes tended to occur more frequently, including paraphrasing, providing information, and closed questioning, in contrast to more complex behaviors, such as interpretation, confrontation, and self-disclosure (Lin, Kelly, & Nelson, 1996). As consultation continued, nearly half of the responses by counselors included providing information. The authors concluded that the consultative and counseling practices are quite similar, a finding earlier reported by Schmidt and Osbourne (1981), and suggest that more formal training in consultation is needed in order for consultants to differentiate these skills (Lin et al., 1996).

Consultants can engage the consultee and ultimately form a successful consultative relationship by using both verbal and nonverbal cues to indicate their respect and interest. For example, Egan (1994) describes specific nonverbal techniques that consultants can use to indicate warmth, empathy, and genuine respect, which can easily be recalled using the acronym SOLER: The letter S stands for facing the other person *squarely*, the letter O stands for using an *open* posture toward the consultee, the letter L stands for *leaning* toward the person, the letter E stands for maintaining good *eye contact*, and the letter R stands for maintaining a *relaxed* posture that does not appear overly stiff.

Brown and colleagues (2001) state that consultants may indicate personal respect, warmth, and empathy through verbalizations as well. Consultants can convey empathic understanding by restating the verbalizations of the consultee. Perhaps more importantly, the consultant should restate and affectively confirm the consultee's statements without judgment. The establishment of an effective and successful consultative relationship is integral to positive outcomes and the possibility that the consultee will seek out the consultant for assistance in the future. Although consultants must convey verbal and nonverbal cues of empathy, respect, and warmth, consultants must also use concreteness in order to accurately understand the presenting problem. Gazda (1973) emphasizes the importance of the consultant eliciting specific rather than vague, abstract descriptions of the consultee's presenting problem.

Other characteristics of the consultative relationship include reciprocal interactions. The consultant, consultee, and client all reciprocally influence each other according to Bandura's model of *reciprocal determinism* (Bandura, 1977b). Consultants influence the consultee by guiding the consultative process through interviewing, and consultees might influence consultants by stating their role, as well as the role of the student and the setting. It is important, then, to consider the behavioral, personal, and environmental factors that contribute to the relationship, rather than merely examining any one single factor.

Assessment

During the assessment stage of the consultative process, consultee characteristics, the immediate and larger environment, and characteristics of the client are examined with regard to the presenting problem. These three domains influence the definition and analysis of the problem behavior (Brown et al., 2001). Consultees will have varying opinions and perspectives of the problem. For instance, teachers may view the problem as largely child based, whereas educational and mental health professionals, such as school psychologists, typically consider the variables within the larger environment, such as the family (Athanasiou, Geil, Hazel, & Copeland, 2002). These differences in the perception of the variables that may affect the child's behavior or academic progress will affect the selection of later interventions and the perceived efficacy of the intervention. It is important, then, to consider these differences at the outset of the consultative process, so that the consultant and consultee can better understand how their unique perspectives of the problem behavior might affect their selection of interventions.

Defining the Problem and Setting Goals

After assessing client, consultee, and environmental characteristics, the nature of the presenting problem becomes more apparent. In Tables 3.1 and 3.2, a Problem Identification Interview Form and Data Sheet are

Table 3.1 Problem Identification Interview (PII) for BC

Client's name: _____ Sex: _____

Address: _____

_____

School: _____ Grade: _____

Consultant: _____

Consultee: _____

	Year	Month	Day
Date of Assessment:	_____	_____	_____
Birthdate:	_____	_____	_____
Age:	_____	_____	_____

Consultant note: The purposes of the PII are to

· Define the problem(s) in behavioral terms.

· Provide a tentative identification of the behavior in terms of antecedent, situation, and consequent conditions.

· Provide a tentative strength of the behavior (e.g., how often or how severe).

· Establish a procedure for the collection of baseline data in terms of the sampling plan and what behavior is to be recorded, who is to record it, and how it is to be recorded.

The consultant should question and/or comment in the following areas:

1. Opening salutation

2. General statement to introduce discussion (e.g., "Describe Diane's hyperactive behavior," or "Let's see, you referred Johnny because of poor self-concept, lack of progress, and rebellious behavior. Which of these do you want to start with? Describe Johnny's rebellion (poor self-concept or lack of progress in the classroom").

Record responses: _____

_____

_____

_____

_____

3. Behavior specification (e.g., "What does Charles do when he is hyperactive?" or "What does Mary do when she is disrespectful?" A precise description of the behavior of concern to the consultee or client, e.g., "What does _____ do?")

a. Specify examples: _____

_____

Important: Ask for as many examples of the problem behavior as possible.

Table 3.1 (Continued)

b. Specify priorities: _____

_____

_____

_____

_____

Important: After eliciting all the examples that the consultee or client can give, ask which behavior is causing the most difficulty and establish a priority.

(*Note:* To help prioritize problems, ask the consultee or client, "On a scale of 0 to 10, where 0 = no problem and 10 = severe problem, how severe is the problem for you?")

4. Behavior setting (a precise description of the settings in which the problem behaviors occur, e.g., "Where does _____ do this?")

a. Specify examples (e.g., home, where in home): _____

_____

_____

_____

_____

Important: Ask for as many examples of settings as possible.

b. Specify priorities: _____

_____

_____

_____

_____

Important: After eliciting the examples that the consultee or client can give, ask which setting is causing the most difficulty and establish priorities.

(*Note:* Settings may be ranked in the same manner as behaviors.)

5. Identify antecedents: What happens right before the problem behavior occurs? (e.g., "What happens before Mary makes an obscene gesture to the rest of the class?" or "What happens before George begins to hit other children?")

Record responses: _____

_____

6. Sequential conditions analysis: When during the day does the behavior occur and/or what is the pattern of antecedent–consequent conditions across several occurrences of the problem behavior? (e.g., "When does Mary ...? Who is Mary with ...? What is Mary supposed to be doing when ...?")

Table 3.1 (Continued)

Record responses: _____
_____
_____
_____
_____

7. Identify consequent conditions: What happens after the problem behavior has occurred? (e.g., "What happens after Mary . . .?" or "What do the other students do when Charles climbs on the radiator?" or "What do you do when George hits other children?")

Record responses: _____
_____
_____
_____
_____

8. Summarize and validate antecedent, consequent, and sequential conditions (e.g., "You've said that you and Timmy argue after you have asked him to do something, and he refused. The argument continues as long as you try to talk to him. Is that correct?" or "You've said that at bedtime you tell Ava that it is time for bed, and that she doesn't answer you. You tell her again, and she says, 'Oh, Mom.' You remind her a third time, and she asks for 10 more minutes. You get mad, threaten to tell her father, and take her physically down to her room. She leaves her room approximately twice, asks for a drink of water, and finally falls asleep. Is that how it goes?")

Record responses: _____
_____
_____
_____
_____

9. Behavior strength

a. *Frequency:* How often a behavior occurs (e.g., "How often does Kevin have tantrums?")

b. *Duration*: Length of time that a behavior occurs (e.g., "How long do Craig's tantrums last?)

Record responses: _____
_____
_____
_____
_____

Table 3.1 (Continued)

10. Summarize and validate behavior and behavior strength:

a. "You have said that Jason makes you angry and upset by wetting his bed."

b. "That he wets his bed approximately four times a week."

c. "Is that right?"

Record responses: _____

_____

_____

_____

11. Tentative definition of goal—question consultee (e.g., "How often would Patrick have to turn in his work to get along okay?" or "How frequently could Charles leave his seat without causing problems?")

Record responses: _____

_____

_____

_____

12. Assets question: Determine what the student is good at (e.g., "Is there something that Mary does well?")

Record responses: _____

_____

_____

_____

13. Question about approach to teaching or existing procedures (e.g., "How long are Charles and the other students doing seat work problems?" or "What kind of . . .?")

Record responses: _____

_____

_____

_____

14. Summarization statement and validation (e.g., "Let's see, the main problem is that Charles gets out of his seat and runs around the room during independent work assignments. He does this about four times each day. Is that right?")

Table 3.1 (Continued)

Record responses: _____

_____

_____

_____

15. Directional statement to provide rationale for data recording (e.g., "We need some record of Sarah's completion of homework assignments, how often assignments are completed, what assignments are completed, and so on. This record will help us to determine how frequently the behavior is occurring, and it may give us some clues to the nature of the problem. Also, the record will help us decide whether any plan we initiate has been effective.")

Record responses: _____

_____

_____

_____

16. Discuss data collection procedures. Data may be collected in four ways:

a. *Real-time recording*

    Advantages:

        Provides unbiased estimates of frequency and duration.

        Data are capable of complex analyses such as conditional probability analysis.

        Data are susceptible to sophisticated readability analysis.

    Disadvantages:

        Demanding task for observers.

        May require costly equipment.

        Requires that response have clearly distinguishable beginnings and ends.

b. *Event or duration recording*

    Advantages:

        Measures are of a fundamental response characteristic (i.e., frequency or duration).

        Can be used by participant-observers (e.g., parents or teachers) with low rate responses.

    Disadvantages:

        Requires responses to have clearly distinguishable beginnings and ends.

        Unless responses are located in real time (e.g., by dividing a session into brief recording intervals), some forms of reliability assessment may be impossible.

Table 3.1 (Continued)

May be difficult with multiple behaviors unless mechanical aids are available.

c. *Momentary time samples*

Advantages:

Response duration of primary interest.

Time saving and convenient.

Useful with multiple behaviors and/or children.

Applicable to responses without clear beginnings or ends.

Disadvantages:

Unless samples are taken frequently, continuity of behavior may be lost.

May miss most occurrences of brief, rare responses.

d. *Interval recording*

Advantages:

Sensitive to both response frequency and response duration.

Applicable to a wide range of responses.

Facilitates observer training and reliability assessments.

Applicable to responses without clearly distinguishable beginnings and ends.

Disadvantages:

Confounds frequency and duration.

May under- or overestimate response frequency and duration.

Record responses: _____

_____

_____

_____

_____

17. Summarize and validate recording procedures (e.g., "We have agreed that you will record the amount of time that Doug's tantrums last by recording the start and stop times. You will do this for 3 days and you will use this form. You will also record what happens before the behavior occurs and what you do after it has occurred. Is this okay with you?")

Table 3.1 (Continued)

Record responses: _____

_____

_____

_____

_____

18. Establish a date to begin data collection.

Record responses: _____

_____

_____

_____

_____

19. Establish date of next appointment.

      Record response: Date _____

                        Day _____

                        Time _____

                        Place _____

20. Closing salutation.

Source: (From *Behavioral Consultation in Applied Settings: An Individual Guide,* by T. R. Kratochwill & J. R Bergan, 1990, pp. 97–106.) New York: Routledge (formerly Plenum Press) with kind permission from Springer Science and Business Media.

provided, respectively. Research suggests that the problem-definition stage is the most important in the consultative process and the most predictive of later outcomes (Bergan & Tombari, 1976). In order to accurately define the problem, the consultant and consultee should spend time assessing the factors (environmental characteristics, consultee characteristics, and client characteristics) that may be related to the presenting problem. After a thorough assessment of these factors, the problem is defined in specific behavioral terms with accompanying objectives (Brown et al., 2001; Zins & Erchul, 2002). During this time, baseline data may be collected regarding the frequency, duration, and intensity of the problem. In addition, antecedents of the behavior and consequences that maintain the behavior are identified.

Table 3.2 Problem Identification Interview Data Sheet (PIIDS) for BC

Date: _____

Observer: _____

Client: _____

Reliability: _____

Consultee: _____

Observer: _____

Consultant: _____ Session #: _____

Interview Objective:	Occurrence:	Response:
1. Opening salutation		
2. General statement		
3. Behavior specification		
a. Specify examples		
b. Specify priorities		
4. Behavior setting		
a. Specify examples		
b. Specify priorities		
5. Identify antecedents		
6. Identify sequential conditions		
7. Identify consequences		
8. Summarize and validate		
9. Behavior strength		
10. Summarize and validate		
11. Tentative definition of goal		
12. Assets question		
13. Question about existing procedures		
14. Summarize and validate		
15. Directional statement about data recording		
16. Data collection procedures		
17. Summarize and validate		
18. Date to begin data collection		
19. Establish date of next appointment		
20. Closing salutation		

Note: From *Behavioral Consultation in Applied Settings: An Individual Guide*, by T. R. Kratochwill & J. R Bergan, 1990, pp. 107–108. New York: Routledge (formerly Plenum Press) with kind permission from Springer Science and Business Media.

Table 3.3 Intervention Rating Profile for Consultee and Client

The purpose of this questionnaire is to obtain information that will aid in the selection of classroom interventions. These interventions will be used by teachers of children with behavior problems. Please circle the number that best describes your agreement or disagreement with each statement.

1. This would be an acceptable intervention for the child's problem behavior.   1 2 3 4 5 6
2. Most teachers would find this intervention appropriate for behavior   1 2 3 4 5 6
    problems in addition to the one described.
3. This intervention should prove effective in changing the child's problem   1 2 3 4 5 6
    behavior.
4. I would suggest the use of this intervention to other teachers.   1 2 3 4 5 6
5. The child's behavior problem is severe enough to warrant use of this   1 2 3 4 5 6
    intervention.
6. Most teachers would find this intervention suitable for the behavior   1 2 3 4 5 6
    problem described.
7. I would be willing to use this intervention in the classroom setting.   1 2 3 4 5 6
8. This intervention would *not* result in negative side-effects for the child.   1 2 3 4 5 6
9. This intervention would be appropriate for a variety of children.   1 2 3 4 5 6
10. This intervention is consistent with those I have used in classroom settings.   1 2 3 4 5 6
11. The intervention was a fair way to handle the child's problems.   1 2 3 4 5 6
12. This intervention is reasonable for the behavior problem described.   1 2 3 4 5 6
13. I liked the procedures used in this intervention.   1 2 3 4 5 6
14. This intervention was a good way to handle the child's behavior problem   1 2 3 4 5 6
15. Overall, this intervention would be beneficial for the child.   1 2 3 4 5 6

Source: Martens, B. K. & Witt, J. C. (1982). Intervention Rating Profile for Consultee and Client. From Martens, B. K., Witt, J. C., Elliot, S. N., & Darveaux, D. X. (1985). Teacher judgments concerning the acceptability of school based interventions. *Professional Psychology: Research and Practice, 16*, p. 193.

Intervention or Strategy Selection

When selecting interventions, it is important to keep in mind that there are several avenues through which a problem may be solved. This is referred to as *equifinality* (Katz & Kahn, 1978). Thus, during this stage, the consultant and consultee brainstorm possible interventions that may be effective in targeting the problem. It is also important to consider strategy integrity (Reynolds, Gutkin, Elliot, & Witt, 1984) and strategy acceptability (Witt, Elliot, & Martens, 1984) when exploring possible interventions (see Table 3.3). *Strategy integrity* is the extent to which interventions can be changed or adapted without impacting their effectiveness. When selecting alternative interventions, the consultant should consider the skills of the consultee, as well as the ease with which they are able to implement intervention strategies (Brown et al., 2001). *Strategy acceptability* is the extent to which the consultee believes that the intervention strategy is acceptable. Research suggests that acceptability of an intervention is associated with whether the intervention is actually implemented (Reimers, Wacker, & Koeppl, 1987). Further, consultees tend to prefer interventions that are time-efficient, nonintrusive, and viewed as effective (Elliot, 1988).

Implementation

During the implementation stage of the consultative process, it is helpful to review the roles and responsibilities of the participants in implementing the intervention. Other issues to be covered during this stage include identifying potential reinforcers, designating the time and day the intervention should be implemented, and producing a written outline delineating each person's responsibilities. During the actual implementation of the intervention, consultants and consultees should be in frequent contact to ensure that it is done accurately, as well as to address any difficulties or concerns that may arise during the implementation process (Brown et al., 2001; Zins & Erchul, 2002).

Evaluation

During and after the implementation of the intervention, the effectiveness of the intervention must be determined. The evaluation of the intervention occurs formatively and summatively. Formative evaluation occurs during the intervention implementation, while summative evaluation occurs after the consultation ceases. Formative evaluation during the intervention implementation is useful because the plan can be modified or adapted according to the needs of the consultee. Thus, if an intervention is not working as expected, the consultant and consultee can agree upon a new method of intervention or, if necessary, return to an earlier stage in the consultative process, such as the intervention selection stage. Specific to consultation in the schools, formative evaluation should be relatively effortless for teachers. Typical procedures used in formative evaluation include single-subject methodologies, such as single phase, reversal, or multiple baseline designs (Zins & Erchul, 2002). In contrast to formative evaluation, summative evaluation is a formal process whereby the effectiveness of the intervention is evaluated (Brown et al., 2001).

Additionally, issues of intervention generalization, fading, and follow-up should be addressed. After the client has achieved positive behavior gains, the generalization of the behavior to other settings can be considered. Generalization occurs when the client applies the knowledge or behavior learned in one setting to other settings. According to researchers, the factors involved in maintaining positive behavior gains are not well understood (Zins & Erchul, 2002). However, researchers have identified ways to plan for generalization when developing interventions, including identifying reinforcers in the naturally occurring environment that maintain the behavior, especially those that encourage independence in the client, such as self-monitoring or self-management (Meichenbaum & Turk, 1987).

The fading of the reinforcement strategies should also be considered during the evaluation phase of the consultative process. Fading occurs when artificial or external reinforcers are gradually removed and replaced by naturally occurring reinforcers in the environment. In order to promote positive behavior maintenance, external reinforcers are gradually removed, rather than being removed all at once, since extinction of the desired behaviors may occur when external reinforcers are suddenly removed. Examples of fading in the school setting may include increasing the length of time between when the desired behavior is evidenced and the time a child earns a reward, or increasing the difficulty of earning a reward. If the client's behavior regresses during the fading process, the previous reinforcement contingencies should be reinstated until the behavior returns to previous levels. Finally, the consultant should follow up with the consultee to ensure that the interventions are being implemented accurately. Follow-up procedures include observations of the intervention implementation, as well as functional assessments when intervention goals are not yet attained (Zins & Erchul, 2002).

Termination

Procedures for terminating the consultative relationship should be discussed at the outset of the consultative process. Termination typically occurs when the consultant and consultee agree that the client has attained the established goals or the consultee has demonstrated self-sufficiency in the implementation of the intervention. Throughout the consultative process, the consultant ensures that the consultee becomes competent in delivering the interventions independently. In this way, the consultee becomes more independent and less reliant on the consultant. Here, the termination of the relationship may be signified by the ability of the consultee to implement the interventions independently. As previously mentioned, consultants should discuss the process of termination at the beginning of the consultative process so that consultees understand the boundaries and limits of the relationship. Another suggested guideline is that consultants may allow the consultee a short period of time to implement the interventions without the consultant's input. Finally, at the termination of the consultative process, the consultant may provide a report summarizing the results of the intervention, as well as garner feedback from the consultee regarding the consultative process. This process serves as a signal to the consultee that the end of the relationship is occurring or will soon occur (Dougherty, Tack, Fullam, & Hammer, 1996). However, researchers have also identified specific reasons for an early termination of the consultative relationship. Early termination may be necessary when consultation has not advanced as expected (Gallessich, 1982), or when a serious issue arises that requires an immediate intervention (Caplan, 1970).

Although termination is an important aspect of consultation, it is less emphasized in the literature when compared to the available research on the entry process. In a review of the disengagement literature, Dougherty et al. (1996) discuss several important characteristics of the disengagement process that have yet to be explored. These include an examination of the emotional and psychological underpinnings of the disengagement process, such as the relationship between the consultant and consultee. The researchers assert that although a strong relationship in the beginning typically yields fruitful results, it may also contribute to a difficult consultant–consultee separation. Other areas in need of research include such variables as the length of the consultative relationship, the type of consultant (i.e., internal vs. external), and consultant roles (i.e., process vs. content expert).

Each step in the consultative process, from entry to disengagement, is integral to successful outcomes, treatment integrity, and consultee satisfaction. The relationship between consultant and consultee is emphasized throughout the process, and this relationship is one of the most important aspects of the entire process. Although successful outcomes may not consistently occur with a good relationship, the consultee will be more likely to seek the consultant for assistance in the future.

Behavioral Consultative Processes

Similar to other consultation models, the four steps in the BC process include problem identification, problem analysis, plan implementation, and evaluation. The consultant and consultee discuss the desired outcomes or changes resulting from the proposed interventions, as well as when and where the intervention will occur and who implements the intervention. They will also set an expected date by which the behaviors should have changed as a result of the proposed intervention. What follows is a description of the steps unique to the BC process.

During the *problem identification step*, the consultant draws upon test data, observations, records, and interviews, for example, to glean information about the client and establish the objectives of consultation. Thus, the problem identification step in the consultative process allows the consultant to better understand the needs of the consultee with respect to the client (Bergan & Kratochwill, 1990). During this stage the consultant and consultee work together to clarify the presenting problem. Because the definition of the problem will lead to interventions, it is important that the definition of the problem behavior is succinct and presented in measurable, objective terms.

Consultees sometimes have difficulty describing the problem in clear and specific terms and often use vague or nonspecific terms to describe the behavior. Thus, during the initial problem identification stage, the consultant must assist the consultee in accurately describing the behavior in measurable terms (Gutkin & Curtis, 1999). Through the verbal communication process, the consultant can use elicitors, emitters, paraphrasing, and summarizing to improve problem identification. Further, the consultant and consultee should agree upon the presenting problem behavior so that both are able to record the behavior as necessary. For example, the target behavior that is described as a classroom disruption may be redefined as "the number of times the student speaks without raising his or her hand during class or without being called upon by the teacher." In this way, the target behavior is specific and easily measured.

During the second step of the consultative process, *problem analysis,* the consultant seeks to identify the variables in the environment and in the client that are contributing to the maintenance of the problem. One of the first steps of this stage is to collect baseline data on the target behavior. When analyzing the problem behavior, the consultant looks at the antecedents and consequences of the behavior over time. Much of this information is gathered through observations of the client in his or her environment (Zins & Erchul, 2002).

Bergan and Kratochwill (1990) also discuss the importance of identifying the client's skill deficits during the problem-analysis stage. Skill deficits may be identified through observations, examination of work samples, and interviews. Identifying skill deficits allows the consultant to plan appropriate interventions later that assist in incrementally increasing the client's skills. For example, a child with poor social skills who has difficulty initiating conversations with peers may need to first learn common ways to introduce topics of conversation. As a part of the problem-analysis stage, consultants can also encourage the consultee to identify his or her strengths and other available supports, which may be used as part of the intervention (Zins & Erchul, 2002).

After the target problem has been identified and analyzed, the consultant and consultee should brainstorm possible interventions in order to prepare for *plan implementation.* Zins and Erchul (2002) set forth principles to consider when consultants and consultees select interventions in the school setting, including the following:

1. Positive intervention approaches should be developed before the use of behavior reduction techniques unless the behavior is extreme.
2. Choose interventions that are the least intrusive and complex. Modifying variables in the child's environment may be easier and less intrusive than helping the client to learn a new skill or behavior.
3. When clients must learn new skills, ensure that the strategies complement existing routines as much as possible.
4. Seek additional resources, such as tutoring or community resources, which may be used if the intervention is not effective in altering the client's behavior.
5. Consultants should provide ongoing support and reinforcement to consultees because they are learning new ways to interact with the client.
6. Choose interventions that are time-efficient, nonintrusive, and perceived to be effective by consultees.
7. Change should be targeted at the highest level of the organization possible.

Regarding the *implementation stage* of the consultative process, Bergan and Kratochwill (1990) discuss several integral components. They assert that both the consultant and consultee should agree upon the nature of the problem, complete the skills analysis, design a plan, and arrange for a follow-up session with the consultee. When designing a plan, these researchers discuss the following steps: (1) establish objectives, (2) select interventions, (3) consider any barriers to implementation of the intervention, and (4) select appropriate assessments. The consultee is expected to carry out the intervention plan during the implementation stage, although the consultant should remain available for monitoring and additional suggestions and/or revisions of the plan. Specifically, the consultant takes the lead in teaching the consultee behavioral skills of reinforcement or modeling, as well as teaching the consultee how to conduct observations. An important part of this stage is formative evaluation, in which the progress of the client is continually monitored to ensure that he or she is benefiting from the proposed intervention plan.

Finally, the *evaluation stage* is characterized by determining the effectiveness of the intervention, generalization, fading, and follow-up. The information shared between the consultant and consultee during this time include whether the goals of the intervention have been met by the client, the overall effectiveness of the plan, and a determination of whether the consultant–consultee relationship can be safely terminated (Bergan & Kratochwill, 1990). In the case of unsuccessful interventions, a new plan may need to be made and implemented.

When evaluating intervention effectiveness, the same procedures used during the baseline data collection phase can be replicated. The evaluation plan should be devised prior to intervention implementation. The effectiveness of the intervention should also be evaluated in order to ensure treatment integrity and to identify potential side effects. When evaluating intervention effectiveness, there are two possible outcomes. One is that the intervention resulted in a successful attainment of treatment goals, and the process can then shift to follow-up monitoring, generalization, and fading. On the other hand, the intervention may have not resulted in a change or successful outcome. In this case, the consultant and consultee may have to repeat the problem-solving process to reach alternative treatment intervention options (Zins & Erchul, 2002).

Once the effectiveness of the intervention has been evaluated, generalization of the intervention, follow-up, and fading of the reinforcement contingencies can be implemented. According to researchers, the factors that help to maintain positive behavior gains are not well understood (Zins & Erchul, 2002). However, researchers have identified ways to plan for generalization when developing interventions, including identifying reinforcers in the naturally occurring environment that maintain the behavior, especially those that encourage independence in the client, such as self-monitoring or self-management (Meichenbaum & Turk, 1987).

Consultant Roles

Researchers have delineated various roles of consultants, acknowledging that consultants usually perform more than one role. In some instances, consultants may act as experts and in others as organizers. In synthesizing the literature on the roles of consultants, Brown et al. (2001) described seven basic roles of consultants, including process observer, process collaborator, content collaborator, content/process collaborator, process expert, content expert, and content/process expert. They assert that the roles can be differentiated based on their relationship to process/content or intrusiveness. Process/content consultation emphasizes joint problem solving and decision making in the consultative relationship. The consultant may observe the consultee's methods of practice, while assisting the consultee in identifying his or her own strengths and weaknesses in regard to a problem. In this way, the consultant engages in consultation in a passive manner. Intrusiveness in consultation refers to the level of intrusion the consultant uses in the process. Further, in this role, consultants may introduce their own values into consultation to make changes. Although there are several consultant roles, they will vary based on the model of consultation used and may be affected by the consultant's training and the expectations of the consultee (Brown et al., 2001).

Consultee Characteristics

Although often overlooked as a variable in the consultative process, characteristics of the consultee are also important to consider when selecting a consultative approach. Several consultee characteristics that influence the consultative process have been identified in the literature, including the consultee's perception of the consultant, professional experience, ethnic background, personality, and the mood of the consultee. Effective consultation involves examining the contribution of the interaction of these variables, rather than focusing on one contributing factor, which is consistent with an ecobehavioral perspective of consultation (Brown et al., 2001). Overall, consultee characteristics are relevant to the consultative process and should be considered in the context of the setting, as well as those characteristics of the consultant and client.

Consultee Perception

Several studies have indicated that the consultee's perception of the consultant can affect the consultative process. For example, a recent qualitative case study that examined teachers' use of school psychologist consultative services revealed that teachers are more likely to seek assistance from peers or supervisors than from school psychologists. Additionally, teachers were either unaware of the availability of such services or held misperceptions of the services. Further, years of teaching experience did not affect their use of school psychologist consultative services. This research, then, revealed the importance of using collaborative problem-solving relationships among teachers and educational and mental health consultants because teachers may not be naturally inclined to use consultative services (Koopman, 2007).

Other factors may affect the consultee's perception of the consultant, including age, gender, personality, and ethnicity, among others. For example, the age of the consultant, whether young or old, can impact the perception of the consultee. The consultee may view a young consultant as lacking experience, for example. Brown and colleagues (2001) discuss how to handle consultees' questioning of consultants' background and experience. They suggest that consultants be direct with consultees and provide accurate, factual information regarding their consultative experience. In addition, consultants may gently probe into consultees' reasoning behind their curiosity regarding consultants' background in order to dispel any misperceptions the consultee may have about the consultant or the consultee process.

Professional Experience

Research suggests a relationship between consultees' professional experience levels and their acceptance of consultants; specifically, the effect of consultees' teaching experience on their perceptions of consultants. Some research indicates a positive relationship between years of teaching experience and the use of consultants (Baker, 1965; Gilmore & Chandy, 1973). However, other research suggests that the years of teaching experience matters less than the years of teaching experience in that particular school setting (Gutkin & Bossard, 1984). Further, recent qualitative research suggests that years of teaching experience on the part of consultees do not relate to their use of consultation services (Koopman, 2007). Hughes, Barker, Kemenoff, and Hart (1993) found that experienced teachers tended to use referral services for special education services more than less-experienced teachers. Using 12 vignettes describing problem behaviors in the classroom, experienced teachers were more likely to refer children for special education evaluation than less-experienced teachers, who were more likely to use consultative services. Thus, there appears to be some disagreement in the literature with respect to the effect of teaching experience on consultees' perceptions and the use of consultation services.

Ethnic Background

Consultees and consultants also may be mismatched in their ethnic background, which can have an effect on rapport building and the success of the consultative relationship. Demographic studies indicate that educational or mental health professionals such as school psychologists tend to be an ethnically and linguistically homogeneous group (Curtis, Hunley, Walker, & Baker, 1999; Reschley & Wilson, 1995). Researchers have investigated the impact of ethnic incongruence between school psychologists and consultees with respect to the preferred types of service delivery (e.g., assessment, consultation, and counseling; Loe & Miranda, 2005). Using the School Psychology Family Practices Questionnaire (SPFPQ), school psychologists answered questions related to professional practice and training issues as related to family-oriented psychological services and cultural diversity (Loe & Miranda, 2005).

The researchers found that ethnic incongruence occurs in one third or more of assessment, consultation, and counseling services, with the highest prevalence rates of ethnic incongruence in assessment and consultation. Ethnic incongruence with consultees can impact consultants' clinical judgment and diagnostic decisions. Although over 90% of the school psychologists in this study reported that they had received diversity training, the impact of the training on providing culturally sensitive and competent services is not well understood. Thus, it is imperative that consultants be aware of how their understanding of their own cultural biases, ethnicity, and communication style may impact consultation effectiveness (Loe & Miranda, 2005).

Personality

Several consultee personality characteristics have been identified in the literature that relate to the consultative process. The personality characteristics of authoritarianism and introspection in the consultee are related to their preferred model of consultation. Mischley (1975) found that consultees who present with authoritarian characteristics are more likely to prefer a client-centered model of consultation. However, introspective consultees are more likely to prefer a consultee-centered model. In another study, teachers who rated themselves as dogmatic preferred behavioral consultants to mental health consultants, rating BC as more facilitative (Slesser, Fine, & Tracy, 1990). Mental health consultants emphasize rapport and building a relationship with the consultee by using reflective and empathic statements, whereas behavioral consultants use a systematic problem-solving approach that focuses on the immediate problem.

Slesser and colleagues (1990) also examined the role of locus of control in school consultation. Teachers first completed the Internal-External Locus of Control Scale, viewed videotapes of psychological school-based consultation, and then completed the Short Form Facilitativeness Inventory and Consultation Outcomes Questionnaire (SFFICOQ). Results indicated an interaction between locus of control and method of consultation. Teachers who rated themselves as having an external locus of control reported significantly higher satisfaction and better consultative outcomes in mental health consultation. However, there was not a significant difference between teachers with external or internal locus of control for BC satisfaction and outcomes. Further, teachers rated BC as resulting in better outcomes than mental health consultation when locus of control is not considered. Overall, teachers tend to rate behavioral consultants as more effective than mental health consultants.

Mood of the Consultee

Finally, the affective state of the consultee can impact the consultative process. Caplan and Caplan (1993) discuss the impact of the emotional state of the consultee on the outcome of consultee-centered consultation, asserting that consultees in crisis situations are more likely to seek out consultative services than those who have lesser concerns. Thus, consultees who are experiencing anxiety over crises may be more apt to follow through with consultative suggestions.

Effectiveness of BC and CBC

Empirical evidence, demonstrated primarily in single-case study designs, indicates that BC is effective in promoting positive behavior changes (Brown et al., 2001; Guli, 2005; Kratochwill & Van Someren, 1995; Medway, 1979, 1982; Sheridan, Welch, & Orme, 1996; Wilkinson, 2005; Zins & Erchul, 2002). In a review of 18 parent consultation studies, in which academic (homework completion), social and emotional (social skills), and behavioral (aggression) concerns were targeted, Guli (2005) found that the CBC model was more effective in producing positive changes in the school setting than were other forms of BC. Effect sizes for the parent consultation studies ranged from moderate to large, suggesting that the use of parental cooperation emphasized in the CBC model may improve outcomes when used in BC.

Although the use of BC may result in clinically significant treatment outcomes, there are several methodological issues to consider. As previously mentioned, intervention effectiveness is usually determined using case study designs in which one or two participants are studied. However, using a small sample size limits the generalizability of the research findings. Other methodological concerns identified in the consultation literature include problems related to replication, treatment integrity, and clearly identifiable procedures (Guli, 2005; Wilkinson, 2005). Suggestions to improve the rigor of consultation effectiveness studies include using between-subjects research designs, multiple baselines in single participant research, the reporting of effect sizes, reliability and validity data in each study, and study replication (Guli, 2005).

In addition to single-subject research designs, there are barriers to the implementation of effective consultative strategies. Examples include lack of consultant training, difficulty identifying the target behavior(s), and lack of consultee training, among other factors (Kratochwill & Van Someren, 2005). Overall, while researchers suggest that BC is a useful indirect mode of service delivery, replicating studies that use more diverse populations and problems are needed in order to provide stronger evidence for its effectiveness.

CASE STUDIES USING BEHAVIOR THEORY
BC/Child Example 1

Evan is a 9-year-old third grade student who has been diagnosed with Asperger's disorder, which is an autistic spectrum disorder characterized by severe and sustained impairment in social interactions and functioning, and restricted, repetitive patterns of behavior, social interest, and activities. Evan transferred into the school district from a private school because his previous school was unable to adequately address his behavioral issues. Upon transitioning to the school district, Evan's IEP (Individualized Education Program) was written to include receiving "pull-out" special education services for 40% of the school day, with the remainder of the day (60%) spent in the regular education classroom.

In his special education program, Evan has been working on his socialization and expressive language skills. Evan has also been receiving school guidance services twice a week to practice his social interaction skills. Evan is intellectually adept and he does need to interact with regular education students to learn to model appropriate behavior, so he spends time in a regular education setting to develop his social skills as well as to enhance his academic skills.

However, in the regular education classroom, when Evan becomes frustrated he tends to crawl under his desk. When reprimanded by the teacher, he becomes overwhelmed, and sprints out of the door of the classroom, and at times leaves the school building. Evan's parents, his teachers, and the school psychologist have convened a meeting to determine what modifications are required to be made to Evan's educational program in order for him to make reasonable educational and behavioral progress.

Discussion Questions

1. Identify and explain the types of historical information that the school psychologist will need to further elucidate the presenting problem.
2. What specific characteristics of the behavior are apparent?
3. What additional information is needed to determine appropriate intervention strategies?
4. What is the school psychologist's role in monitoring the effectiveness of the interventions?

BC/Child Example 2

Emily is a student in middle school who has been an "A" or "B" student throughout her school career. Mr. and Mrs. Brown describe Emily as their "star child" because of her personality characteristics of high achievement motivation, tenacity, and attention to detail. Emily is attentive and well behaved in school, and she submits homework that is always complete, neat, and on time.

Until recently, school was considered to be an area of success for her. However, Emily is now, for the first time, evidencing difficulty in her math class. Emily's math teacher, Mr. Caesar, is presenting fractions and decimals to the class, and although Emily is working diligently in class and submitting her homework, it is clear that she is not understanding her math assignments. Mr. Caesar, in order to get a better sense of what might be the problem, engages in several curriculum-based measurement (CBM) probes to ascertain Emily's mastery of the seventh grade math curriculum to date. Much to his surprise, Emily has mastered only 40% of what the class has covered so far, although she earned a "B" for the first marking period. Upon looking back at his grade book, Mr. Caesar realizes that her high grade was largely due to her submission of on time, neat, and correct homework. Mr. Caesar then begins to administer CBM probes reflecting concepts presented during the previous school years, and finds that Emily's instructional level is at about that of a fourth grader.

Mr. Caesar schedules a conference with Emily's parents, and her mother arrives to meet with Mr. Caesar. She explains that she usually assists Emily with her homework, which provides an explanation regarding Emily's proficiency on these tasks. However, Emily's mother is having increasing difficulty helping her daughter understand the progressively abstract concepts presented in her seventh grade math class. Further, Mrs. Brown is shocked to learn about Emily's poor mastery of math concepts during the previous grades. She explains that because Emily was earning "Bs" in her math classes at school, she assumed that Emily was doing fine. Mr. Caesar and Mrs. Brown speculate that Emily's good conduct, excellent work completion, and diligence in completing her homework has been the source of her good grades in the past. However, neither is sure what to do to assist Emily as she continues to slide into poorer mastery of the mathematics material.

Discussion Questions

1. Using behavioral terms, what is the definition of the problem in this scenario?
2. How would conducting observations of Emily in her math class assist the consultant and consultee in formulating ideas to help Emily?
3. What would be some intervention strategies that could be used to assist Emily, taking into account the evidence-based strategies presented in the literature?
4. What role should Mrs. Brown play in the consultative process? Is Mr. Brown's participation necessary for an optimal consultative outcome?

BC/Child Example 3

Patrick is a 7-year-old boy who attends a private Montessori school. Approximately 2 years ago, at the suggestion of his pediatrician, he was seen by a child psychologist, who diagnosed Patrick with an adjustment disorder with mixed anxiety and depressed mood and an expressive language disorder. Patrick has been seeing a therapist twice a month for the last 2 years to assist him in managing his anxious, depressive symptoms.

At school, Patrick's teacher reports that he appears less mature than other children his age. He has difficulty following directions, sitting still, and concentrating. Additionally, Patrick can be aggressive with other children. He tends to bully other children by hitting, jumping on them, and screaming, for example.

Because Patrick has difficulty following directions and rules, he is not allowed to go on school field trips. A few months ago, Patrick was not allowed to ride the bus for a short time due to safety concerns with respect to him standing up and running on the bus. According to his parents and teacher, Patrick also tends to talk back to his teacher and is very stubborn at school. Teachers must repeat directives several times to Patrick, and he does not always comply. When he does not comply, he becomes argumentative. Patrick's mother reported that she believes that his behavior is maintained because teachers coddle him.

Discussion Questions

1. What, if any, additional information is needed to clarify the presenting problem?
2. Describe the presenting problem in behavioral terms, including how the consultant would proceed through the problem analysis stage.
3. What are possible interventions that could be used with Patrick in the home and school setting? How should the interventions be chosen?
4. Discuss potential barriers to intervention implementation.

BC/Family Example 1

Jaquan is a 7-year-old child who attends Progressive Elementary School in the second grade. Initially his mother reports that Jaquan has always enjoyed school and had relatively no behavior difficulties until this year. However, Jaquan's records document a history of hyperactivity and behavioral difficulties for which he was placed on the psychostimulant medication, Ritalin, between the ages of 2 and 3. His mother indicates that medication increased Jaquan's hyperactivity and thus she declined to renew his prescription. Due to Jaquan's behavior difficulties, the pre-referral child study team met and began a remedial behavior plan for Jaquan that was designed to decrease his attention-seeking behaviors, loud outbursts, and oppositional behaviors. Jaquan has received ongoing behavioral interventions (without an IEP) for 2 years in both kindergarten and first grade.

Jaquan's mother admits that he can be "hyper" at school even with support, and is even more hyper at home. Teachers describe Jaquan as somewhat immature and demanding a large amount of one-on-one attention. Additionally, Jaquan can be oppositional toward adults and has difficulty sharing and cooperating with peers. Jaquan is extremely persistent and has difficulty discontinuing a behavior that he desires, whether positive or negative. His parents are concerned about his lack of sustained attention and his oppositional behaviors at home and at school.

Discussion Questions

1. Based on the information described in the case study, describe the presenting problem.
2. How would the school psychologist, parent, and teacher assess the effectiveness of the behavioral interventions currently being used with Jaquan?
3. What specific suggestions would you provide to Jaquan's teacher to help him in the classroom environment?
4. What can the teacher do to encourage cooperation and consistency between the school and the home?

BC/Family Example 2

Tyrone is a 10th grade student at Achievement High School, in a school system that boasts high numbers of very successful students in an affluent community. Tyrone's parents are both accomplished professionals; Tyrone's father works as a principal in a neighboring school district, and his mother is a superintendent for another school system in the county. Tyrone has always been a very average student, earning largely "Cs" in his academic classes, but excelling in art and design. Further, Tyrone is described by his teachers as a well-liked adolescent who is involved in such activities as Art Club and a social service club that specializes in volunteering throughout the community.

As Tyrone prepares to begin his junior year of high school, his parents have requested a conference with the school principal, the school counselor, one of the district's school psychologists, and a group of teachers from his former and future school year. After the team assembles, Tyrone's parents express their concern about their son's future. They explain that they feel Tyrone will not be accepted into a good college with his "C" grades and would like to request a full psychological evaluation. When Tyrone's teachers and the principal respond with confusion, indicating that they feel Tyrone is performing just fine in school, his parents protest that in such a high-achieving school system, there is no reason that their son should not be earning all "As."

The school counselor then begins to review, with Tyrone's parents, the list of Tyrone's accomplishments at school, including his talents in art and design and his philanthropic interests. Tyrone's parents feel, however, that their son cannot make a "decent living" as an artist, and communicate to the team that while art is a worthy hobby, something has to change in order for Tyrone to start performing better at school. Tyrone's parents suspect an undiagnosed learning problem and are pushing for an evaluation before the start of school.

Discussion Questions

1. What should be the response of the team to Tyrone's parents' request that a psychological evaluation be conducted immediately?
2. Who, among the team, should work as a consultant?
3. If Tyrone's parents are the consultee, what issues need to be considered when selecting appropriate interventions?
4. What techniques should be utilized when preparing to engage in collaborative problem solving between the consultant and consultee?

BC/Family Example 3

Rachel is a second grade student who was recently diagnosed with attention deficit hyperactivity disorder, inattentive type, by the school psychologist. Rachel has been evidencing symptoms of the disorder at both home and school, causing difficulties in her functioning in both settings. At home, she has difficulty in organizing herself, including the items in her room, as well as her books and written materials. Rachel's mother also reports that Rachel has trouble beginning and following through with her homework assignments. Rachel's mother reported that she must check her homework for completion.

At school, Rachel has difficulty regulating her emotions while completing academic work. For example, she may tear or choke up during a math lesson. When completing academic tasks that she finds to be difficult, Rachel will appear sad, put her head down, and cry. According to the teacher, she engages in this behavior approximately once per week and the crying lasts between 5 and 30 minutes. Rachel's teacher also reported that she has difficulty completing tasks independently and frequently requests assistance from the teacher during class. She frequently appears to be "in a fog," for example, daydreaming or staring into space. Unfortunately, this passive-off-task behavior impacts negatively upon her work completion rates.

The IEP team recommended several classroom interventions, including presenting material in different modalities, repeating directions, and seating Rachel by an academically successful peer. However, Rachel continues to struggle both behaviorally and academically. Rachel's teacher and mother are concerned that the interventions are not effective and that she needs a more restrictive placement.

Discussion Questions

1. How would the consultant elicit specific information regarding the nature of the presenting problem?
2. Provide an operational definition of the presenting problem based on the available information.
3. Brainstorm possible interventions.
4. How could the consultant assess the effectiveness of the current interventions used with Rachel?

BC/Educator Example 1

Michael is a second grade special education student diagnosed with mental retardation, and is receiving self-contained educational support services. In addition, he is encopretic, with leakage from his underwear becoming an increasing problem. In the classroom, Michael's special education teacher has implemented a behavior modification program, whereby he is able to earn points during the week for appropriate toileting, and cash in his points each Friday for selected rewards. Unfortunately, this program has not been successful in improving Michael's independent toileting skills.

Michael's mother has called the school psychologist threatening to sue both the teacher and the district over her son's educational and health services. Michael's mother related that the teacher had called her to explain about Michael's increasing number of accidents, and how the teacher and the school nurse had decided that if Michael had a bowel movement in his pants, he would be instructed to clean himself up and then be placed in a diaper. The teacher explained to Michael's mother that it was necessary for Michael to assume responsibility for himself, and that his accidents were directly related to his mother's lack of consequences at home for his encopresis.

Discussion Questions

1. How can the consultant mediate the relationship between the teacher and the parent?
2. What is the role of the consultant in this situation?
3. Who is the consultee and who is the client?
4. Because the current behavioral modification program has not been effective, what additional suggestions would you give to the teacher and the parent?

BC/Educator Example 2

Mark Jones is an 11-year-old sixth grade student who has been identified and found in need of special education services for a specific learning disability in reading. Mark is currently enrolled in a regular education class with in-class support in reading. In addition, he has been diagnosed with ADHD, and is receiving psychostimulant medication therapy.

His mother, Mrs. Jones, has just received a copy of her son's progress report, which indicates failing grades in math, science, and social studies, due to lack of homework completion. Mrs. Jones has met with Mrs. Smith, Mark's regular education teacher, to attempt to develop a system whereby Mrs. Smith will ensure that Mark has entered the assignments in his homework book. Additionally, Mrs. Smith will check that the appropriate books have been selected to take home each day. Mark's mother, Mrs. Jones, will then oversee that work is completed and returned in a green folder to be handed in to Mrs. Smith daily.

Mrs. Smith has stated that she feels Mark is old enough to assume this responsibility, and since homework is posted on the board daily, he has no excuse for not completing the work. Mrs. Smith reports that she does not have the time to check all students' homework books daily. Mrs. Smith also indicated that if Mark requires additional assistance beyond what is given to his classmates, he should be placed in a more restrictive special education program.

Discussion Questions

1. Describe the presenting problem.
2. Using a BC model, identify and explain the steps that the consultant would use with the classroom teacher to clarify the presenting problem and develop interventions.
3. What could the teacher do to enhance Mark's independence in task completion within the classroom setting?
4. How would intervention effectiveness be measured in this scenario?

BC/Educator Example 3

Nick is a 14-year-old who has been diagnosed with Asperger's disorder. Among other difficulties, Nick has been the victim of teasing and bullying by his peers since kindergarten. This school year in particular, Nick has had difficulty interpreting the bullying behavior of his peers. Although he is teased by his peers for being "different," Nick also teases other children. He has difficulty coping with the bullying behavior of others, which may manifest in verbal or physical outbursts. Socially, Nick reports being interested in others, but is not able to name any true friends. He continues to have difficulty understanding the meaning of friendship and the requisite social and emotional reciprocity that is a part of relationships with others.

Nick also experiences anxiety regarding his school performance. He becomes worried before a test, when an assignment is due, or when he has many questions to ask during class, for example. When he has a question for a teacher, he may ask the question at a busy time or during class when the teacher is moving along with the lesson. Thus, he has some difficulty reading social situations. When anxious, he may experience a meltdown in which he may cry or have a behavioral outburst.

Nick's IEP goals include increasing his skills in coping with anxiety in the classroom, through such techniques as writing down questions on a piece of paper and then approaching the teacher at a later time, waiting his turn to ask a question, and finding a good time to ask the teacher a question. Although several suggestions have been made to Nick, he continues to struggle with understanding the feeling of being anxious, as well as identifying appropriate methods to cope with his anxiety. Nick is also worrying about his upcoming transition to high school. His teacher would like to help him succeed, but she has difficulty understanding how to help him in increasing his social and emotional behavioral repertoire.

Discussion Questions

1. Describe the steps in the behavioral consultation process that you, as the consultant, would use to assess the problem.
2. Name interventions that could be used to help Nick cope with anxious feelings in the classroom setting.
3. Considering the implementation stage of the consultation process, what are some barriers that may affect the teacher's ability to implement the interventions?
4. How can the consultant remove or inhibit the barriers?

BC/Systems Example 1

Brandon is an eighth grade student who has been receiving special education services due to a significant reading disability. Last year, at his annual review, his mother questioned his achievement levels in reading, but was assured by his teachers that he was making good progress. During the current school year, Brandon's mother continued to be concerned about his reading and written communication skills and chose to have him evaluated at the local university's child study center.

The results from that evaluation reflected 3 months' growth in reading since his last evaluation, 3 years ago, and 6 months' growth in his written communication skills. In light of his above-average ability, Brandon's mother is demanding that he receive daily reading instruction using a direct instruction approach as recommended by the local university's child study center. In addition, Brandon's mother wants her son to receive the direct instruction for 2 hours daily, 5 days a week throughout the summer. If the district refuses to provide this service within 30 days, she will pursue due process procedures against the school district.

Discussion Questions

1. What is the school psychologist's role as the consultant in this situation?
2. Who is the consultee in this scenario?
3. What is the problem?
4. How could CBC be used in this example?

BC/Systems Example 2

Mrs. Donati is a tireless advocate for her son, Jeff, who was diagnosed with cerebral palsy and Downs syndrome as a very young infant. Jeff received early intervention services within the first few months of his life, and has developed into a young man who has a lovely personality and is responsible for several household tasks, including feeding the family dog and taking out the trash. As Jeff has turned 14, he has moved into eighth grade at the junior high school, and has been experiencing difficulty for the first time in his educational programming.

In explanation, Jeff has been fully included in the regular education curriculum for grades K–7, despite a recent cognitive assessment that estimated his Full Scale IQ to be 45 and evaluated his inability to read. However, the multidisciplinary team at the junior high school has met with Mrs. Donati to share with her their concerns regarding their belief that full inclusion is no longer a feasible or appropriate option for Jeff. The team is concerned that Jeff needs instruction in functional life skills, bathroom independence, and occupational readiness, and believes that these skills cannot be taught in the regular education setting.

However, Mrs. Donati believes that the best way for Jeff to learn how to be an independent adult is for him to be educated in a class with nondisabled peers. She firmly believes that the district is not meeting their requirements in providing Jeff the least restrictive environment in addition to the specialized instruction that he needs. Mrs. Donati will not agree to the district's suggestion to educate Jeff in a self-contained special education classroom, while the multidisciplinary team refuses to integrate Jeff into regular education classes in the eighth grade, arguing that his needs cannot possibly be met.

Discussion Questions

1. Who is the most appropriate consultee in this example—Mrs. Donati, the MDT (Multidisciplinary Team), or both?
2. How would the goals for consultation change depending upon who is the consultee?
3. How can the consultant help the consultee define the problem in behavioral terms?
4. What changes does the system need to make?

BC/Systems Example 3

Sarah recently moved with her family from another state, and now attends the fourth grade in the Meets All Needs School System. After about a month of school, Sarah arrived with a packet of information that she explains her mother asked her to give to her teacher. The teacher examines the paperwork, and then shares it with the principal at the end of the day. Apparently, Sarah was identified as being mentally gifted at her previous school. Sarah's teacher and principal study Sarah's educational records from the other school system, quickly determining that while Sarah obviously met the guidelines to be diagnosed as mentally gifted in the other state, her scores on an individually administered test of intelligence (reported in her school records) do not meet the threshold for Sarah to be included in the gifted program in her current school.

When questioned about Sarah's performance in the classroom, Sarah's current teacher reports that she does not believe that Sarah is a mentally gifted student. Apparently, Sarah has some "holes" in her knowledge in several subject areas, and seems not to have been exposed to several topics that are presented in the third grade in the Meets All Needs School System. However, Sarah's teacher admits that in other areas, Sarah appears to perform far beyond the rest of the class. Sarah's teacher tells the principal that she believes in order for a child to be mentally gifted, he or she needs to be performing uniformly well in all areas, and Sarah is not. Another concern raised by Sarah's teacher is that Sarah often seems to daydream during class, and doesn't always seem motivated to achieve her very best. Sarah's teacher concludes that Sarah must not be gifted because she does not possess sufficient achievement motivation. Sarah's principal returns to her office to think about all of this information. She then calls for a meeting of the school psychologist, school counselor, and Sarah's teacher, hoping that this group can determine what is the best course of action.

Discussion Questions

1. Explain why this case study can be analyzed from a BC approach.
2. What is the role of Sarah's parents in the BC process?
3. Who is the client in this case study?
4. What should the goals be for this case using a BC orientation?

SUMMARY

In this chapter, the BC model of consultation was presented, including CBC. Information was provided regarding the importance of verbal communication in the BC process. The general stages of consultation were then reviewed, including formal entry, establishing an effective relationship, assessment, problem definition and goal setting, intervention or strategy selection, intervention implementation, intervention evaluation, and termination. Additionally, BC processes were summarized, along with consultant roles and consultee characteristics. In the next chapter, social cognitive theory consultation will be reviewed and discussed, along with case studies related to that theoretical model.

CHAPTER 4

Social Cognitive Theory Consultation

INTRODUCTION

Although the behavioral model of consultation (BC) and the social cognitive theory model of consultation (SCTC) both encourage behavioral change in the client, there are several differences between the two approaches. While the behavioral model uses operant learning to promote change in the client, the social cognitive theory model focuses on changing the cognitions of the consultee and client in order to change their behavior. In the consultative model of social cognitive theory (SCT), variables within the person (cognitions), variables demonstrated by the person (behavior), and variables outside the person (the environment), are all considered to impact the functioning of the consultant, consultee, and the client. Overall, the purposes of both BC and SCTC are to promote positive change, but differences lie in their conceptualization of the consultee's and client's functioning.

Assumptions of Social Cognitive Theory

Bandura (1978), the creator of SCT, developed his theory in response to traditional behaviorism, arguing that not all learning could be detected simply through observing behavior. Instead, some learning occurs through observing others, and this knowledge may not be acted upon immediately, but instead stored for future use. Thus, based upon this recognition, Bandura (1978) proposed his SCT, suggesting that while people's behavior can be changed through operant conditioning—*external forces*—as the behaviorists believe, people's behavior can also be changed through cognitions, or *internal forces*. Further, since people's behavior influences their future behaviors and cognitions, as well as the environment, all are *reciprocal determinants* of human behavior because these factors act in concert and cannot be separated.

Thus, the social cognitive theory model of consultation arises from the theories of Bandura (1977a, 1977b, 1978), in which he proposed that the interplay of individuals' behavior, cognition, and the environment form the basis of human functioning. Moreover, the interrelationships among these factors influence both the consultee's and the client's functioning (Bandura, 1978). In this type of consultation, motivation to combat the problem, as well as to establish self-efficacy and independence in the consultee is highlighted (Bandura, 1977a; 1977b). Further, the goals of consultation are to alter or influence the relationships among person, environment, and interpersonal factors, while enabling the consultee to more effectively address the future problems that may arise in that client or others (Bandura, 1978).

Much of the information in this chapter reflects the work of Brown and Schulte (1987) and Brown, Pryzwansky, and Schulte (2001). Readers are encouraged to consult these original works for further information about the SCTC model. Brown and Schulte (1987) outline the assumptions and values of SCTC. An overarching theme of SCTC is to promote positive changes within three variables—behavior, cognitions, and environment—rather than focusing on a single targeted area. Brown and Schulte (1987) assert that there are two philosophical assumptions that underpin the SCTC model: (1) reciprocal determinism and (2) altering the homeostatic relationships among the behavior, cognitive, and environmental variables. The idea of reciprocal determinism in SCTC is that the relationship between behavior, cognitions, and the environment impact the three parties involved in the consultation process: the consultant, consultee, and the client. In order to fully understand the problems evidenced by the consultee and client, all three variables must be considered in the consultation process.

The process of altering the homeostatic relationship occurs in three parts. The first goal of consultation is to alter the relationships among the three variables that are currently preventing the consultee from interacting with the client in an efficacious manner. The second goal is to alter the interplay of the cognitive, behavior, and environmental factors that affect the client's functioning in a particular situation. The third goal of the consultative process is to promote change in the consultee so that he or she may independently and effectively address similar problems in the future.

The Role of Motivation in the Consultation Process

Motivation is an important area of focus in SCTC because the consultant's role in the process is to encourage or enhance the consultee's motivation to develop self-regulatory behavior. Bandura (1977a; 1982b) asserts that motivation in such instances is derived from the anticipation of positive results, which relates to the self-efficacious beliefs of performing tasks and setting goals according to one's own personal standards. Direct instruction, feedback, and observation of models evaluating their own behavior are used to encourage the development of self-regulation (Bandura 1977a; 1977b; 1978).

The role of the consultant in enhancing motivation and behavioral standards is to alert the consultee to positive outcomes of the consultation process, such as improved ability to cope with the client, improved understanding of the consultee's own functioning, and setting goals according to the standards of the SCTC process. The consultant may need to provide direct instruction to the consultee in particular situations in which the standards need to be changed, including: (1) introducing the new skills that the consultee will need to develop, (2) providing exposure to situations that allow the consultee to practice the skills and evaluate his or her performance, (3) delivering feedback to the consultee, and (4) offering opportunities for the consultee to observe appropriate models (Bandura, 1977a, 1977b, 1978). Bandura (1977b) describes other methods through which the consultee can develop new skills and enhance motivation, including physical demonstrations, verbal descriptions, or through media resources, such as books and videos. Additionally, observation of models may encourage the consultee to use and/or develop new responses.

SCTC Process

Bandura (1977b) discusses the importance of the relationship between the consultant and consultee. Here, the ideal consultant is warm and genuine, while projecting competence (Bandura, 1971). At the same time, the consultant builds rapport through shared experiences or interests, thereby promoting a collegial relationship. Bandura's conception of the consultant–consultee relationship is akin to a counseling relationship characterized by genuine concern, empathy, warmth, and openness. The consultant encourages the development of motivation in the consultee through methods described earlier, such as modeling and direct instruction. Additionally, the consultant influences the consultee's behavior through a demonstration of competence (Bandura, 1971). For example, the consultant might demonstrate competence by calling attention to the effects the environment has upon both the consultee and client. Further, the consultant may model intervention techniques that the consultant can use to improve the client's functioning in his or her particular setting.

Other characteristics of the consultative relationship include reciprocal interactions. The consultant, consultee, and client all reciprocally influence each other according to Bandura's model of reciprocal determinism (Bandura, 1977b). Consultants influence consultees by guiding the consultative process through interviewing. Conversely, consultees may influence consultants by explaining their perception of their own role in the consultative process. Finally, similar to other BC models, expectations regarding goals, outcomes, and the length of meetings are discussed at the outset of the consultation process. It is important, then, in SCTC to consider the behavior, personal, and environmental factors that contribute to the relationship rather than focusing on a unitary factor.

Assessment

In SCTC, an assessment of the problem is accomplished through a measurement of the consultee's cognitive processes, especially those related to self-efficacy, in addition to a measurement of behavioral processes and environmental factors (Bandura 1977a; 1978). Then the client's cognitions, motivations, and environment are assessed, with the consultant and consultee remaining collaborative during the assessment. As the process of consultation commences, an important goal of the consultant is to assist the consultee in gaining independence from the consultant. Brown and Schulte (1987) also assert that the assessment process is collaborative, and as such, the consultant should not take primary responsibility for any stage within the consultation process. Further, who performs what role in the process is not determined prior to the start of the consultation process. Rather, the roles of the consultant and consultee depend on the level of expertise each possesses, accessibility to clients, and time availability. Brown and Schulte (1987) further assert that the consultant should not hinder the consultee from learning skills to function independently, which is an important point to consider in the assessment process.

Consultee Assessment

In order to examine the consultee's behavior and current level of functioning, the consultant may conduct observations of the consultee in situations in which the consultee is working with the client. The consultant

Table 4.1   Questions to Ask during the Consultee Assessment

1.	Has the consultee acquired the necessary skills needed to deal with the client's problem?
2.	What is the level of self-efficacy with regard to the behaviors needed to deal with the client's problems?
3.	What is the level of motivation with regard to the presenting problem?
4.	Are there powerful environmental constraints (i.e., informal norms, rules, traditions) that preclude consultee action?

Source: (From A Social Learning Theory Model of Consultation, by D. Brown and A. Schulte, 1987, *Professional Psychology: Research and Practice, 18*, p. 285.) Copyright 1987 by the American Psychological Association. Reprinted with permission of the author.

examines the consultee's self-efficacy (cognition), skills (behavior), and the consultee's environment. The observations of the consultee may be formal or informal, depending upon whether the consultee desires informal observational data or quantified, formal data in order to evaluate the effectiveness of the consultation outcomes, for example. When assessing the consultee, the consultant may ask questions related to the consultee's motivation to solve the problem, beliefs regarding his or her self-confidence in performing the necessary interventions, and ability to implement the required interventions. These questions may be addressed through self-ratings of motivation and self-efficacy, role-playing and interviews, and drawing inferences from statements the consultee makes. See Table 4.1 for specific questions that should be addressed during the consultee assessment.

The consultee assessment also includes an examination of the consultee's environment. Possible concerns in the environment may include behavioral norms and physical attributes of the setting, for example. A classroom located near the gymnasium or band room may present problems related to noise and increased student traffic. At the end of the consultee assessment, the consultant and consultee collaborate to identify areas that need improvement (Brown, Pryzwansky, & Schulte, 2001; Brown & Schulte, 1987).

Client Assessment

An assessment of the client involves the consultee discussing the client's strengths and needs, his or her self-efficacy in coping with the problem, and an examination of the environmental variables that may inhibit the client from actively addressing the problem. First, the consultant collaborates with the consultee to identify the client's behavioral strengths

Table 4.2 Questions to Ask during the Client Assessment

1.	Does the client have skill deficits?
2.	What are the client's self-efficacy beliefs regarding the ability to deal with the presenting problem?
3.	What is the client's appraisal of the importance of dealing with the problem?
4.	Are there powerful environmental variables in the immediate situation that inhibit the client from taking action?

Source: From "A Social Learning Theory Model of Consultation," by D. Brown and A. Schulte, 1987, *Professional Psychology: Research and Practice, 18*, p. 285. Copyright 1987 by the American Psychological Association. Reprinted with permission of the author.

and areas of concern, which may be assessed through techniques such as interviewing, self-ratings, and observations. The most basic question to be asked of the consultee regarding the client's behavior is whether the client has the necessary competencies to function in the presenting situation (Brown & Schulte, 1987; Brown et al., 2001). Table 4.2 provides specific questions to be answered during the client assessment process (Brown & Schulte, 1987, p. 285).

After assessing the client's behavioral strengths and weaknesses, the client's cognitions or appraisal of the problem situation are assessed. During this step, it is important to measure the client's beliefs of self-efficacy, with the goal of finding out what the client's perceptions are of his or her ability to cope with the situation. The client's self-efficacy may be assessed with rating scales (Bandura, 1982a, 1982b; Keyser & Barling, 1981), such as the General Self-Efficacy Scale (GSES; Schwarzer, & Jerusalem, 1995). In addition, Brown and colleagues (2001) suggest simply asking the client about his or her level of confidence in dealing with the problem.

The consultee can assess the client's cognitions or expectations regarding his or her performance using informal interviews (Mischel, 1973). The following interview format is suggested to guide the consultee in eliciting the client's cognitions. First, the consultee can identify the problem behavior by asking the client to: (1) Describe the behavior in words or through role-plays, (2) Identify the parameters of the behavior including time, place, and circumstances, and (3) Identify cues and reinforcers in the environment. The consultee can then suggest alternative, appropriate behaviors that the client might use in the situation by role-playing the appropriate behaviors and/or verbally describing the behaviors (Brown et al., 2001).

In addition, the consultee may ask the client to contribute his or her perception of the positive behaviors that are being evidenced, which may be assessed in the following ways: (1) Self-ratings of confidence in performing the desired behavior, including rating himself or herself on a scale of 1 to 10, (2) Identifying possible outcomes of performing the desired behavior such as environmental and personal rewards, and (3) Asking the client how important it is to him or her to behave appropriately in the situation. Lastly, the consultee reviews the assessment results with the client (Brown et al., 2001).

The third phase of the client assessment involves examining the client's environment. In contrast to behavioral approaches that typically focus on an examination of immediate, proximal environmental cues, the SCTC approach is more expansive. Brofenbrenner's (1979) ecological perspective is used to describe the environmental assessment process. Initially, the microsystem of the client is assessed, including his or her family, peers, or classroom, for example. In this microsystem, antecedents of the behavior, positive and negative reinforcement strategies, and the influence of other behaviors that are present when the problem behavior occurs should be identified (Brown et al., 2001).

In addition to the client's microsystem, the client's relationships with family and friends, for example, need to be considered as a part of the client assessment process. Here, the consultant and consultee examine how the client functions within interpersonal relationships. The overarching goal of assessing the client's environment is to examine the role and extent of positive reinforcement in maintaining the appropriate behavior. An environment that includes some level of positive reinforcement is considered as a supportive one. Other environmental variables include those in the client's ecosystem, such as a paucity of resources (e.g., books, pencils, or other school supplies) in the classroom. After the client's environment is assessed, the consultant and consultee can determine the effect of behavior, cognitions, and environment on the client's functioning (Brown et al., 2001).

Statement of the Problem and Goal Identification

Based on the assessment of the consultee and client, problem statements and goals are identified for both the consultee and the client. With the consultant's guidance, the consultee prioritizes the goals so that the possibility for success exists. The goal is to maximize the consultee's potential for success in working with the client (Brown et al., 2001).

Selecting and Implementing Interventions

Consultants work with consultees to choose appropriate interventions. Ultimately, the consultee should choose the intervention with the assistance of the consultant, who typically has knowledge of research-based interventions. The selection of interventions, then, should be a result of a collaboration between the consultant and consultee, much like the consultation process itself (Bergan & Kratochwill, 1990). Bergan and Kratochwill (1990) suggest the following sequence in selecting an intervention: (1) Generate a list of possible approaches for assisting the client, (2) List the positive and negative aspects of each while considering the consultant's, consultee's, and client's point of view, (3) Identify possible positive and negative impacts on the system (outside the client and consultee), and (4) Select an intervention. Finally, the intervention should be monitored and evaluated based on behavioral and cognitive changes in the consultee and client.

After the intervention is selected, the consultant models the implementation strategy for the consultee, drawing upon Bandura's (1978) findings that individuals can learn behavior by observing others and recognizing the consequences that are related to such behavior. The consultee can then practice the intervention as the consultant provides feedback regarding the consultee's manner of implementation. When the consultee has mastered the implementation of the intervention and both the consultant and consultee are confident in the consultee's ability to implement the strategy, the strategy can be implemented with the client (Brown et al., 2001).

Types of Interventions

The interventions used with the consultee and the client are drawn primarily from the works of Bandura (1977a, 1982b). These interventions concern increasing self-efficacy in the consultee or the client through mastery of a particular behavior. For example, a client (student) may increase his or her self-efficacy after learning to track a behavior, such as frequently getting out of his or her seat during instruction, through self-monitoring techniques. In this instance, the child increases his or her confidence in learning to monitor his or her behavior and inhibit behavioral responses. Self-efficacy, then, can be achieved through performance mastery of a particular behavior.

Self-efficacy can also be enhanced through vicarious learning opportunities in which clients observe appropriate models. A child who has difficulty using audible self-talk techniques to regulate negative emotions

Table 4.3 Examples of SCTC Behavioral Techniques

1. Symbolic modeling—the desired behavior is presented through various media resources such as audio, video, or written materials

2. Performance enactments—the consultant models the desired behavior and then requests the consultee to perform the behavior, while providing coaching and feedback

3. Covert modeling—the consultee imagines him or herself performing the desired behavior

4. Cognitive restructuring—this involves identifying thought patterns that occur prior to, during, or after a problem situation and replacing the negative or inappropriate thought patterns with appropriate ones. Cognitive modeling and feedback is used throughout the process

5. Self-monitoring—a strategy to increase an individual's awareness of the problem behavior by identifying the characteristics of the behavior or by monitoring their own progress toward a goal

Source: (From Behavioral Approaches to Consultation, by D. Brown, W. B. Pryzwansky, and A. C. Schulte, 2001, *Psychological Consultation: Introduction to Theory and Practice* (5th ed.), p. 65.) Copyright 2001 by Pearson Education. Reprinted by permission of the publisher.

may observe a peer successfully using the techniques. Modeling experiences can also be provided through media resources such as videotapes, films, and books, for example (Bandura, 1977a). See Table 4.3 for examples of SCT behavioral techniques as aggregated by Brown et al. (2001).

Verbal persuasion may also be used to enhance self-efficacy beliefs, although this is one of the less effective techniques in comparison to self-monitoring or modeling (Bandura, 1977a, 1982b). Consultants can verbally encourage the consultee or client to enact the new behavior. Another target of self-efficacy intervention is emotional or physiological arousal, since techniques used to decrease emotional arousal prior to the enactment of a behavior can enhance an individual's self-efficacy (Bandura, 1977a). Interestingly, individuals with high emotional arousal are more likely than those with average or low levels of emotional arousal to have low self-efficacy. Cognitive restructuring and desensitization techniques may be used to decrease arousal so that the consultee and client can learn to control or alter their cognitive processes prior to or during a behavioral performance. However, this technique is also considered to be less effective than self-monitoring or modeling techniques in enhancing self-efficacy.

Brown and colleagues (2001) suggest a hierarchy of steps to encourage self-efficacy based on the aforementioned intervention techniques. The consultee or client may have difficulty performing a behavior as suggested by the consultant. Although performance enactments are considered the most important in increasing self-efficacy, the following hierarchy is suggested to guide the process: (1) Use verbal persuasion techniques, such as encouragement and affirmation of the consultee's or client's ability to perform the behavior, (2) Use vicarious learning experiences by having the consultee or client observe an individual successfully perform the behavior, and (3) Use performance enactments through the use of role-playing so that the consultee and client can practice the behavior and achieve success. Finally, techniques that diminish excessively high emotional arousal levels, such as systematic desensitization, are used only when the consultee or client presents with irrational fears or worries.

The consultee's and client's appraisal of his or her performance is also important to consider during intervention implementation. An individual's appraisal of his or her performance and expectations of the situation, such as its difficulty, is linked to both intrinsic and extrinsic rewards, which are subsequently connected to the consultee's or client's motivation to perform the behavior, as well as the achieved outcomes of performing the behavior. Appraisal and expectations may be altered through cognitive restructuring, consultant feedback, and modeling, among other techniques (Bandura, 1977a).

Intervention Monitoring and Evaluation

Bergan and Kratochwill's (1990) model of consultation outlines the specific steps that can be used in monitoring and evaluating the effectiveness of an intervention. The social cognitive theory model of consultation, although concerned with evaluating the behavioral aspects of interventions, also stresses the importance of cognitions. Therefore, when evaluating intervention plans, the focus would also be on consultees' and clients' self-efficacy beliefs, appraisals of the situation, and expectations of outcomes.

The Role of the Consultant in SCTC

In working in a consultative relationship, the roles of the consultant range from process or content observer, to collaborator, or to expert. The role of the consultant differs depending on process or content, as well as the level of intrusiveness in the consultation process (Brown et al., 2001). Behavioral consultants typically assume control of the consultative relationship, performing in an expert role in which they guide the consultation process through the use of verbal structuring techniques (Bergan & Kratochwill, 1990). In contrast, in the social cognitive theory of consultation, the role of the consultant is facilitator or collaborator throughout the entire consultation process.

Specifically, the consultant's role in SCTC is to instill motivation in the consultee to improve self-regulation skills and to assist the consultee in establishing behavioral standards for himself or herself, as well as the client. Bandura (1977a, 1982b) discusses ways in which motivation can be developed and behavioral standards adopted, asserting that motivation stems from expecting positive outcomes, confidence in performing tasks, and meeting goals associated with personal behavioral standards. Behavioral standards can be encouraged through direct instruction and feedback, as well as the observation of others evaluating themselves (Bandura 1976, 1977b, 1978).

In the social cognitive model of consultation, in contrast to behavioral models of consultation, the consultative relationship is viewed as nonhierarchical and collaborative. Although behavioral models also emphasize collaboration between the consultant and consultee, the SCTC model *relies* upon this collaborative relationship. It is essential to the success of the consultation process that positive changes are effected in both the consultee's and client's self-efficacy beliefs, behaviors, and environment. Based on Bandura's theoretical contributions, the SCTC model is also concerned with the concept of reciprocal determinism or the interplay of cognitions, behavior, and environmental variables. As such, the SCTC model differs from BC in its emphasis on cognitions in the consultant, the consultee, and the client.

Effectiveness of SCTC

Unlike BC, little documented research exists regarding the efficacy of SCTC. However, while the SCTC model has yet to be validated (Brown & Schulte, 1987), the interventions used in the SCTC process are supported by research (Bandura, 1977b, 1978, 1982b). Similar to the circumstances in the BC model, SCTC effectiveness may be related to factors within the consultation process (Kratochwill & Van Someren, 1995). The relationship between the consultant and consultee, which is emphasized in SCTC, may impact consultation outcomes and effectiveness. For example, research indicates that teachers have positive perceptions of consultants who allocate ample time for the consultant and consultee to discuss concerns. Interestingly, such teachers tend to view the consultation process as positive despite the presence or lack of intervention effectiveness (Athanasiou, Geil, Hazel, & Copeland, 2002). Moreover, because the SCTC process is collaborative in nature, a breakdown in the consultant–consultee relationship may negatively affect treatment outcomes.

Other factors that may be related to SCTC effectiveness include the role of motivation and self-efficacy beliefs instilled in the consultee during the consultative process. The consultant's role in SCTC is to enhance the consultee's motivation in establishing behavioral standards for both the consultee and the client. This may occur through direct instruction, feedback, and modeling (Bandura, 1977a, 1982b). The success of SCTC relies upon the ability of the consultant to teach the consultee new skills, thus increasing the consultee's motivation and self-efficacy beliefs, which, in turn, contribute to positive consultation outcomes (Brown & Schulte, 1987).

CASE STUDIES USING SOCIAL COGNITIVE CONSULTATION
SCTC/Child Example 1

Billy is a fourth grade student who has had a history of inappropriate behaviors, including physical and verbal aggression demonstrated toward his peers and teachers. His teacher has been using a response–cost behavioral modification system within the classroom, which has been very effective in reducing such behaviors. However, Billy has continued to demonstrate aggressive episodes both on the bus and playground. The principal finds that denying him recess has not been an effective means of managing his behavior, and recently observed a group of classmates goading him into aggression on the playground. During a playground observation, Billy's principal and teacher noted that Billy often mimics the "play-fighting" demonstrated by peers, but does so without his target's knowledge, and to a more severe extent.

When Billy has evidenced poor behavior, the principal keeps him in his office as punishment for the next recess, and notes that during these office visits, Billy works industriously and gets all of his work completed to the principal's satisfaction. During his conversations with Billy, the principal is concerned that Billy does not truly understand why his behavior is considered to be different from his peers, and unacceptable. The principal feels that Billy "is a good kid," but doesn't know what to do to prevent these behavioral episodes from occurring.

Discussion Questions

1. Conceptualize the problem in terms of reciprocal determinism: the presenting problem behaviors, environmental issues, and cognitive factors.
2. Knowing that the behavioral modification system is effective in the classroom, what other intervention techniques would be effective with this child in other settings based on the social cognitive theory model of consultation?
3. Explain the role of motivation in this example.
4. What types of SCTC techniques would be useful for the child to learn?

SCTC/Child Example 2

Jane is a 14-year-old girl diagnosed with Asperger's syndrome, which is an autistic spectrum disorder characterized by severe and sustained impairment in social interactions and functioning, and restricted, repetitive patterns of behavior, social interest, and activities. Jane attends mainstream classes at school. Her guidance counselor recently met with the school psychologist regarding Jane's behavior in school. Although she is involved in the theater arts, which presents many opportunities for social interaction, Jane continues to have difficulty making friends. She sometimes teases, pesters, or touches peers that she likes. These behaviors negatively affect her ability to make lasting friendships.

Jane also experiences some teasing at school and does not always cope with bullying appropriately. Peers at school recently called her a mean name repeatedly. She screamed, "Stop it!" several times, even though Jane recognizes that the strength of her reaction will provoke her peers to continue name calling. In addition, she may laugh at inappropriate times or at situations or ideas that others do not find humorous. When the guidance counselor questions Jane about these incidents, Jane reports that she would like to improve her ability to recognize appropriate times to be silly. Although Jane's guidance counselor is inexperienced in working with children diagnosed with autism spectrum disorders, she is willing to learn new strategies to help Jane succeed with her peers.

Discussion Questions

1. How would you assess the guidance counselor's self-efficacy beliefs?
2. What kind of additional information would be helpful in this scenario?
3. What intervention strategies may be useful for Jane's guidance counselor to learn in order to help Jane succeed socially?
4. Describe ways to increase the guidance counselor's self-efficacy in improving Jane's social skills. Describe ways to improve Jane's self-efficacy and motivation in social interactions.

SCTC/Child Example 3

Alex is a sixth grader who attends a state-certified private school for children with neurological disabilities. In the previous school setting, Alex exhibited behavioral difficulties and had a history of hitting peers and teachers. At the beginning of the current school year, Alex was to transition back to his home school district. However, he had difficulty with this transition, and on one occasion, he planted himself on the floor and refused to do his work. Because Alex exhibited difficulty adjusting to his home school district, it was determined that the private school remained the most appropriate placement. Upon returning to the private school, the school social worker reported that there was a period of 2 weeks in which Alex exhibited behavioral issues such as "meltdowns."

Since that time, she reports that Alex has been generally well behaved. However, he tends to model other students' poor or inappropriate behavior, such as bullying or teasing a new student. This appears to be the result of a desire to fit in socially, rather than actual maliciousness, according to the social worker. Further, Alex may refuse or protest when beginning a new activity or going on a field trip, for example, but often adjusts to a new situation after a short time.

Alex's school uses a schoolwide behavior plan in which students can earn play money to spend at a school store or market every Friday. However, Alex is not motivated by this system. The social worker would like to find new ways to motivate Alex to behave appropriately and reinforce him for doing so while promoting his social development.

Discussion Questions

1. What would be the first step in assessing the current concern?
2. What specific questions would you ask the consultee and client regarding their motivation, appraisal, and skills in dealing with the current problem?
3. Name and describe possible interventions to use with Alex.
4. Why has the token economy system been ineffective?

SCTC/Family Example 1

Matteo is a second grade student who enjoys school and very much likes his teacher, Ms. Ramirez. Ms. Ramirez reports that Matteo has been doing well in school, and seems well liked by his peers. The problem that Ms. Ramirez has brought to the consultant is that she thinks that Matteo, as well as several of his peers, are masturbating in the classroom. Ms. Ramirez feels foolish bringing this issue to the attention of the consultant, but she does not know what she should or should not do.

Ms. Ramirez has done a little research on human sexuality, and understands that it is normal for children to begin exploring their bodies and repeating behaviors that feel good to them. However, she feels that the behavior is "feeding on itself" because several of the children seem to be engaging in it, with no apparent self-consciousness. Ms. Ramirez is concerned that in short order, the whole class is going to be adopting these behaviors, and then what should she do?

Discussion Questions

1. Describe the student's current functioning and/or problem.
2. Who is the client in this situation? As the consultant, how would you assess cognitions?
3. What strategy would you suggest for working with Ms. Ramirez?
4. How does a social cognitive theory conceptualization of this case differ from a behavioral consultation viewpoint?

SCTC/Family Example 2

Mrs. Edwards has contacted the school psychologist to discuss her daughter, who attends a second grade class in the school district. Mrs. Edwards describes her daughter as a very sensitive youngster who is struggling academically this year after being a very successful student in first grade. Mrs. Edwards has met with her daughter's current teacher, and has found her to very inflexible. Mrs. Edwards is afraid to anger the teacher, but sees her daughter beginning to complain of not feeling well almost every morning. However, by late morning, if she is allowed to miss school, she is fine, according to the babysitter.

Mrs. Edwards notes that neither she nor her husband are "yellers" at home, and finds that verbal redirection is enough to change her daughter's behavior when it is inappropriate. However, Mrs. Edwards believes that her daughter's teacher uses yelling in the classroom in order to maintain control of the students, which intimidates her daughter. Mrs. Edwards wonders if she should ask for a change of teacher, even though her daughter is in the middle of the school year, or whether she should just tell her daughter to do her best, and simply chalk the year up to a loss.

Discussion Questions

1. Describe the questions and methods of assessment you would use to assess the teacher's current functioning and behavioral strengths and weaknesses.
2. Brainstorm possible factors involved in the teacher's rigidity. How does this rigidity affect her behavior? Consider the environmental factors as well.
3. Why would Mrs. Edwards's cognitions be a potential target for intervention?
4. What is the student's current functioning?

SCTC/Family Example 3
Harris is a 14-year-old boy who recently transferred to a public school district from an alternative education placement. He has been diagnosed with posttraumatic stress disorder and attention deficit hyperactivity disorder. Harris's adoptive family is very loving toward him. Historically, Harris experienced emotional, sexual, and physical abuse in foster homes, as well as in his biological home. Although Harris often earns good grades and maintains appropriate behavior at school, his teacher and parents have expressed concern regarding his socialization and ability to manage his emotions and behavior. An IEP (Individualized Education Program) meeting was recently held to discuss these concerns.

Harris maintains few friendships. His mother reported that he may be experiencing teasing at school. Harris has a desire to fit in with his peers, but often has difficulty relating to them appropriately. He has difficulty interpreting social cues and makes fun of others without recognizing the effect of his behavior. Harris also has a strong interest in girls. Last summer, Harris had a "summer romance" with a girl who attended his summer camp. His mother reported that the girl and Harris got together a couple of times over the summer to watch a fireworks display, as well as to attend a birthday party. The girl then transferred to his school district in the beginning of the current school year. In his school setting, Harris was somewhat embarrassed by the girl, who is diagnosed with an autism spectrum disorder. Over time, Harris distanced himself from her without considering her feelings.

Harris's family wants him to excel both socially and academically, but feel that his current emotional concerns may impede his academic progress and interpersonal adjustment. The teacher acknowledges Harris's difficulty in making friends, but does not see it as a pressing problem as Harris earns good grades.

Discussion Questions

1. What is the presenting problem?
2. What factors (cognitive, environmental, behavior) are impacting Harris's ability to make friends?
3. How would you assess the teacher's cognitions? The mother's?
4. How do the teacher's beliefs impact her behavior toward Harris?

SCTC/Educator Example 1

Zach is an 11th grade student who has been diagnosed with a learning disability in reading and written language; he is enrolled in an honors science course. His Individualized Education Program requires the following modifications be made to the curriculum for him: typed lecture notes, no credit off for misspelled words, retesting for low test grades in order to determine mastery, and extra time for testing. Mr. Matthews, his science teacher, refuses to permit the modifications in the class saying that it is an honors course, and he is not a special education teacher.

In all of his other classes, Zach is performing well because his teachers make the requested modifications with no difficulty. In fact, his Spanish teacher provides a structured study guide for Zach to follow the week before every test, encouraging him to study with a peer tutor, as well as with his parents. During a trip to the teacher's lounge to use the restroom, the consultant overhears Mr. Matthews complaining about the "special privileges" to some of Zach's other teachers. Although some nod sympathetically, others look uncomfortable as Mr. Matthew adds, "Next, you're going to be telling me the kid should be on the honor roll. Not on my watch!"

Discussion Questions

1. How would you explore the teacher's cognitions?
2. What is the impact of his cognitions on the current situation?
3. What about the environment could support or diminish Mr. Matthews's behaviors?
4. What social cognitive theory strategies would you use to alter Mr. Matthews's beliefs?

SCTC/Educator/Family Example 1

The principal of the Early Childhood Center has contacted the school psychologist to request an evaluation of Beth, a kindergarten student. Beth has not spoken a word in school over the past 4 months, either to the teacher or any classmates. The teacher has contacted Beth's mother, who is very puzzled by her daughter's behavior in school. Beth's mother stated that Beth is a chatterbox at home, but can be shy in new social situations. She is at loss to explain her daughter's silence in school. Both the classroom teacher and principal feel that Beth is autistic and requires a more appropriate and specialized educational placement.

The school psychologist observes Beth in the classroom on two occasions. She observes a youngster seated at a table with five other students. The other students seem comfortable with Beth, and frequently respond on her behalf. The classroom teacher makes a point of asking Beth questions, with Beth maintaining eye contact, but exhibiting no verbal responses. The teacher appears very frustrated with the situation, and points out to Beth that unless she answers the questions, the teacher won't know if she is learning.

During the psychoeducational assessment, Beth refuses to respond to questions asked by the psychologist. However, through the use of a puppet, the psychologist begins eliciting verbal responses from Beth, and at the completion of the assessment, determines that Beth is functioning in the superior range of intellectual functioning with well-developed academic achievement skills.

Information from a behavioral and emotional assessment suggested that Beth was afraid of failing academically, and felt vulnerable and exposed when asked to participate or talk in class. Interestingly, when

Beth's mother and siblings arrive to pick her up after school, the school psychologist observes Beth talking with them in a soft voice, suggesting that Beth feels comfortable speaking when in a familiar, safe environment.

The psychologist then meets with the classroom teacher and principal to review her conclusions regarding her evaluation of Beth, including a diagnosis of selective mutism. The psychologist provides the teacher with reading material about the disorder and suggests a variety of techniques for working with Beth. However, both the teacher and the principal disagree with the psychologist's conclusions, and question the accuracy of her evaluation and conclusion. The principal requests a second opinion and feels that the psychologist has missed the diagnosis.

Discussion Questions

1. What is the presenting problem?
2. Describe how you would approach this situation.
3. Assuming that the teacher and principal believe that an autism diagnosis is more appropriate, how would the consultant go about assessing their beliefs? How do these beliefs or cognitions relate to their self-efficacy?
4. How are their beliefs potentially impacting their interactions (behavior) with Beth?

SCTC/Educator Example 2
Soledad is a 3-year-old girl who is diagnosed with autism. She is enrolled in a structured preschool for typically developing children and children with autism spectrum disorders. The schoolteacher, Mrs. Smith, and the aide are working with Soledad to help her learn and follow the routine in the classroom. With adult guidance and prompting, she is compliant with following directions. However, she does require constant adult prompting or she is quickly off task.

Mrs. Smith previously reported to the school psychologist that they are working with Soledad to help her learn and follow the routine. Mrs. Smith also stated that Soledad is able to stay seated for a few minutes, but needs adult prompting to stay on task because she is disorganized and requires significant structure. Soledad exhibits multiple self-stimulatory behaviors in the classroom. Soledad also has communication delays, both verbal and nonverbal.

Soledad tends to be nonsocial at school and displays minimal interest in her peers. However, she does show much interest in the adults in the room. She spontaneously offers hugs and kisses to her aide and teacher multiple times per day. Her engagement with others is reported to be intermittent; she may interact for brief moments, but otherwise is largely aloof and unaware of her classmates.

Discussion Questions

1. Conceptualize the presenting concern in a social learning theory framework.
2. What interventions is the teacher currently using with Soledad? How would you assess the teacher's self-efficacy beliefs?
3. What aspects of the child's microsystem are impacting her functioning in the school setting?
4. Brainstorm possible problem statements and goals.

SCTC/Systems Example 1

The high school guidance counselor calls the school psychologist requesting an immediate consultation. Susan, an 11th grade high school student, is in the guidance counselor's office, threatening suicide. Susan has disclosed to the counselor that her stepfather has been sexually assaulting her, and after finally telling her mother about the abuse, her mother has kicked her out of the home. Susan has nowhere to live, is hysterical, and says she can't go on.

To add to this crisis, several of Susan's friends have been evidencing symptoms of anxiety and irritability in their classes. The students in Susan's immediate peer group seem preoccupied, and aren't focusing on the academic material in their classes. For example, when reminded to return to the task at hand in her Algebra class, Susan's best friend, Amy, says, "How can I focus on this stuff when there are real-life problems going on?"

Discussion Questions

1. Who is the consultee and who is the client in this example?
2. What consultee questions can you use to assess the guidance counselor's current beliefs regarding this crisis situation?
3. What client questions need to be answered?
4. How should Susan's peer group be addressed, or should they?

SCTC/Systems Example 2

Paula is a sixth grade student who attends Any Middle School. Paula evidences difficulty experiencing and expressing her emotions. Although she has friends, she worries about making mistakes in her friendships and being forgotten by her girlfriends. In addition, she experiences some depressive symptomatology, such as negative self-talk, worrying about grades, difficulty with concentrating, as well as eating and sleeping disruptions. Paula qualifies as emotionally disturbed under special education law (IDEA [Individuals with Disabilities Education Act]). Her grades are often in the average range, but at times can drop dramatically when depressive symptoms are exacerbated.

The family physician has recommended that Paula receive counseling to address her depressive symptomatology and emotion regulation difficulties. School psychologists in this particular school district do not typically provide counseling services. The guidance counselors are willing to provide Paula with short-term behavioral therapy, but do not feel they can address her emotional problems.

Discussion Questions

1. Describe the problem.
2. How would you assess the problem?
3. What are the school district's beliefs (cognitions) with respect to counseling services within school? How do these beliefs impact their behavior?

SCTC/Systems Example 3

Carl is a 15-year-old boy who has been diagnosed with autism and attends mainstream classes with a full-time aide. His mother recently met with the school psychologist to discuss ongoing concerns regarding Carl's peer socialization and daily living skills. Carl has low social interest and prefers to play by himself at home. Carl attends a social skills group, but has difficulty joining in discussion and play with the other children. Carl did not want to join his school's choir because of the social demands associated with peer interaction. However, Carl is able to participate in the adult choir at church.

Although Carl has expressed a desire to be independent and move out of his parents' house when he is old enough, he has difficulty performing the daily living skills necessary for independent living. His difficulty in performing these skills appears due to a lack of motivation rather than an inability to perform the tasks. He presents with good personal hygiene and is able to use the bathroom, shower, and tie his shoes independently. However, he has difficulty cleaning up after himself and cooking simple meals. Carl's mother expressed concern regarding his ability to take care of himself, especially when he is older.

Carl's mother has requested a meeting with his teachers, principal, and the school administration. She wants Carl to participate in daily living skill activities throughout the school day, but the district does not perceive it as a necessity because Carl is successful academically. The district's daily living skill program is typically reserved for lower functioning children.

Discussion Questions

1. What consultant characteristics are essential to working with the school district?
2. What consultee questions would you ask? What are the environmental constraints to providing Carl with daily living skill opportunities?
3. What information would you need from Carl?
4. How do the school district's cognitions affect their behavior in the current situation?

SUMMARY

In this chapter, SCTC was reviewed. Information was provided regarding the assumptions of SCT and the role of motivation in the consultation process. The SCTC process was then described, including its characteristics and the nature of the consultative relationship, the assessment process, the statement of the problem and identification of goals, the selection and implementation of interventions, and the monitoring and evaluation of interventions. Additionally, the role of the consultant in SCTC was discussed, and a summary of the effectiveness of SCTC was provided. In the next chapter, Adlerian consultation will be presented, along with case studies that can be used to practice this consultative model.

CHAPTER 5

Adlerian Consultation

OVERVIEW

Alfred Adler was an Austrian psychologist who cofounded psychoanalysis with Sigmund Freud and a group of colleagues. Adler is well known for rejecting Freud's view of the nature of human functioning, subsequently developing his own theory of individual psychology. In constructing his theory, Adler used the following central concepts: (a) Humans are social beings and their behaviors are embedded in their social contexts, (b) behavior is based on one's subjective reality, and in order to understand behavior you must look at the individual's idiosyncratic experience, (c) individuals function holistically and should not be viewed from a reductionistic perspective, in which aspects of functioning are isolated and examined independently, (d) in order to understand personality, one must examine the characteristic patterns and beliefs about a person's view of the self, others and the world, all of which create a person's *lifestyle*, (e) all aspects of behavior are goal-directed and purposive, (f) human beings have a need to belong, and (g) individuals have the power of choice in controlling their attitudes and behaviors (Brown, Pryzwansky & Schulte, 2006; Dinkmeyer, Carlson, & Dinkmeyer, 1994).

Adler's writings were not translated into English until the 1950s, so his seminal work is reported on and expanded by authors such as Heinz and Rowena Ansbacher and Rudolf Dreikurs.* While Adler's work focuses on children and their development, he especially understood the critical experience of schooling, as noted in his 1929 *Individual Psychology in the Schools* publication. In particular, Adler highlighted the

---

* Works by these authors as well as those of Dinkmeyer et al., (1994), Dinkmeyer and Carlson (2006), and Brown et al. (2006) have been adapted for this chapter. Readers are encouraged to consult these works for further understanding of this consultative model.

importance of early experiences in the development of personality. He described the importance of inborn feelings of inferiority that children face as they compare themselves to older children, adults, and the world around them (Stein & Edwards, 1998).

These feelings of inferiority serve to propel the child forward to strive to acquire the skills he or she views as reflecting competence. As the child grows, his or her experiences in the family social environment influences the choices he or she makes in developing lifestyle patterns. By 5 or 6 years of age, the child has acquired a sufficient amount of experience so that he or she is able to develop a prototype of his or her goals and style of life (e.g., personality). Early goals contribute to the development of the final goal, which is a subjective, fictional representation of the individual and his or her future that serves to drive behaviors in the present (Stein & Edwards, 1998).

Children who are supported in their family environment and given the opportunity to develop their strengths will develop courage, the ability to make decisions, and empathic social interests. In healthy individuals, the tasks of life (i.e., work, community, and love) are handled through active, flexible problem solving (Adler, 1927/1957, 1992). Such children are then able to use their feelings of inferiority as a stimulus for continued development, striving for superiority over personal and social difficulties rather than superiority over others. Moreover, social interest is seen as an indicator of mental health (Stein & Edwards, 1998).

However, Adler contended that for children who are not supported, are deprived of having their basic needs met, are abused, hated, excessively pampered, or have a disability (e.g., organ inferiorities), mental health problems may develop (Brown et al., 2006; Dreikurs, 1953). Discouraged, these children cope with their feelings of inferiority by reliving or masking their feelings. Instead of confronting difficulties, they will falsely bolster their feelings, resulting in a fragile feeling of superiority. At other times, they may use psychological symptoms (e.g., depression, anxiety) as a means to explain failures.

In an attempt to develop their life path, children who misbehave reportedly do so to reach one or more of four goals: attention, power, revenge, or confirmation of inadequacies in order to disengage from social interactions, which would be a symptom of mental health. For example, Adler believed that children seeking attention are actually striving to obtain recognition. Further, children who have a goal for power may either appear domineering and aggressive, or may passively entice others into engaging in power struggles. Children who seek revenge punish others in an effort to get even. Finally, children who desire to withdraw from social connections fear that interacting with others will highlight their inadequacies. Dreikurs (1968) reported that one or more of these goals are evident in the misbehavior of children up to the age of 10 years. However, in other cases, chronological age may not be the best indicator, since the presence of developmental delays may keep these goals relevant after age 10 (Croake & Myers, 1985). The misbehavior of older children and adults can also be explained by these four goals, but their manifestation may be more complex.

In addition to attempting to reach the four goals, adolescents work to attain three additional goals: excitement, peer acceptance, and superiority. According to Adler, those adolescents with excitement goals demonstrate misbehavior to avoid routines, frequently engaging in drugs and alcohol use, sexual activity and other high-risk behaviors. Adolescents with peer acceptance goals will constantly attempt to gain widespread peer acceptance. Both of these misbehavior goals have the potential to become power struggles with parents and teachers. Further, adolescents with superiority goals strive to prove they are the best (or better than most) in their grades, honors, athletics, and so forth. However, this group can use their talents destructively, putting others down in the attempt to distinguish themselves from peers (Dinkmeyer & Carlson, 2006).

According to Adler, the decision to adopt a lifestyle is based on the child's or adolescent's perceptions of his or her limitations. For example, if a challenge is seen as only a temporary setback rather than devastation, then a more positive psychological outcome will result. Adler believed that the more unsupported the child or adolescent, the more discrepant his or her fictional final self goal would be from his or her actual self goal. In this way, the child's or adolescent's (mis)perceptions guide his or her views about the self, others, and the world, resulting in patterned behaviors that comprise one's personality (Dinkmeyer et al., 1994).

Adler maintained that lifestyle or personality choices are made both at the conscious and unconscious level, with these two systems working in conjunction with one another. Adler's description of the importance of birth order, and the potential psychological significance that this social experience may have for the individual child or adolescent, exemplifies how the conscious and unconscious experiences work together. When considering the role of the unconscious, Dreikus (1953) prefers the term *unadmitted*, as he argues that lifestyle choices are knowable but are often explicitly ignored. For example, the finding that no one discards a behavior that is useful to him or her, or acknowledges one that is not, captures the concept of *conscious ignoring*. In fact, much of Adlerian practice is focused on understanding the driving significance of a person's conscious and unconscious goals.

Adlerian Consultation (AC)

In Adler's theory, a primary goal of consultation is to prevent mental health problems through encouragement (Adler, 1957). Expressing belief in the individual's ability and worth rather than reinforcing behavioral accomplishments is the kind of support needed by children in order to develop into healthy individuals. In fact, Adler believed that the positive rewards used in behavioral systems actually discourage healthy development because behavioral systems value actions rather than people in their own right (Brown et al., 2006). Adlerian consultation provides the opportunity to educate teachers and parents about the importance of encouragement, which is the first step toward prevention of unhealthy lifestyle patterns.

Assumptions of AC

As previously stated, in AC, encouragement is assumed to provide the needed support for healthy development. Brown et al. (2006) describe how Adler used clear, unambiguous language with teachers and parents to show how to express and use encouragement in interacting with children in schools. When communicating with children, it is important that teachers and parents keep the following principles in mind: (1) demonstrate acceptance, (2) separate the act and the actor, (3) value effort over outcomes, (4) consider current functioning as more important than past events, (5) emphasize intrinsic motivation, and (6) value the person instead of his or her behavior (Dinkmeyer & Carlson, 2006).

Adler contended that the way in which teachers and parents use language to address difficulties demonstrated by children is critical in establishing how children will view their worth. Of particular importance is not only accepting the individual, but also communicating about problems in a way that conveys acceptance. For example, teachers can discuss a child's difficulties by first identifying the child and then the accompanying difference or variation (e.g., culture, disability). This framework is evident today in the "person first" nomenclature in which children are being described as having a disability, instead of being disabled (Snow, 2007).

Adler also advised that it is important to separate the act from the actor; teachers and parents can demonstrate and communicate care to a child, and still not like his or her behavior. Since th–is is an important distinction, it should be stated explicitly. Further, effort and improvements in participation should be valued rather than the outcome of such behaviors. Similarly, grades should be discussed in terms of participation and improved learning rather than performance outcomes, such as percentage correct. Again, individual growth is seen as the most important factor to consider (Dinkmeyer & Carlson, 2006).

Following his theory, Adler recommended that teachers and parents focus on current functioning instead of prior behavior, believing that it is not helpful to comment on poor past behavior, as it devalues the importance of the child's current functioning. Similarly, pointing out improvement from the past in a manner that highlights historic poor performance is not seen as being helpful in improving future functioning. Adler argued that highlighting the temporal nature of success is likely to leave students feeling as though they cannot sustain the current level of approval (Stein & Edwards, 1998).

Additionally, orienting students to their feelings about success is an important foundation to encouragement. Adler recommended that moving appraisals of worth from an external source (e.g., how I think you did) to an internal source (e.g., how do you feel about your work?) is of critical importance to establishing a system of self-encouragement. If feelings of worth are contingent upon the environment, then the environment will dictate worth, which is not a useful or safe situation for children because the environment may withdraw approval (Brown et al., 2006). In Table 5.1, examples of praise versus encouragement are provided.

Stages of the AC Process

Initiation of the Relationship

In AC, the consultation relationship is critical to the success of the process. Such relationships are voluntary and nonhierarchical because the consultant and consultee are equal collaborators working together to solve a problem of a third party. Interactions should be free from judgment, and they also should be characterized by empathy and mutual respect (Dreikurs & Cassel, 1971). As the consultative relationship is established, the consultant seeks to determine the lifestyle (e.g., personality) of the consultee, since this knowledge will impact the course of consultation and the roles that will be assumed by both the consultant and client.

Assessment of the Problem

In assessing the problem, consultants may use both interviews and observations. Often, interviews are highly structured and include questions for

Table 5.1 Differences between Praise and Encouragement

| PRAISE | | | ENCOURAGEMENT | | |
UNDERLYING CHARACTERISTICS	MESSAGE SENT TO CHILD	POSSIBLE RESULTS	UNDERLYING CHARACTERISTICS	MESSAGE SENT TO CHILD	POSSIBLE RESULTS
Focus is on external control.	"You are worthwhile only when you do what I want." "You cannot and should not be trusted."	Child learns to measure worth by ability to conform; or child rebels (views any form of cooperation as giving in).	Focus is on child's ability to manage life constructively.	"I trust you to become responsible and independent."	Child learns courage to be imperfect and willingness to try. Child gains self-confidence and comes to feel responsible for own behavior.
Focus is on external evaluation.	"To be worthwhile, you must please me." "Please me or perish."	Child learns to measure worth on how well he/she pleases others. Child learns to fear disapproval.	Focus is on internal evaluation.	"How you feel about yourself and your own efforts is most important."	Child learns to evaluate own progress and to make own decisions.
Rewards come only for well done, completed tasks.	"To be worthwhile, you must meet my standards."	Child develops unrealistic standards and learns to measure worth by how closely he/she reaches perfection. Child learns to dread failure.	Recognizes effort and improvement.	"You don't have to be perfect. Effort and improvement are important."	Child learns to value efforts of self and others. Child develops desire to stay with tasks (persistence).
Focuses on self-evaluation and personal gain.	"You're the best. You must remain superior to others to be worthwhile."	Child learns to be overcompetitive, to get ahead at the expense of others. Feels worthwhile only when "on top."	Focuses on assets, contributions, and appreciation.	"Your contribution counts. We function better with you. We appreciate what you have done."	Child learns to use talents and efforts for good of all, not only for personal gain. Child learns to feel glad for successes of others as well as own successes.

Source: (From *The Growing Teacher: How to Become the Teacher You've Always Wanted to Be*, by J. Carlson and C. Thorpe, 1984, Englewood Cliffs, NJ: Prentice Hall, Inc. (pp. 39–40).) Copyright 1984 by Prentice Hall. Reprinted with permission from the author.

parents and/or teachers concerning the details of the child's movements throughout the day and a description of their reactions to those events. Consultants may use the Diagnostic Student Interview, a structured questionnaire designed to illustrate and explicate the child's lifestyle patterns and perceptions thereof. It is recommended that consultants gather data regarding the use of encouragement, children's opportunities to have impact upon and assume responsibilities in their environment, as well as natural and logical consequences for behavior, each of which will be discussed in detail in the following section (Brown et al., 2006, Dinkmeyer & Carlson, 2006).

Setting Goals and Interventions

The intervention selection process is determined by the goal of the misbehavior. If only one misbehavior goal is identified, then that goal is the focus of intervention. If there are several misbehavior goals identified, then the consultee selects the goals that interventions should target. Once the target is selected, consistency is emphasized. In addition to matching goals and interventions, direct instruction in social skills, for example, may be needed for the client. Commonsense interventions are suggested to parents and teachers in order to avoid the need to train individuals in theoretical concepts. Finally, consultants provide support to the consultee throughout the process (Dinkmeyer & Carlson, 2006).

In the AC process, consultants accept and expect resistance, understanding that teachers, parents, and the client may all resist change. At times, more than one person in the system may be resistant. In AC, there are many reasons for the consultant to encounter resistance from consultees or clients, including fear of the client getting better, fear of discovering a sensitive family dynamic (e.g., drug use, divorce), and so forth. Consultants often reference their own feelings of frustration in order to guide their interpretation of the level of resistance encountered in the consultative relationship. When resistance occurs, consultants do not address it directly, but rather seek to clarify the complaints by the consultee, and in turn transfer the responsibility of solving those complaints to the consultee (Dinkmeyer & Carlson, 2006).

Analyze the Results

In the AC process, follow-up sessions are designed to review progress, address new concerns, and to provide support to consultees. The AC relationship is typically terminated when the consultee feels that the intervention has met his or her goals. If the consultee is resistant to making changes and there is no progress, however, the consultant may terminate the relationship (Dinkmeyer & Carlson, 2006).

AC in the Schools

In other forms of consultation, often the primary goal is to address the needs of the client or third party. However in AC, the consultee is not viewed as simply the translator or conduit for information and change processes provided by the consultant to reach the client. Instead, the consultee's attitudes are targeted for change as well (Dinkmeyer & Carlson, 2006). By establishing that the consultee retains responsibility for the problem as well as its solution, the consultee (who needs the help) can get the help (from the consultant) to make the changes in himself or herself (the consultee), so that he or she can help himself or herself while helping another (the client) (Dinkmeyer et al., 1994).

Dreikurs (1968) applied Adler's view of changing the consultee's attitudes and skills when he suggested that school and family systems should seek advice from children regarding the way in which the environment (e.g., classroom, family) is functioning. Dreikurs (1968) also believed that it was important for children to take responsibility for their space (e.g., desk, bedroom, etc.) and decision making. Glasser (1998) provides an example of this principle in his writings about quality schools, in which he describes a quality school as one in which children participate in creating the expectations (e.g., rules) of the classroom and school building. When adults value the choices that children make, according to Glasser (1998), children learn to value themselves.

A related concept is the idea of natural and logical consequences. Without risking a child's safety, Adler believes that the natural environment should provide corrective feedback to the child. For example, a child choosing not to wear a coat to school will result in the natural consequence of being cold. In this instance, there is no need for parental punishment or corrective feedback about making a poor choice. Similarly, a logical consequence is applied by the natural and social environment where the infraction occurred, and is one in which the punishment fits the crime. For example, writing on a school desk would result in the child being responsible for either cleaning the desk or buying a new one. Conversely, taking away recess or library privileges for misbehavior on the bus would not be a logical consequence. As described by Ansbacher and Ansbacher (1956), these rules are predetermined as part of the classroom code of conduct, and consequences are administered without anger, negative emotions, or punishment. In Table 5.2, examples of differences between punishment and logical consequences are provided.

Types of Consultation

Developmental Consultation

Within AC, the most preferred type of consultation, *developmental consultation*, is used when the goal is to create a learning environment for the consultee that ultimately informs the way in which he or she should work with the client (Dinkmeyer & Carlson, 2006). This may include explicit examples of how to show care and value to children, or experiences that illustrate natural and logical consequences.

Remedial Consultation

The second type of consultation, *remedial consultation*, is used when it is evident that a crisis is pending and steps need to be taken to avert a negative outcome (Dinkmeyer & Carlson, 2006). Remedial consultation requires identifying the client's goal of misbehavior. By observing the impact of the client upon others, the consultee describes the behavior of the client to the consultant. For example, mildly annoying behaviors are likely an attention-seeking goal, whereas aggressive behaviors are likely a power goal. Typically, the feelings elicited in the consultee regarding the client's misbehavior are sufficient for diagnosing the goal.

However, further evidence may be required by talking with the client (child). For example, if one asks the client (child), "If you could be an animal, what would it be?" although the answer is not significant, the answer to the follow-up question, "Why would you want to be that animal?" provides insight. If the client (child) picks a cat, because cats can do whatever they want and everyone leaves them alone, then social withdrawal is the goal. Similarly, asking the client (child) "What animal would you not like to be?" and "Why would you not like to be that animal?" provides insight into the goal of the client's misbehavior. Once the diagnosis is made, feedback to the consultee is provided. Tentatively, through questioning the consultee, the consultant suggests the client's behavioral goals. The tentative format allows the consultee to reject or resist accepting the interpretation, which can be used to help clarify the goal motives of the consultee. Interestingly, the consultee's acceptance of the goal is not an immediate objective.

Table 5.2 Major Differences between Punishment and Logical Consequences

PUNISHMENT			LOGICAL CONSEQUENCES		
CHARACTERISTICS	UNDERLYING MESSAGE	LIKELY RESULTS	CHARACTERISTICS	UNDERLYING MESSAGE	LIKELY RESULTS
1. Emphasis on power of personal authority.	Do what I say because I say so! I'm in charge here!	Rebellion. Revenge. Lack of self-discipline. Sneakiness. Irresponsibility.	1. Emphasis on reality of social order.	I trust you to learn to respect yourself and the rights of others.	Self-discipline. Cooperation. Respect for self and others. Reliability.
2. Rarely related to the act; arbitrary.	I'll show you! You deserve what you're getting!	Resentment. Revenge. Fear. Confusion. Rebellion.	2. Logically related to misbehavior; makes sense.	I trust you to make responsible choices.	Learns from experience.
3. Implies moral judgments.	This should teach you! You're bad!	Feelings of hurt, resentment, guilt, revenge.	3. No moral judgment. Treats student with dignity.	You are a worthwhile person!	Learns behavior, may be objectionable (not to self).
4. Emphasizes past behavior.	This is for what you did—I'm not forgetting! You'll never learn!	Feels unable to make good decisions. Unacceptable in eyes of teacher.	4. Concerned with present and future behavior.	You can make your own choices and take care of yourself.	Becomes self-directed and self-evaluating.
5. Threatens disrespect, either open or implied.	You'd better shape up! No one in my class acts like that!	Desire to get even. Fear. Rebellion. Guilt feelings.	5. Voice communicates respect and good will.	It's your behavior I don't like, but I still like you!	Feels secure in teacher's respect and support.
6. Demands compliance.	Your preferences don't matter! You can't be trusted to make wise decisions!	Defiant compliance. Plans to get even another time. Destruction of trust and equality.	6. Presents a choice.	You can decide.	Responsible decisions. Increased resourcefulness.

Source: (From *Systematic Training for Effective Teaching (STET): Teacher's Handbook* by Dinkmeyer, McKay, and Dinkmeyer, 1980, Step Publishers, Bowling Green, Kentucky.) Reproduced with permission from the author.

Crisis Consultation

Finally, in *crisis consultation*, an extreme event has already happened, and the consultant is being asked to respond. In such instances, stress levels are often very high, and consultees may be overly willing or resistant to intervention (Dinkmeyer & Carlson, 2006). Moreover, it is important to determine the type of consultation within AC that is being requested. The consultant should consider the type of consultation desired, as well as the optimal time for effective change. In summary, although change can happen at any time, the most effective type of consultation is developmental, since the goal is to assist the consultee in developing knowledge and new skills.

EFFECTIVENESS OF AC

Unlike other forms of consultation, such as BC, there is limited empirical support for AC. As noted in chapter 2, most consultation research does not examine approaches where inferences about the cause of behaviors are employed. Further, the individual focus of AC does not lend itself to control sample comparisons. Of the limited research available, there are some case studies concluding that this type of consultation is successful with teachers (Mortola & Carlson, 2003; Schneider, 1983; White & Mullis, 1998) and parents (Kottman & Ashby, 1999). Researchers examining the use of AC in teacher encouragement have also found an improvement in student on-task behaviors (Hillman & Shields, 1975; Rathvon, 1990). Despite its lack of substantial empirical support, however, Dinkmeyer (2006) maintains that Adler's individual psychology is "exceptionally suited" as a consultative model. Barriers to providing AC include the limited ability to measure outcomes in an age where evidence-based decisions drive school setting conclusions. Moreover, most graduate training programs in education and related fields have a limited focus on teaching Adlerian concepts.

CASES IN ADLERIAN CONSULTATION
AC/Student Example 1

Marcus is a 12-year-old male who attends the sixth grade at Average Middle School. Marcus's difficulties at school include frequent disruptive classroom behaviors, continued discipline referrals, and a decline in academic performance as reported by teachers, parents and the school principal.

Marcus lives with his parents, his younger sister, Kelly, and his paternal uncle. According to Marcus's mother, her pregnancy with Marcus was complicated by severe kidney infections requiring hospitalization, where she was prescribed a variety of sulfur-based medications. Consequently, Marcus was born without enamel on his teeth, an expected but unfortunate result of the medications. Additionally, Marcus's mother reports that since he was a toddler, Marcus has always had a difficult temperament characterized by irritability and restlessness. Marcus's mother describes him as an overly sensitive young man who can become emotional, tearful, and at times aggressive when he is confronted with issues that he finds uncomfortable. She advises that when Marcus becomes upset, "leaving Marcus alone is the only thing that works with him."

Marcus's teachers and counselor indicate that Marcus is ostracized by his peers. When questioned, Marcus confirms these perceptions, stating that his peers view him as "bad." On one occasion, while being escorted by a teacher to in-school suspension, Marcus threatened self-injurious behavior and thus was taken to the counselor's office. The counselor, who had worked with Marcus in the past, initiated appropriate intervention after consulting with the school psychologist and principal. During the intervention, Marcus was tearful and responded angrily toward the counselor, stating he was "just joking." He also reported that he was suspicious of the intent of the counselor's stated desire to help him. After a formal assessment was recommended and conducted at the local Child Psychiatric Hospital, Marcus returned to school. Marcus's teachers report nothing has changed, and that Marcus continues to act defiantly in the classroom.

Discussion Questions

1. What is the goal of AC in this case?
2. What stage of consultation is this?
3. Explicitly state the personality and social environmental issues with Marcus' teachers and parents.
4. In what way will encouragement be used with the teacher? With his parents?

AC/Student Example 2

Luciano is a 16-year-old male who irregularly attends the 10th grade at Distressed Public High School. His mother, Ms. Illiano, reports that Luciano is noncompliant with household rules, engages in physical fights with her and his younger brother Frank (who is 7 years of age), and is using illegal substances. Specifically, Luciano has a documented history of using inhalants such as spray paint and nonstick spray-on oil. When questioned, Luciano admits to having friends who are known drug users and dealers. However, he denies current drug use. All of Luciano's friends are over the age of 18 and none are working or attending school.

Ms. Illiano has a documented history of coping with stress through alcohol use. She has previously attended, but not completed, three counseling programs for alcohol and substance abuse, and is currently enrolled in her fourth drug treatment program. Ms. Illiano says that her success in treatment depends heavily on Luciano's behavior, as he is a significant source of stress for her. She often feels as though Luciano is trying to get back at her, and admits that parenting in the home is limited. From her report, it is difficult to tell if there are established rules within the household.

Discussion Questions

1. What is the goal of AC in this case?
2. What stage of consultation is this?
3. What type of misbehavior goal does Luciano exhibit?
4. How will natural and logical consequences work in this case?

AC/Student Example 3

Sally is a 12-year-old female student who attends seventh grade at Any Junior High School. Sally has always been known to earn excellent grades, complete chores at home, and requires limited supervision from her parents. Sally recently won the school spelling bee and is planning to compete at the district bee. As an excellent student, Sally's teachers have begun to allow Sally some class time to prepare for this important event. Recently, the parent–teacher organization (PTO) hung a banner that heralded Sally's win.

The school counselor has become concerned because Sally's name recently appeared on a request for peer mediation. Also, when Sally added her name to the sign-up sheet for the counselor's social group, the Lunch Bunch, regular attendees began crossing their names off the list, writing "snob" next to Sally's name. Sally's peers have reported that Sally "thinks she's something she's not." Sally's teacher says that others are jealous of the attention Sally receives and she has advised Sally to remain focused on her goals and to ignore the behavior of her classmates.

Discussion Questions

1. What stage of AC is this?
2. What type of misbehavior goal does Sally exhibit?
3. Explicitly state the personality and social environmental issues.
4. In what way can encouragement be used?

AC/Family Example 1

Jen is a 10-year-old female in the fifth grade. She is diagnosed with a learning disability and has received special education since the first grade. Jen has a small group of friends and an active social life. Jen is aware of her learning disability and tends to befriend others who also learn differently, demonstrating great consideration for the learning differences others experience.

Jen's teachers report that she is somewhat at risk for exploitation by her peers. In explanation, Jen's easygoing nature leaves her open to manipulation from others. For example, Jen's favorite social activity is dancing. However, some of her peers have reported that Jen "dances for boys." Jen admits to "dancing" only for boys with whom she is not friendly as a way to interact with new people. She also adds that she tends to dance at her bus stop and only between classes, "never when we are supposed to be listening in our seats."

A discussion with Jen and the school counselor has highlighted her naïveté as to how others may misinterpret or misrepresent her socially appropriate interests. Jen's mother is aware of Jen's perceptions of her behavior, but she worries that others are taking advantage of her daughter. However, Jen's mother reports that she is not going to discourage a "normal, healthy interest in exercise," and she wants Jen's teachers to instead focus on Jen's learning needs.

Discussion Questions

1. What is the goal of AC in this case?
2. What type of misbehavior goal does she exhibit?
3. In what way can encouragement be used?
4. How will natural and logical consequences work in this case?

AC/Family Example 2

Alicia is a 14-year-old female who is in the eighth grade. Alicia currently resides in a foster placement with her half brother, three foster brothers, and a foster sister. Alicia's biological parents are both incarcerated on drug charges, and Alicia's early childhood history is characterized by neglect. Prior to her foster placement, Alicia and her siblings lived on the street, attended school sporadically, and prided themselves on their independence.

Alicia's foster mother reports that Alicia is streetwise and focuses on drug use and sexual behavior when talking to others. Additionally, Alicia's foster mother reports that Alicia enjoys the response she elicits from adults when she talks about her life history. In fact, she will often ask adults if they are surprised at her "knowledge about the world," adding that most are surprised. When adults are unresponsive, Alicia will embellish her stories to the point of being outrageous. Often social agencies and schools respond to her reports, a sequence that Alicia obviously enjoys, but have led to nothing more than the conclusion, "while she has been exposed to many things, there is no evidence of direct abuse." Alicia's foster mother is most interested in how to help Alicia adjust to a stable family life.

Alicia's teachers report that she demonstrates limited social skills. Her actions tend to be somewhat impulsive and at times indicate a clear devaluation of self. Alicia's peers neither reject nor seek to be with her—with interests so discrepant from theirs, it is like she is "invisible to them." Likewise, Alicia seems disinterested in peers and spends most of her time with adults. When she finds teachers unresponsive, she will seek out the counselor, reporting "flashbacks about sex and drugs." A bright girl, Alicia's grades are Bs and Cs, and her rates of acquisition and retention of class material are average.

Discussion Questions

1. What is the goal of AC in the case of Alicia?
2. Explicitly state the personality and social environmental issues for Alicia and her foster mother.
3. In what way can encouragement be used?
4. How will natural and logical consequences work in this case?

AC/Family Example 3

Tyler is a 7-year-boy who was referred for a special education evaluation by his mother, despite a "B" average and appropriate rates of acquisition and retention of material in the curriculum. However, in order to allay his mother's concerns, the school agreed to conduct the multidisciplinary evaluation. Consistent with teacher reports, grades, and standardized test scores, Tyler was found to fall within the low average range and progressing through the curriculum as expected. He was not eligible for special education services; however, the team recommended some supportive interventions in the general education classroom to maintain his current progress.

Sure that Tyler could be an "A+" student, his mother became convinced that Tyler had undiagnosed AD/HD. Therefore, she asked her pediatrician to prescribe a medication trial to see if Tyler's grades would improve. After a month of medication, Tyler's teachers noted a minimal increase in attention skills but no increase in his academic skills. The pediatrician saw no benefit in continuing the medication, so it was discontinued.

At present, Tyler's mother reports that she has just finished researching celiac disease, and believes that removing wheat from Tyler's food may improve his grades. Consequently, Tyler's mother is requesting that the school provide a special diet for Tyler and that his teacher requires parents to provide snacks that are Gluten-free for special occasion celebrations, such as holiday parties and birthdays.

As the school complied with this request, Tyler's mother added that she thinks he may be allergic to the trees in the nearby woods. She is therefore asking for an improvement in the air quality provided with the current air-conditioning system. Tyler's teacher is now requesting help to manage the mother of a well-adjusted, average young boy who is functioning well in school.

Discussion Questions

1. What stage of consultation is this?
2. What type of misbehavior goal is exhibited?
3. In what way can encouragement be used?
4. How will natural and logical consequences work in this case?

AC/Educator Example 1

LeShaun is a ninth grade student who is beginning his first year at Competitive High School. At school, LeShaun appears to be mild mannered, shy, and withdrawn. Recently, LeShaun's teachers and the support staff have noticed a decrease in his ability to perform basic self-help activities. For example, he will ask his peers what he should order from the school cafeteria for lunch. Often, he requests teacher support for mundane tasks, asking what color to label a science graph or how to title an English assignment. Recently, in gym, he reported that he could not dress himself and requested assistance from the coaching staff.

When school officials contact his parents, they confirm similar "regressive" behaviors at home. They asked LeShaun directly about this strange behavior, and he reported that school stress is interfering with his ability to make decisions. Specifically, he fears making the "wrong" choices. He reasons that by consulting with those around him, he may be saved from this fate. Also, he believes that other people like to tell him what to do, so the arrangement is mutually beneficial. Although LeShaun's grades have remained in the "B" and "C" range, all parties are unsure who is doing LeShaun's work both in and out of class. While LeShaun admits to being afraid of being wrong, he judges this new behavioral style as an effective solution.

Discussion Questions

1. What is the goal of Adlerian consultation in LeShaun's case?
2. What type of misbehavior goal does he exhibit?
3. In what way can encouragement be used?
4. How will natural and logical consequences work in this case?

AC/Educator Example 2

Mindy is a 6-year-old girl who attends kindergarten at the Excellent Elementary School. She lives with her foster parents, her biological brother James, who is 2½ years old, and her foster brother Ben, who is a medically fragile 9-year-old. Mindy has lived in her current foster placement for 8 months. Over the last 2 years, there have been three previous foster placements, and she has been placed in respite care on and off throughout her life.

Mindy's biological mother is reported to have a significant drug and alcohol abuse history, and to carry the diagnosis of mental retardation (mild) and panic attacks without agoraphobia. Mindy's biological father is also reported to have problems with drugs and anger. Mindy's developmental history is characterized by abuse. Specifically, as an infant, she was diagnosed with failure to thrive, and her medical records indicate she may suffer from fetal alcohol syndrome (FAS). While living with her parents, Mindy was sexually abused, witnessed the stabbing of her nephew, which resulted in her father's imprisonment, and was hospitalized for malnutrition around the time of her brother's birth. Mindy has participated in sexual abuse recovery counseling (ages 4 to 6); however, she often reveals the details of her abuse publicly, and seems to enjoy the shocked responses of teachers.

To date, she remains preoccupied with death, often talking about killing others and/or dying. At age 4, Mindy took an overdose of Tylenol, presumably as a suicidal gesture. She is also preoccupied with food and will steal food items from teachers and other students. Mindy's foster parents report that she will hoard food in her closets, although there are no restrictions on eating in the home.

Mindy and her brother have visitation with their biological mother every other Tuesday. During these visits, it is reported that Mindy's mother gives more attention to her brother, James. Mindy is reportedly very jealous of attention given to James by both her biological mother and by her foster mother. Mindy's medical records indicate that she has tried to hurt James on several occasions, including overturning his high chair and playpen and covering his face with a pillow. For these reasons, Mindy is closely supervised at home. It is important to note that Mindy is not particularly affectionate toward her foster brother Ben, but also has not been aggressive with him.

Although reports indicate that Mindy historically experienced a significant delay in her speech and gross and fine motor skills, at this time, speech and motor skills are within normal limits. Mindy's kindergarten teacher reports that she is overwhelmed by working with Mindy. She feels angry, and does not believe that she is "equipped to handle such a problem child" or to respond to concerned parents who are taken aback by Mindy's reports about her past experiences.

Discussion Questions

1. What is the goal of Adlerian consultation in Mindy's case?
2. What type of misbehavior goal does she exhibit?
3. In what way can encouragement be used? Provide details for this complex case.
4. How will natural and logical consequences work in this case?

AC/Educator Example 2

Ernest is a 10-year-old male who attends the fourth grade. His family moved to the United States 6 years ago illegally. Both of Ernest's parents hold several part-time jobs and work long hours. The family lives in a poor neighborhood that is riddled with street violence. Ernest does not associate with neighborhood children; he has only one acquaintance in school with whom he will occasionally sit at lunch.

At school, Ernest declines to participate in free play, sports, or other social activities occurring during the school day. Often, Ernest will return to the classroom at lunch and read books or draw while the other students and teachers are not present. Left alone, Ernest will complete a minimal amount of school work and seems to fade into the classroom environment. When participation is required, Ernest often feigns illness or remains passively off-task. Recently, his teachers have noticed that Ernest's low level of participation has morphed into refusal. They are also concerned that Ernest has such little interest in interacting with his peers.

Discussion Questions

1. What type of misbehavior goal does Ernest exhibit?
2. Explicitly state the personality and social environmental issues for Ernest and his teachers.
3. In what way can encouragement be used?
4. How will natural and logical consequences work in this case?

AC/Systems Example 1

An alternative education school is designing a schoolwide behavior program to address the needs of the adjudicated youth they serve. All students attending the school have committed crimes. The teachers feel they need to establish an environment where students learn that illegal and aggressive behaviors will not be tolerated; student behavioral control is the first priority so that academic needs may be addressed. To this end, the teachers feel they need a behavioral system where there are clear rules, consequences that are administered consistently by all administrators, and strong sanctions for inappropriate behavior such as cursing, disrespect, and threats or actual violence.

In many ways, these teachers fear the students who attend the school. It is their perception that previous verbal threats made by students toward the faculty were handled inappropriately, and they believe that administrators coddled the students when it was time to implement consequences. Worried about their safety, these teachers plan a demerit system that calls for sanctions and suspensions. However, the principal trying to recruit students to the program notes that community and state agencies want systems that promote positive behaviors through support.

Teachers are unsure how they can control the students' behavior without punishment for poor conduct. Also, teachers report that they dislike a behavioral system that rewards youth for "simply acting like you are supposed to behave." The lead teacher approaches you for advice on how to word behavioral sanctions in a positive way so that the teachers are meeting the requests of the principal and their need to control student behavior.

Discussion Questions

1. What is the goal of Adlerian consultation in the case of the Alternative Education School?
2. What stage of consultation is this?
3. What type of misbehavior goal is assumed?
4. State explicitly the personality and social environmental issues for the teachers and the social context relevant to the system.

AC/Systems Example 2

A local elementary school is interested in establishing a bullying prevention program to help deter low-level aggressive behavior and to improve civility by implementing a conflict mediation program at school. The school faculty has reviewed the curriculum, and supports its premise and implementation. However, teachers are concerned about two contingencies the school board may attach to the program, thus undermining its effectiveness.

First, the school board is insisting on retaining a zero-tolerance policy regarding verbal threats. Alternately, the faculty feels that the purpose of the program is to increase assertiveness and promote appropriate communications between students. Currently, there are students who do not meet the desired behaviors, and to dismiss this group from school and prevent them from participating in the program does not seem like a sound decision. The school board counters that this long-standing school policy has deterred students from engaging in negative disrespectful behavior in the past.

Second, the school board is also considering making participation in the bullying prevention program a privilege for students who meet certain academic requirements. Specifically, only students who are able to complete their academic tasks, as evaluated by their teachers, may attend the program as a reward for work completion. School board members reason that since academic instruction is the first task of the district, extracurricular socialization experiences should be provided in a manner that does not interfere with instruction. The school principal has approached you regarding the way in which the school board should be addressed regarding this issue on behalf of his teaching staff.

Discussion Questions

1. What is the goal of Adlerian consultation in the case of the elementary school that wants to implement a bullying program?
2. What type of misbehavior goal are they trying to prevent?
3. In what way can encouragement be used?
4. How will natural and logical consequences work in this case?

AC/Systems Example 3

The administration of a local school system has been taken over by a state watchdog agency because of inadequate yearly academic progress demonstrated by students in grades 2 and 4 through 8. The agency wants the school system to develop a strategic plan to address both the behavioral and academic issues of the students in the district.

Interviews with the relevant stakeholders reveal that the superintendent is primarily focused on student behavior. He reasons that school must be populated by students who can comport themselves in an appropriate manner so that they can benefit from the educational environment. The superintendent believes that setting up a caring environment is the only way to attract students. He further argues that good school attendance is the key to promoting academic skill development in students.

The watchdog agency is flexible in allowing the district to set their remediation plan; however, it is clear that the benchmark for improvement is demonstrating improvement in academic skills, especially those on state standardized tests, regardless of attendance. Therefore, it is believed that the superintendent's goals are too limited to meet the minimum standards for improvement necessary for the school system's survival.

Discussion Questions

1. What is the goal of Adlerian consultation in the case of the failed school?
2. Explicitly state the personality and social environmental issues that the school system is going to have to address.
3. In what way can encouragement be used?
4. How will natural and logical consequences work in this case?

SUMMARY

In this chapter, information was presented regarding the use of AC in school systems. First, AC was defined, followed by information underscoring the importance of the social environment in this consultative approach. According to Adler, inadequate environments characterized by hostility, rejection, and/or neglect lead children to choose attitudes and behaviors reflective of maladjustment and psychological disturbances. The underlying assumptions of AC were subsequently presented. The stages of AC, including initiation of the relationship, assessing the problem, setting goals and interventions, and analyzing the results were all considered from both individual and environmental vantage points. Information regarding the roles and responsibilities of the consultant and consultee in AC, and the specifics of school-based practice were reviewed. Finally, the effectiveness of AC was explored. In the next chapter, organizational and systems consultation (OSC) will be discussed, along with the presentation of case studies in which this approach may be practiced.

CHAPTER 6

Organizational and Systems Consultation

INTRODUCTION

The concept of system dynamics models of organizational operations was first introduced in the industrial/organizational psychology literature during the 1950s (Rouwette & Vennix, 2006). Later, in the 1970s and 1980s, studies began to emerge suggesting that organizational development theory, traditionally applied to business settings, could be also applied to schools (Schmuck, 1995). Several theorists in the field of school psychology, including Zins, Curtis, Graden, and Ponti (1988), Zins & Ponti (1990), Schmuck (1995), Illback & Zins (1995), and Illback & Zins(2007), among others, have written about this topic, advocating for organizational and systems consultation (OSC) to promote organizational developmental change in educational settings. Similarly, in the discipline of school counseling, a number of researchers, including Kurpius and Rozecki (1992),West and Idol (1993), and White and Mullis (1998) have also encouraged the use of OSC in educational settings.

Within the last decade, changes in federal policy and the vast increase in empirically based interventions (EBIs) developed to facilitate student academic and behavioral success have created a zeitgeist in which schools are better equipped to address the needs of all children. However, according to Graczyk, Domitrovich, Small, and Zins (2006), certain organizational factors, which can be established through OSC, must be in place to facilitate both the adoption and sustainability of EBIs in school systems. The implementation of OSC frequently requires making organizational changes, particularly in establishing programs and policies designed to prevent problems rather than react to them, whether they are at the administrative level (e.g., crisis prevention programs) or at the child level (e.g., structuring the classroom to prevent behavioral outbursts).

A theoretical perspective that supports the use of OSC is Bronfenbrenner's (1979) ecological–developmental perspective, in which the ecology of children is viewed as a series of concentric contexts in which they function, including: (1) the immediate social-culture environment, such as the family, classroom, and peer group (microsystem), (2) the larger social-cultural environment, such as the school, extended family, extended peer network (exosystem), and (3) the distant social-cultural environment, such as the regional and state educational systems, the neighborhood, and the community. Nastasi (2006) explains that these influences are reciprocal (macrosystem), with the individual influencing the ecological system through child–parent and student–teacher interactions, for example. Similarly, these influences are evolutionary, with prior experiences affecting later functioning and interactions in both similar and new contexts. In using this theoretical perspective, OSC can be implemented at various concentric contexts, depending upon the problem or issue that is being addressed.

Organizational change (OC) in educational systems tends to occur slowly, and must, since there is evidence that efforts to promote rapid, systemic changes in organizations often result in resistance and failure (Derr, 1976; Illback & Zins, 1995). In reviewing the stages of OC, McDougal, Conan, and Martens (2000) and Adelman and Taylor (2007) report that there must be some *organizational readiness*, or a willingness to receive change (see Figure 6.1). First, the motivation and capability of a critical mass of stakeholders to make change must be sought (Adelman & Taylor, 2007). Then, support demonstrated by top management, active participation of administration and staff, and their commitment to the goals and processes of the project must be achieved (see Table 6.1; Fullan, Miles, & Taylor, 1980; McDougal et al., 2000; Rosenfield, 1992). Illback & Zins (1995) describe this stage as the *diagnosis phase*, in which all parties affected by the change work collaboratively to develop a clear vision of where the process is headed, also understanding that plan formulation is an incremental process (McDougal et al., 2000).

In stage two, *implementation support*, the involvement, understanding, and support of administration continues, training of systems members occurs, initiation of pilot sites are established, and project implementation is guided by external consultants assisting internal facilitators and team members (Fairweather, Sanders, & Tornatzky, 1974; Fullan et al., 1980; McDougal et al., 2000; Rosenfield, 1992). Illback & Zins (1995) describe the processes of planning, initiation, and implementation as

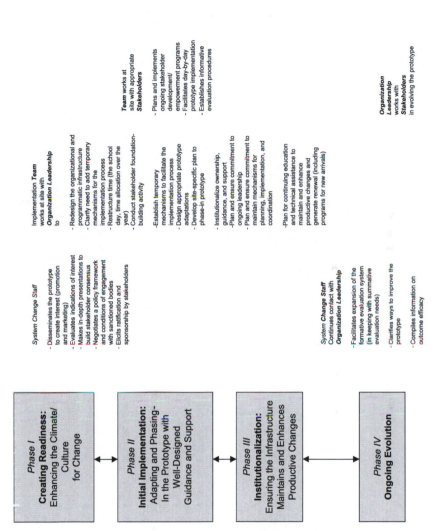

System Change Staff
- Disseminates the prototype to create interest (promotion and marketing)
- Evaluates indications of interest
- Makes in-depth presentations to build stakeholder consensus
- Negotiates a policy framework and conditions of engagement with sanctioned bodies
- Elicits ratification and sponsorship by stakeholders

Implementation **Team** works at site with **Organization Leadership** to
- Redesign the organizational and programmatic infrastructure
- Clarify need to add temporary mechanisms for the implementation process
- Restructure time (the school day, time allocation over the year)
- Conduct stakeholder foundation-building activity

- Establish temporary mechanisms to facilitate the implementation process
- Design appropriate prototype adaptations
- Develop site-specific plan to phase-in prototype

- Institutionalize ownership, guidance, and support
- Plan and ensure commitment to ongoing leadership
- Plan and ensure commitment to maintain mechanisms for planning, implementation, and coordination

- Plan for continuing education and technical assistance to maintain and enhance productive changes and generate renewal (including programs for new arrivals)

Team works at site with appropriate **Stakeholders**
- Plans and implements ongoing stakeholder development/ empowerment programs
- Facilitates day-by-day prototype implementation
- Establishes informative evaluation procedures

System Change Staff
Continues contact with **Organization Leadership**

- Facilitates expansion of the formative evaluation system (in keeping with summative evaluation needs)

- Clarifies ways to improve the prototype

- Compiles information on outcome efficacy

Organization Leadership works with **Stakeholders** in evolving the prototype

Phase I
Creating Readiness: Enhancing the Climate/ Culture for Change

Phase II
Initial Implementation: Adapting and Phasing-In the Prototype with Well-Designed Guidance and Support

Phase III
Institutionalization: Ensuring the Infrastructure Maintains and Enhances Productive Changes

Phase IV
Ongoing Evolution

Figure 6.1 Prototype implementation and scale-up: Phases and parallel and linked tasks. (From Systemic Change for School Improvement, by H. S. Adleman & L. Taylor, 2007, *Journal of Educational and Psychological Consultation, 17,* p. 62.)

Table 6.1 Stages of Organizational Change and the Activities Related to Each Stage

FAIRWEATHER ET AL. (1974)		FULLAN ET AL. (1980)/ ROSENFIELD (1992)	
STAGES	**PRINCIPLES/ ACTIVITIES**	**STAGES**	**ACTIVITIES**
1. Approaching-persuading phase	Developing "brand awareness" Foot-in-the-door Principle of participation	1. Entry and start-up/ initiation	Organizational readiness exists Supported by top management Participation by administrators and staff before implementation Resources mobilized and committed
2. Adoption phase	Outside intervention Action-oriented intervention Principle of group action or implementation	2. Transition, initial use/ implementation phase	Administrative active support Sustained work and training Develop internal consultants Monitor program integrity and participant concerns
3. Diffusion stage	Resistance to change is proportional to social status and role change required Principle of experimental input Principle of activating diffusion centers	3. Institutionalization	District commits funds Included in operating budget Run largely by internal staff Permeates the system: expands from pilot program to other sites

Source: (From Using Organizational Change Procedures to Promote the Acceptability of Preferral Intervention Services: The School-Based Intervention Team Project, by J. L. McDougal, S. M. Clonan, & B. K. Martens, 2000, *School Psychology Quarterly, 15,* p. 152.)

occurring during this time, with changes being carried out through the use of a well-designed infrastructure that provides guidance and support (Adelman & Taylor, 2007). In this stage, it is important to accurately define the goals of OSC, because only when plans have a requisite level of specificity will institutionalization and generalization occur, in which changes are adopted throughout a system (Illback & Zins, 1995).

In stage three, *diffusion*, support is garnered for the expansion of the model, from pilot sites to other locations (Fairweather et al., 1974). At this time, staff resistance may be a significant problem, although it can be lessened through internal consultants' work to sustain the project as well as expand it. When there is an infrastructure to maintain and enhance productive change (Adelman & Taylor, 2007), ideally, institutionalization and generalization will occur, although lasting significant change takes quite a while, probably at least 2 to 3 years (Fullan, 1982; Lippit, Langseth, & Mossop, 1985; Illback & Zins, 1995).

Finally, in stage four, *ongoing evolution and creative renewal* occur through mechanisms used to refine changes made and provide continuous support. In this phase, stakeholders become part of a learning community in which renewal is creatively pursued (Adelman & Taylor, 2007). It is also necessary to distribute program evaluation data so that participants receive feedback regarding program implementation, efficacy, and recommendations for future practice (McDougal et al., 2000).

Given the extensiveness of this process and the large number of personnel involved, it is not surprising that OC efforts implemented through OSC seem to fail as often as they succeed. Zins & Ponti (1990) report that OC efforts frequently fail due to several factors:

1. The organizational assessment did not fully identify the problem or the needs of the system.
2. The issue of readiness for change was not considered.
3. The intervention strategies were inadequately specified and implemented.
4. The consultee system was not sufficiently included in developing the change plan.
5. Program evaluation plans were not developed or the results of such evaluations were not used.
6. There was poor or no follow-up.
7. Sufficient time was not allowed for the change to occur. (Fullan et al., 1980).

However, there is an increasing interest in adoption of OSC in recognition of the many problems facing domestic school systems and the need to develop alternative methods for providing educational services to students with special needs (Zins & Ponti, 1990), because there is evidence (Fuchs & Fuchs, 1994; Winzer, 2000) that special education programs often fail to individualize instruction, use curriculum that is diluted or nonexistent, and implement models of service delivery that are poorly directed and fragmented (Wasburn-Moses, 2006). Other reasons that explain the heightened interest in OSC include: (1) an expanding body of evidence supporting the process of consultation (Gutlin & Curtis, 1990), (2) a movement toward prevention-oriented programs in which consultation is the primary means of service delivery (Phillips, 1990; Zins & Forman, 1988; Zins & Wagner, 1987), (3) an avenue of facilitation for the implementation of data-based interventions, and (4) a need for an organizing framework to increase continuity and coordination among interventions (Gutkin, 1986; Zins & Ponti, 1990). The use of OSC may also help avoid Type III error, which is concluding that a program is not effective, when in fact the measurement of program effectiveness was affected by inadequate implementation of the program. Consultants can utilize OSC to determine whether programs are truly ineffective, or whether there is a relationship between the levels of program implementation and program outcomes (Kalafat, Illback, & Sanders, 2006).

Systems-level applications (positive behavior support [PBS] Sugai et al., 2000; curriculum-based assessment; [CBM] Deno, 1985, 1995; social and emotional learning; [SEL] Zins & Elias, 2006), in which OSC plays a vital role, are being used increasingly in multitiered service delivery, response to intervention (RTI), models to foster the social and academic success of all children and adolescents (Hojnoski, 2007). In RTI models, assessment, early intervention, and evidence-based practices are synthesized in a systemwide prevention effort in regular education settings (Greenberg et al., 2003; Knotek, 2005; Hojnoski, 2007). The emphasis in RTI on multiple level problem solving fits well with OSC because educational and mental health professionals, such as school psychologists, school counselors, and social workers, can work consultatively with special and regular education teachers to assist them in integrating their previous understandings of a student-focused etiology of learning problems into an ecologically-oriented instructional model (Knotek, 2005). While RTI will be discussed in more detail in the following chapter, readers should note that OSC methods can be used in implementing and sustaining the evidence-based interventions associated with the model.

Another use for OSC is to address issues of equity for families in school systems, which requires organizational change and strategic planning involving the families, the community, and school systems. As mentioned in the first chapter, Wizda (2004) argues that one of the most important roles for consultants is to help build schools' capacity to meet the needs of an increasingly diverse population. Many of the methods used to improve multicultural awareness and understanding can be developed through OSC, including establishing research-based programs that are responsive to the needs of diverse students and their families (Rogers, 2000), identifying and eliminating roadblocks to equitable parental participation (Ochoa & Rhodes, 2005), and educating staff members regarding the mismatch between the values and expectations of home and school that commonly plague culturally diverse students (LaRoche & Shriberg, 2004).

Recognition of diversity through OSC also extends to sexual differences, in which school systems engage in equitable practices in working with lesbian, gay, bisexual, and transgender (LGBT) families and youth. Jeltova and Fish (2005) recommend that Havelock and Zlototow's (1995) model of OSC can be used to create environments that are friendly to LGBT families, children, and adolescents, including involving all parties that hold power within a system, identifying resistance to systemic changes, following an agenda to create a welcoming school atmosphere for all, developing functional patterns of communication and dissemination of information within schools, and identifying overt or tacit discriminatory practices. Additionally, OSC can be used to create programs encouraging: (1) education of school professionals, parents, and students about what it means to be LGBT; (2) collaboration and communication with diverse families; (3) recognition of discomfort, lack of competence, or lack of experience in working with LGBT families; (4) advocation for families; (5) information regarding appropriate reactions to witnessing harassment; and (6) identification of incidence, forms, and effects of harassment (Jeltova & Fish, 2005).

In consideration of the issues discussed in the previous paragraphs, and in order for school-based consultation to be as effective as possible, some researchers have argued that consultants must adopt an orientation emphasizing a systems perspective, considering the layers of functioning described by Bronfenbrenner (1979) instead focusing on individuals, which only allowed for interventions on one level (Zins & Ponti, 1990). White and Mullis (1998) add that since a holistic conceptualization of students' problems is often necessary for effecting lasting change, OSC is a time-efficient, systems-conscious method that can be used to positively impact large numbers of students. In this chapter, two general consultative models that have been proposed in the adoption of a systems perspective will be reviewed and discussed, along with the evidence that exists in support of such approaches.

ORGANIZATIONAL DEVELOPMENT CONSULTATION

Organizational development (OD) is a purposeful, continuous effort in which systems study themselves in order to promote improvement in system norms, structures, and procedures. In schools, the goals of OD are to improve interpersonal processes and student performance through OSC (Schmuck, 1995). Frequently, problems in schools that seem to be child-focused are actually building, systems, or community problems that need to be addressed at multiple levels using a problem-solving process to encourage systematic, multifaceted intervention and substantive change (Knoff, 2000). Organizational development consultative (ODC) approaches can be used to assist schools in clarifying their overall problems and their rationale in supporting intervention strategy choices, selecting explicit standards in order to support strength and fidelity of implementation, monitoring standards and evaluating feedback regarding implementation quality, analyzing the organizational obstacles impeding high-quality implementation, and choosing strategies to overcome such impediments. Innovations in ODC are developed, revised, and perfected until successful implementation is realized in each concentric context (Gottfredson, 1993).

Traditionally, ODC has been implemented by specialists trained in group dynamics who hold advanced degrees in business, education, or the social sciences, and who are external to the organization. However, Schmuck (1995) argues that ODC procedures are more likely to be employed in school systems if a group of members internal to the organization function as consultative facilitators. The success of strategic planning and program implementation relies upon a team of facilitators who use participative management to forward goals, and who see organizational change as natural, necessary, and ongoing in a healthy system (Knoff, 2000).

The following is suggested for the team of facilitators (Schmuck, 1995):

1. Appoint a coordinator to serve at least part-time.
2. Include at least 10 members throughout the school system who perform different roles, including teachers, counselors, and school psychologists, etc.
3. Designate team members to work part-time (10% to 15% of their time) as facilitators.
4. Allow team members to respond to requests instead of assigning duties, but do advertise the group's services and offer demonstrations.

5. Do not assign team members to consult with groups with whom they regularly interact.
6. Give the team its own budget.
7. Train team members to provide consultative services in temporary small groups of two to four.
8. Provide time and opportunities for continuing education for the team.

Schmuck (1995) describes the process goals of ODC as building upon organizational strengths and circumventing organizational weaknesses. In pursuing such goals, there is an emphasis upon clarifying communication, improving meetings, solving problems, making decisions, and resolving conflicts. These goals can be pursued at the systems level, including a focus on one-to-one relationships, small working groups, relationships among members in such groups, whole organizations, and relationships between these organizations and their external stakeholders. However, goals can also be set for educational content, such as curriculum change (innovation in subject matter), group and organizational restructuring (establishing new role relationships and creating teams), and staff development (introducing new knowledge, skills, and values to individual educators).

Problem Definition, Assessment, and Diagnosis

Theorists such as Gottfredson (1984; 1993) and Gottfredson, Rickert, Gottfredson, & Advani (1984) have developed an ODC approach, program development evaluation (PDE), in which school systems can begin by defining a problem and following a process that culminates in implementing organizational innovations for lasting change. In following this model, consultants who wish to become systems change agents must first come to understand a problem, both empirically and practically (including developing a conceptual model, reviewing the relevant source literature, and utilizing a blueprint for problem solving in which interventions can be linked to functional problem analyses; Dwyer, Osher, & Wagner, 1998; Knoff, 2000). Included in this process is a needs assessment in which the following occurs: (1) measurement of the extent to which those in the schools and community see the problem as an important concern that needs to be addressed; (2) measurement of the scope and dynamics of the problem (including incident and impact data in the school and community); (3) an identification of school and community personnel, committees, and task forces currently involved in addressing the problem; and (4) evaluation of the recent interventions and programs that have been implemented in an attempt to resolve the problem and their short- and long-term impact (Knoff, 2000).

Lowman (2005) has written about the contribution of Harry Levinson to the importance of diagnosis in organizational assessment. Levinson, a clinical psychologist, was one of the first theorists to think systematically about organizational assessment and intervention, arguing that without competent assessment there can be no assurance that the treatments selected will be effective in remedying the perceived problem or encouraging long-lasting change (Levinson, 2002). Consultants using ODC can use two kinds of diagnostic processes, including assessment of organizational dysfunction (Lowman, 1993) and assessment of organizational health and intended optimization (Lowman, 2005). In both diagnostic processes, Levinson advocates for the use of psychodynamic principles in determining what data should be collected, by whom, and perhaps more importantly, what psychological processes occur among those from whom data are being collected. In summary, the results of the assessment should guide the development of the corrective action so that a plan is formulated based upon an understanding of what an organization needs and how the intended changes relate to those needs (Lowman, 2005).

Development of Implementation Standards

In the PDE method, implementation standards are specified for each intervention, including the quantity and quality of services or activities for each intervention component. When possible, standards are followed based upon empirical evidence developed from previous studies reported in source literature, and are concrete, realistic, and under the direct control of the implementer. However, when such information is not available, it is recommended that the implementer estimate the amount of the intervention required to produce the desired changes in the target behavior, and later gather data regarding the effectiveness of the intervention (Gottfredson, 1993).

Measurement and Evaluation of Implementation Standards

Each standard is measured through data collection methods, such as logs and recorded observations, and the resulting information is then incorporated into the job descriptions of service providers. Gottfredson (1993) suggests that data on the strength and fidelity of the interventions, as compared to the standards, should be frequently summarized for those implementing the strategies or program. Feedback on interventions appears to be particularly helpful when provided at natural breaks in service delivery, such as during holidays, so that changes can be initiated and evaluated during the next stage of implementation (Gottfredson, 1993).

When implementation standards are not being met, organizational obstacles preventing strong implementation of interventions should be assessed. Such a process is termed *force field analysis* (Lewin, 1951), and is used to identify the environmental forces impeding innovation. Typically, a number of logistical issues are uncovered that require that the organizational standard operating procedures be altered. Harder to change, however, are beliefs and attitudes held by organizational members that retard innovation. Gottfredson states, "These obstacles sometimes stop an innovation cold, but more often they weaken the innovation by reducing staff motivation and willingness to join the effort" (1993, p. 278). Since the process of overcoming these organizational obstacles is a long and difficult one, the development of a coalition of resource people, such as a cross-disciplinary force of professionals and community members, can be helpful in encouraging commitment to change from systems members (Knoff, 2000).

INTERVENTION ASSISTANCE CONSULTATION

Developed by Zins, Curtis, Graden, & Ponti (1988) and expanded upon by Illback & Zins (1995), intervention assistance consultation (IAC) is a systemswide model of service delivery developed to respond to individual student needs through a structured use of problem-solving strategies employed in the child's least restrictive educational setting before referral to a more restrictive placement. These researchers initiated this consultative model in order to: (1) provide help to students before potentially stigmatizing labels needed to be used, (2) emphasize prevention and early detection of problems, and (3) provide an opportunity for educators and caregivers to examine their initial perceptions of and attributions for problems before such perspectives became solidified in the form of a referral for a psychological or psychoeducational evaluation (Zins & Ponti, 1990).

Individual versus Team Approach

During the past 20 years, there has been a movement emphasizing internal consultative teams working collaboratively in school systems, with stakeholders such as educators, parents, and community members demonstrating active participation (Illback & Zins, 1995). Although most intervention assistance programs involve the use of a problem-solving team consisting of special and regular educators, administrators, and educational and behavioral support personnel, Zins & Ponti (1990) argue that in large groups, communication can be complex, and there are extensive costs in terms of efficiency, time, and resource allocation. Small teams can effectively use consultative processes to promote change in school systems, such as in the case of prereferral intervention teams meeting students' needs through prevention and intervention (Kerwin, 1995). Further, a single consultant and consultee can develop effective solutions to most problems. In the IAC process, while the majority of issues are addressed through individual consultation, the expertise of the team is also available when needed (Zins & Ponti, 1990).

Training in Consultation and Data-Based Interventions

Although the use of consultation has recently become much more extensive, individuals need to be trained in consultative methods in order for approaches such as IAC to be effective. Training can occur during in-service days in school systems by inviting an outside expert to teach educators about IAC, with brief booster sessions held periodically afterward, or through soliciting the help of a local expert to train other staff in consultation skills. In both methods, an intensive training program is recommended in which participants receive both didactic and experiential training with an applied focus (Zins, 1989). Individuals with previous experience, expertise, and/or training, or those with a particular interest in consultation should receive in-depth training and instruction in facilitating others' consultative skills, such as regularly scheduled peer review activities (including problem solving, case presentations, and discussions of pertinent professional literature; Zins & Ponti, 1990).

Another area of competency necessary for individuals using the IAC method is knowledge of the design and implementation of data-based interventions. Optimally, the IAC team will have diverse areas of expertise in specific academic and behavioral domains. However, additional training may be necessary in skills such as applied behavior analysis and recent empirical advances in certain curricular areas (Zins & Ponti, 1990).

Leadership and Team Membership

In the IAC method, most team members will serve on a voluntary basis, while others may be appointed to positions based upon their organizational role, such as school psychologists or school counselors. Zins &

Ponti (1990) advocate for all members to be volunteers who either have or can acquire the necessary skills for the IAC process. Further, incentives for participating, such as release time or continuing education credits should be offered to acknowledge the often substantial investment of team members. Because many problems expand beyond the purview of schools, agencies outside of the school system should also be invited to participate on the team in order to encourage lasting change (Hazel, 2007).

Recordkeeping

Since IAC is a formal organizational function, written documentation should be completed providing evidence of efforts made to assist educators and students. These written records should include clear problem identification, baseline data, detailed intervention procedures, monitoring of treatment integrity, and outcome data. Such information can be helpful in documenting prior assistance efforts and how they were implemented, as well as in supplying data to help frame evaluation questions and the development of interventions should a later assessment be necessary (Zins & Ponti, 1990).

Permission to Intervene

Addressed briefly in the first chapter, the issue of permission to intervene in consultation is an ethical issue that is often ambiguous. When working directly with a child, parental permission must be granted, but in other cases, professional judgment must be exercised in order to determine whether parental permission is necessary. Zins & Ponti (1990) encourage erring on the side of caution, and when in doubt, obtaining permission. According to the IAC model, parents are always informed of a teacher's concerns regarding their child before the IAC process begins (Zins et al., 1988).

Diagnostic Interventions

Before planned intervention may be undertaken, a diagnosis of the organization and environment should occur in order to gain an understanding of the personnel, technologies, processes, and structures of the system. Because diagnosis is more than a single event and often requires the efforts of organizational members to engage in problem solving and goal setting as a part of the diagnostic process, a time- and labor-intensive process, ownership of and commitment toward correcting a problem is encouraged (Illback & Zins, 2007).

In diagnosing for change, it is necessary to determine: (1) the present state of the organization and what is currently occurring, (2) the likely future state of the organization sans any change strategies, (3) the ideal or preferred state of the organization from the perspective of the organizational members, (4) the restraints that are blocking movement from the present to the ideal state of the organization (Hersey & Blanchard, 1982; Katz & Kahn, 1978), and (5) the resources necessary, such as personnel, time, and money, to effect change. The central goal of the diagnosis phase is to identify the problem situation by determining the discrepancy between the current and ideal state, to analyze these data, and to develop and implement intervention strategies to rectify this discrepancy (Illback & Zins, 1995).

Multiple methods are typically used in diagnosis, and are tailored to assess specific situations. Illback & Zins (1995) advocate for the use of four general methods of data collection, including (1) direct observation, (2) analysis of written records and documents, (3) interviews, and (4) the use of questionnaires, surveys, or rating scales. In conducting direct observations, members of the organizational consultation team can observe an event, such as a faculty meeting; a case, such as the process of a multidisciplinary evaluation from referral to placement; or a person, such as following an individual for a day to develop data regarding his or her daily routines. During these observations, other individuals, as they relate to the object of the observation, would be monitored, as well as the effects of the observed event, case, or individual upon other constituencies.

In examining and analyzing written records or documents, organizational team members can procure data relevant to the explanation of the problem, such as school board meeting minutes, student files, newspapers, state and federal legislation, and budget reports. Interviews may also be conducted, in which individuals relevant to the explanation of the problem, such as administrators, teachers, support staff, parents, and students, offer their perspective regarding the issue being investigated. Finally, questionnaires, surveys, and rating scales can be used to investigate issues such as morale, leadership, relationships, and climate, among others. The consultation team can develop such instruments, or may use those that have been already developed, such as the *Organizational Climate Description Questionnaire* (Halpin, 1966; Illback & Zins, 1995).

Process Interventions

While any number of strategies can be implemented to improve the functioning of a school organization, sometimes strategies such as process interventions are needed to improve the working relationships among school employees. In OD, the major focus is upon human relations and the concepts, values, and techniques described in the group dynamics literature. In these areas, interventions are typically targeted at addressing concerns such as communication, decision making, leadership, team building, and the behavioral characteristics of individuals. Small groups or whole school systems can be the focus of interventions, with information sharing, working through differences (thereby enhancing collaboration), and participative decision making (leading to commitment) parts of the IAC process (Friedlander & Brown, 1974; Illback & Zins, 1995). Unlike diagnostic interventions, process interventions focus upon only one component of the system and are likely to create more lasting change than traditional training and education processes, since new attitudes, behaviors, and relationships are adopted within the work setting (Beer, 1980; Illback & Zins, 1995).

The specific techniques used in process interventions include survey feedback, group development and team building, intergroup development and system building, and process consultation. In the survey feedback approach, data are systematically collected on the school's functioning and need for change, including attitudes about morale, organizational climate, job satisfaction, roles in problem solving and decision making, concerns regarding specific problems, and so forth. In gathering such data, techniques include interviewing and questionnaires, and summarized information is reported back to the members of the organization, with motivation for change induced through recognition of discrepancies between ideal and actual practices in the school's functioning (Goldstein, 1978). Another intervention used is group development or team building, involving: (1) identifying work difficulties within participants, (2) identifying interpersonal difficulties among participants, (3) developing better work procedures, attitudes, and interaction patterns (French & Bell, 1978), and (4) reducing barriers to group effectiveness and efficiency, thereby improving the functioning of the group.

In intergroup development and system-building techniques, the goal is to increase the understanding and collaboration between independent work groups, such as administrators and teachers (Beer, 1980). Groups within the organization provide information to each other regarding performance, conflict situations, and tensions (French & Bell, 1978), explore methods of improving collaboration, and work toward improving the accuracy of the perception of the other groups. A fourth intervention, process consultation, is often used in schools, with activities designed to help individuals understand the process events occurring in the environment, including communication patterns, decision making in groups, leadership, and conflict. In this strategy, group members learn about their problem-solving skills and decision-making operations (Illback & Zins, 1995).

Technostructural Interventions

In educational organizations, the interrelationships between the technology of work and worker productivity and satisfaction are an important area of study. Schools are complex structures that define roles, responsibilities, and the basis of decision making for its individuals. State and federal regulations and judicial mandates dictate policies for school systems; boards of education utilize policy guidelines and action formats to reach decisions; and school districts create internal administrative procedures to carry out the decisions that are made. Beer (1980) identifies five areas of structural intervention—reward systems, performance management, control systems, job design, and organizational design (Illback & Zins, 1995).

Both explicit (pay scales, tenure, and promotion) and implicit reward systems (recognition for effort) serve to regulate individual behavior in organizations, and research suggests that modulating such reward systems can induce substantive, enduring change (Luthens & Kreitner, 1975). For example, although the job performance of teachers is typically not rewarded through merit pay, rewarding excellence through rewards and verbal praise can be very motivating to encourage change.

In managing job performance, the focus is upon creating systems for delineating, describing, measuring, and modifying job behaviors. Goal attainment scaling can be used to set goals and measure programs, involving the identification of treatment or performance goals in a measurement system allowing for cross-domain comparisons and flexible data aggregation (Kiresuk & Sherman, 1968; Illback & Zins, 1995). Another approach, performance appraisal, includes collecting performance data and communicating the findings to individuals or groups. When included in an organizational routine, feedback from performance appraisals seems to improve worker satisfaction and productivity (Beer, 1980). Finally, in performance review and development, job functioning is described as a developmental process, with a reduced emphasis upon outcomes. Areas of strength and weakness in role functioning are identified by supervisor and supervisee, and process goals and activities for improvement are implemented (Beer, 1980; Illback & Zins, 1995).

Organizations use control systems to manage resources. Although financial resources tend to be systematically allocated, there appears to be no clear procedure by which schools manage their human, technological, and informational resources. Thus, some educational organizations have instituted human resource accounting systems to inventory their human assets and account for their use (Flamholtz, 1974; Illback & Zins, 1995).

Further, job design interventions involve the characteristics of work tasks that affect quality of work life and productivity issues, with the expectation that organizational members will be happier and more productive when they believe their jobs are significant, responsible, varied, and likely to result in satisfaction. Jobs can be redesigned to alter work tasks, modify the work unit in comparison to other units, or change the physical or psychological environment in which the work is completed (Illback & Zins, 1995).

Finally, organizational design is a global technostructural intervention in which five fundamental issues need to be considered:

a. What are the characteristics and needs of the population(s) to be served? b. How important is responsivity to external changes (e.g., from the community) to this organization? c. When new problems or circumstances emerge, how does the organization process and assimilate this information, and what are its characteristic response modes? d. How efficiently and effectively are human, financial, informational, and technological resources being allocated at present, and what would a more desirable situation look like? e. How much effort is currently being expended to coordinate programs, and to what degree are these management efforts effective? (Illback & Zins, 1995, p. 231)

Based upon the problems that are identified through the answers to these questions, consideration may be given to restructuring the organization.

Individual Interventions

In this domain, interventions are used when a problem is seen as isolated and requiring the behavior change of a particular person or group of people. Although organizational problems may exist, it is also true that some individuals simply fit poorly with the expectations for their role.

Thus, Illback & Zins(1995) argue that the best technique for establishing person–situation congruence is to find and place the right individual in the right job. For example, in selecting teachers, instead of relying upon an interview to judge competence, work samples, paper and pencil measures, an observation of teaching, structured interviews, and a review of relevant background data could be used, potentially improving the fit between an individual and a teaching position.

However, when individuals in a school system do not perform adequately, there may be cause for a deficiency evaluation, remediation, or termination. These methods should include a process in which problem behaviors are identified, recommendations for improved performance are given, timelines for remediation are established, and statements regarding due process and ultimate consequences are provided.

For those who are not performing poorly enough to be terminated, continuing professional development is an excellent means of assisting teachers in acquiring new skills (Illback & Zins, 1995). Sheridan and Henning-Stout (1994) state, "Perhaps the greatest opportunity for a consultant to influence organizational practices is through formalized staff development. In-service programs can be implemented to effectively increase the knowledge base of all school staff" (Sadker & Sadker, 1982, p. 103). In addition to staff development opportunities, strategies oriented toward the personal growth and development of educators (e.g., personal counseling), and self-supervision may be helpful in remedying individual problems (Illback & Zins, 1995).

Program Evaluation and Accountability

Although often overlooked, evaluation plans are a necessary component in the success of intervention programs. In IAC, unless evaluation and accountability procedures are built in, the team cannot ascertain whether individual interventions are effective or whether the IAC program is meeting its goals. Therefore, accountability involves establishing goals, maintaining routine recordkeeping, and consistently documenting intervention designs and outcomes. Zins & Ponti (1990) recommend that after IAC is implemented, multidisciplinary team referral, psychoeducational assessment, and educational placement rates should be tracked. Additionally, the number and types of problems presented, the percentage of time devoted to consultation in comparison to other services, the outcomes of the interventions initiated, and the range of consultees participating (including their satisfaction and perception of consultative effectiveness) in the IAC process should also be monitored.

EFFECTIVENESS OF OSC

A little more than a decade ago, Forman (1995) contended that while many factors related to consultation have been explored in research studies, organizational variables, such as the authority structure, the decision-making structure, the reward structure, and the communication structure of school systems have not been adequately investigated. Thus, in the last decade, theorists have attempted to operationally define OSC in school systems, and researchers have begun to conduct outcome studies regarding the effectiveness of these approaches.

Gottfredson, Gottfredson, and Hybl (1993) described the use of the OD consultation method in a 3-year program designed to improve student behavior in middle schools. In this program, the PDE method was used to provide a context for achieving strong implementation in addressing the causes of misbehavior at different levels, including: (1) clarification of school rules, (2) increased consistency in rule enforcement, (3) improved classroom management and organization, (4) increased communication with parents regarding student behavior, and (5) reinforcement of appropriate behavior. Consultants worked with teachers and administrators to identify concrete performance standards for each program component and to monitor the implementation of new strategies, with frequent feedback used to foster implementation. Gottfredson et al. (1993) reported that schools with the most effective improvement teams ensured strong treatment fidelity, with corresponding significant increases in appropriate student conduct.

Additionally, although many school systems have adopted IAC, little data exist in which the short- and long-term effects of such approaches have been evaluated (Illback & Zins, 1995). Numerous researchers (Illback & Zins, 1995; Zins et al., 1988; Zins & Ponti, 1990) have identified a need for studies in establishing the effectiveness of OSC. There is much that we still do not know about the effect of organizational factors upon the behavior of consultants, consultees, and clients, and additional research must be completed before concluding that OSC is indeed effective. Nevertheless, as we continue to develop our understanding of the importance of organizational developmental change in educational settings, it is clear that the usefulness of such OSC approaches has only begun to be recognized.

CASE STUDIES IN ORGANIZATIONAL/SYSTEMS CONSULTATION
OSC/Child Example 1

The high school principal contacts the school psychologist, school counselor, and social worker, requesting that they have a conference with the school nurse. The principal has stated that they have an awkward situation involving the senior class valedictorian, Maria, who is scheduled to graduate in 3 months with her peers. The principal indicated that the school nurse suspects that the student in question is pregnant, and has been so for 5 to 6 months, and since time is a factor, the meeting should occur right away.

The team of consultants arranges to meet with the school nurse, who is worried about what she should do. Upon discussing the matter with the school nurse, the consultants find that the nurse has privately spoken with the student, who denies that she is pregnant. The nurse is now concerned about the safety of the student and the safety of her fetus. Because the student is 18 years of age, the nurse is unsure whether the student's parents should be contacted, and does not know how to proceed regarding this situation. She is also worried that the lack of action demonstrated by school staff will signify tacit approval of Maria's pregnancy to other students at the school.

The team of consultants indicates to the nurse that they will look into the matter, and respond to her concerns as quickly as they can. When examining the district's policy and procedures manual, the consultants find that there are no provisions for handling student pregnancies. Thus, the consultants conclude that they have three problems:

1. What should be done (if anything) about Maria's pregnancy?
2. Should the school discuss the matter with Maria's family?
3. What policies need to be established so that similar events can be handled sensitively and deftly in the future?

Discussion Questions

1. Who is the consultee, and who is the client?
2. Why do the consultants need to consider the Family Education Rights and Privacy Act (FERPA) (20 U.S.C. § 1232g; 34 CFR Part 99) or the Buckley Amendment, when making their decisions?
3. How is this case study an example of an organizational problem?
4. What are the proximal and distal recommendations that should be made in order to address this problem?

OSC/Child Example 2

Doug is a kindergarten student who has been recently diagnosed with a significant hearing loss. He now uses hearing aids in both ears and is receiving special education support services. His medical specialist has recommended that Doug be provided with an auditory trainer for use in the classroom. According to the National Institute on Deafness and Other Communication Disorders, auditory trainers are "electronic devices that allow a person to focus attention on a speaker and reduce the interference of background noise. They are often used in classrooms, where the teacher wears a microphone to transmit sound and the child wears a headset to receive the sound. Children who wear hearing aids can use them in addition to the auditory trainer" (http://www.nidcd.nih.gov/health/voice/auditory.asp).

Doug's parents forwarded their physician's letter requesting the implementation of the auditory trainer and have requested an Individualized Education Program (IEP) meeting to include the auditory trainer in their son's IEP. The special education supervisor has indicated that the superintendent refuses to pay for an auditory trainer, so the school system must deny the parent's request for the auditory trainer. The school will, however, permit its use in the classroom if the parents provide the trainer for use at school. The school psychologist takes his concerns to the district's child study team because he is unsure if this response is correct and what steps should next be taken.

Discussion Questions

1. What diagnostic interventions need to be undertaken in order to understand the systems obstacles in this case?
2. To what extent does the systemic knowledge of assistive technology devices have an effect upon the outcome of this case?
3. What role does the consultant play in this problem or solution?
4. Should the role of the superintendent in this scenario be addressed, and who would be expected to accept this responsibility?

OSC/Child Example 3

Becky is a fifth grade student who has cerebral palsy. She is a bright and personable child, and according to her teacher, is performing very well in all of her classes. In order to maximize her inclusion with other children in her class, Becky has a personal aide who accompanies her to the bathroom and to her "special classes" (physical education, art, and music), in order to make the small accommodations necessary to assist her in participating fully in these classes. As the year winds to a close, Becky's parents meet with her teacher to discuss Becky's transition to the middle school.

At this meeting, Becky's parents discover that the middle school, an older building, has three levels and no elevator. Becky's teacher worries aloud that it will be difficult to ensure that all of Becky's academic classes will be on the first floor, and says it will be impossible for Becky to be included in physical education, art, music, and technology because these classes are held on other floors of the building. Additionally, the sixth grade class lockers are located on the third floor, which would prevent Becky from accessing a locker. Consequently, Becky's teacher suggests that it might be better for Becky to begin attending a private school that "will be more responsive to her needs."

Becky's parents are upset and return home to talk about this problem. They feel that Becky has been achieving very well in the public school system, and to remove her from a setting in which she has been thriving would be unwise. Additionally, Becky's friends are all planning to attend the middle school, and Becky's parents worry that depriving Becky of her social contacts at school would be tremendously upsetting to their daughter. Uncertain of their options, Becky's parents schedule a meeting with the assistant superintendent in the district. They have not told Becky about this problem because they hope to be able to resolve it without her knowledge.

Discussion Questions

1. Who could serve as a consultant in this scenario?
2. What may be the unforeseen consequences of a decision made in this situation?
3. How does educational law relate to this problem?
4. What are the school district's reasons for suggesting that Becky attend another school? Are they defensible?

OSC/Family Example 1

Juan is a 16-year-old sophomore in high school, who has been measured to have a level of intellectual functioning that falls within the superior range, but with a significant reading disability. Juan would like to go to college, and is particularly interested in eventually working in the fields of architecture or engineering. As a sophomore, Juan takes an advanced math class, but struggles greatly with his reading skills, particularly in his history and English classes. Juan has historically received itinerant special education services to support him in reading, according to his IEP.

Although Juan excels in his math and science classes, he typically receives grades of "C" and "D" in his English and history classes. Juan's parents, Mr. and Mrs. Rivera, are very concerned that Juan will not be accepted into college with these grades, and wonder why, if Juan is receiving special education support, that Juan is not at least earning "Bs" in all of his classes. Mr. and Mrs. Rivera have been doing some research regarding accommodations that can be made for students with reading disabilities, and have discovered that there are assistive technology devices that can be used to help children and adolescents succeed in school.

Mr. and Mrs. Rivera have requested an IEP meeting to (1) complain that the school did not provide an assistive technology evaluation for their son, (2) request that the school immediately provide Juan with a Kurzweil reader (which scans the text and reads it out loud to the student, who wears earphones), and (3) request that training be provided to their son in effectively using assistive technology. Mr. and Mrs. Rivera are also requesting that Juan be given a laptop to use during the school day. The school psychologist, the school counselor, Juan's regular and special educators, the school principal, and the special education coordinator are meeting with the Rivera family to discuss their concerns and requests.

Discussion Questions

1. What evidence supports the Riveras' request?
2. What is the role of assistive technology in supporting children and adolescents with special needs?
3. How should information be gathered regarding intervention fidelity and effectiveness?
4. What should be done if feedback shows that performance standards are not being met?

OSC/Family Example 2

A group of parents who have children in a district program for elementary grade students with autistic spectrum disorder have requested a meeting to express their displeasure regarding the district's failure to provide an empirically based curriculum, and appropriate teaching methods and behavioral interventions for their children. The parents have alleged that the district is using antiquated teaching and behavioral management methods to work with this group of children, and that the teaching staff does not have the necessary training to enable them to work successfully with autistic youth. The parent group has stated that they will initiate due process procedures on an individual basis unless the district revises their educational programming for these youngsters.

The curriculum committee convenes a meeting at the behest of the school district superintendent, and decides to appoint a subcommittee to investigate evidence-based practices in teaching and behavior modification for children with special needs, with a recommendation for the selection of a curriculum that would meet the needs of students with disabilities. The subcommittee has no idea where to start, and is unsure which resources would be helpful to consult. Additionally, one of the subcommittee members has been asked to meet with the parents' group to assuage their concerns and promise them that help is on the way. This individual has no idea what to say, and leaves the meeting with the parents feeling as though they are angrier and more dissatisfied than before. The curriculum group, as well as the special subcommittee, feels ill-equipped to tackle this task.

Discussion Questions

1. Who are the consultant, consultee, and client in this case study?
2. In OSC, problems that appear to be child-focused are often actually systems problems. Is this the case in this scenario?
3. How can this problem be viewed as a positive change for the school system?
4. How can the OSC team avoid making the Type III error in evaluating the effectiveness of the new program?

OSC/Family Example 3

At the end of the first month of school, Mr. and Mrs. Frank, along with a special education advocate, are seated in the office conference room of the elementary school building when the school principal (Ms. Camilla) arrives at work. Upon questioning the school secretary, who has arranged for the Franks to wait for the principal, Ms. Camilla discovers that the Franks have come to discuss the special education programming for their son, Mitchell. Ms. Camilla sits down with the Franks and their advocate to discuss their concerns, and discovers that

Mitchell has apparently been moved to a less-intensive special education service delivery program without the approval of his parents.

Apparently, at the end of the previous school year, Mitchell's special education teacher believed that Mitchell was essentially working independently and required significantly less assistance than the other children in the program. Based upon Mitchell's success and independence in completing his work, his teacher believed that he would only require itinerant special education services for the following school year. Thus, instead of providing Mitchell with instruction in a resource room, a special education teacher would meet with Mitchell at the beginning and end of each school day to review any concerns he had and to ensure that his school work and homework were being done accurately. The teacher, after consulting with the special education director, had sent home a letter with Mitchell explaining her rationale for recommending a less intensive special education program and enclosed a change-of-placement form, which the Franks were to sign to signify their assent to this change. The teacher had sent Mitchell's file to the itinerant special education teacher, who had added Mitchell to her caseload.

However, the Franks never received the letter and did not assent to the change of placement. The principal surmises that Mitchell either lost or misplaced the letter, which never reached his parents. However, the Franks are very angry that Mitchell has been "downgraded" to a less intensive program and feel that he is owed compensatory instructional time. They have requested that the principal call the special education teacher to set up a preconference hearing. The Franks, upon consulting with their advocate, have decided to seek recourse through due process procedures.

Discussion Questions

1. What is the role of the consultant in this scenario?
2. How is this example a systems-level consultative problem?
3. How does educational law pertain to this problem?
4. What kind of intervention would be appropriate for this case?

OSC/Educator Example 1

Emily is a fourth grade student who was diagnosed as having a learning disability in reading and mathematics while she was in the second grade. Consequently, for the past 2 years, she has been receiving pullout special education services for reading and mathematics. This year, in spite of the special education support, she has continued to struggle and has failed to make satisfactory academic achievement gains during the fourth grade school year. Emily's classroom teacher, Miss Edwards, recently met with Emily's parents and informed them that she is recommending that Emily be retained.

Emily's parents are irate that the school year is almost over and the teacher is now bringing her concerns to them. Emily's parents have contacted the superintendent of the school district to complain, and he has, in turn, referred the issue to the school psychologist. Before scheduling a meeting with Emily's parents and teachers, the school psychologist speaks with the school principal in order to understand the nature of the problem. The principal confides to the school psychologist that in addition to the fact that Emily's teacher is not the strongest educator in the school, she has been absent for much of the year because of a maternity leave. When she returned from her leave, she found that Emily had not mastered much of what is expected of children in the fourth grade curriculum. Upon conferencing with the special education teacher, Emily's teacher discovered that the substitute had great difficulty managing the behavior of the students in the classroom, and thus academic issues were a secondary concern.

The school psychologist schedules a meeting with Emily's regular and special education teachers, the principal, the special education director, and Emily's parents. She recognizes that this problem has multiple levels, and thus plans to begin the meeting by viewing this issue from an OSC perspective.

Discussion Questions

1. Is it appropriate for the school psychologist to acknowledge the systems nature of this problem, or should she exclusively focus on the problem as it pertains to Emily?
2. How could this problem be defined and diagnosed?
3. What are appropriate interventions for this problem?
4. What are the long-term ramifications of this problem?

OSC/Educator Example 2
Eric is a first grade student who has been diagnosed with apraxia, which is a motor speech disorder. Children with apraxia have great difficulty planning and producing the precise, highly refined, and specific series of movements of the tongue, lips, jaw, and palate that are necessary for intelligible speech. Eric's teacher reports that his poor communication skills are negatively impacting both his social development and his educational

achievement. She is particularly concerned that Eric's poor intelligibility is interfering with his ability to learn to read, since he is having difficulty pronouncing the phonemes necessary to decode new words.

In accordance with his IEP, Eric currently receives speech therapy twice weekly for 20 minutes, and after conversing with his teacher and learning of her concerns, his parents have requested that speech services be increased significantly, ideally to 5 days of service each week. They explain that after consulting the website of the Childhood Apraxia of Speech Association of North America, they learned that children with apraxia who have severely unclear or little speech and are more severely affected will require more therapy than those who have milder apraxia. Eric's parents agree with the suggestions given by experienced speech and language pathologists that a child with moderate to severe apraxia of speech have individual speech therapy three to five times per week.

The IEP team is brought together with the purpose of revising Eric's IEP. However, when Eric's parents request the increase in speech and language services, the speech therapist states that her present schedule does not provide any time to increase Eric's therapy sessions, and suggests that Eric's parents obtain private speech therapy services outside of school. Eric's parents are bewildered at this suggestion, since they thought that the school was to provide such services, but they agree to check their health insurance policies to determine whether they can receive speech and language therapy outside of school. The other team members look at each other and are obviously perplexed regarding whether it is appropriate for the speech therapist to make such a request.

Discussion Questions

1. What is the problem in this case study?
2. How is this case an example of an accountability issue in the school system?
3. Who should function as the consultant in this scenario?
4. How can the school system support Eric and his parents as they work toward improving his disability?

OSC/Educator Example 3

Mr. Innovation has been hired as the new school counselor for the middle school in the Helpful School District. He is fresh from graduate school and has many ideas for programs he would like to implement in his new role. One of Mr. Innovation's foremost goals is to implement a comprehensive developmental guidance curriculum in which he visits classrooms once a week on a rotating basis, focusing on strengthening students' skills in anger management, socialization, citizenship, and so forth. A few weeks before school begins, he meets with the school principal, who cautiously supports Mr. Innovation's initiatives, but also wonders aloud whether Mr. Innovation will be able to "fit it all in." Although puzzled regarding the principal's response, Mr. Innovation is still excited about the opportunities he has to positively impact children's growth and development.

Two weeks before school starts, Mr. Innovation meets with the guidance team, who share with him the responsibilities he will have in his new job. The other school counselors describe their job responsibilities as scheduling students for classes, supervising standardized test administration, chairing student assistance and IEP teams, and handling the routine emergencies of the school. When Mr. Innovation describes the initiatives he would like to implement, the other counselors appear to be wary and explain to him, "This isn't that type of school." Mr. Innovation is taken aback, and when he asks to what they are referring, the counselors state that while all of these new ideas from his training program sound good, they simply don't have time to be counseling students in the classroom. Mr. Innovation protests, saying that working with children to prevent problems was the reason he became a school counselor. One of the counselors looks at the other and says, "Well, I guess this isn't going to be your ideal job."

Discussion Questions

1. What is the problem in this scenario?
2. How can OSC be used to address this problem?
3. Can Mr. Innovation serve as a consultant?
4. What are the systemic barriers to introducing change?

OSC/Systems Example 1

Dr. Overworked, the district school psychologist, has found his responsibilities steadily increasing throughout the year until he is no longer able to meet mandated timelines associated with initial and annual psychoeducational evaluations. He has explained the nature of his dilemma to Mrs. Owens, the special education and psychological services supervisor, who has indicated that no funds are available to contract for additional psychological services. Dr. Overworked then called the assistant superintendent to explain his problem and Mrs. Owens' response to his query. The assistant superintendent counsels him to do "the best you can" and reminds Dr. Overworked that the district cannot afford a complaint filed regarding failure to meet mandated timelines.

Consequently, Dr. Overworked finds himself in a very uncomfortable situation, with new evaluations exceeding mandated timelines and both staff and parents complaining about his lack of availability. He is unsure what to do, and since there are no other school psychologists in the district, does not have anyone else to consult regarding the discrepancy between work demands and the time available to complete his responsibilities. Dr. Overworked has reached the point that he is beginning to suffer from insomnia due to work-related stressors. When visiting his primary care physician regarding this problem, Dr. Overworked finds that he has also developed high blood pressure. Dr. Overworked's physician counsels him to make some substantive changes in his life to avoid long-term repercussions to his health.

Discussion Questions

1. Is this a systems-level problem?
2. How or could this problem have been prevented?
3. What would planned organizational change look like in this scenario?
4. What is the role of the assistant superintendent in this problem?

OSC/Systems Example 2

A representative from the state Department of Disabilities (DOD) has called on behalf of Mrs. Jackson, whose son, Jayson, is receiving services in a special education program for students with severe neurological disabilities, located in a neighboring school district. The representative has explained that Jayson has a severe epileptic disorder, in which he experiences uncontrolled seizures if he becomes overheated. After consulting with the family's caseworker, Jayson's mother has presented a letter to the bus coordinator from her son's neurologist requesting that he be transported back and forth to school in an air-conditioned bus.

The bus coordinator has failed to respond to the request, and since warmer weather is fast approaching, Jayson's mother is becoming increasingly concerned. Consequently, Mrs. Jackson has contacted both Jayson's home school district and host school district, and has asked to be put in touch with someone who can assist her. Mrs. Jackson has been transferred to several individuals' voice mail accounts, including principals, psychologists, social workers, and special education directors, but either these individuals have failed to return her calls or they have pled ignorance and suggested that Mrs. Jackson call someone else.

Mrs. Jackson then contacted the DOD to see if she could obtain some help, since she was unable to find someone in either school district to assist her. Because Jayson's health is in jeopardy, the representative from the DOD immediately contacted the home school district to see what could be done to resolve this dilemma in the short term and address Jayson's transportation needs in the long term. The administrative office secretary has fielded the call and wonders to whom this call should be transferred?

Discussion Questions

1. Why has a breakdown in communication occurred?
2. Whose responsibility is it, or should it be, to ensure that Mrs. Jackson receives the help she and her son require?
3. How should the conduct of the personnel who have failed to return Mrs. Jackson's calls be addressed?
4. What is the role of the DOD representative in this case?

OSC/Systems Example 3

Mrs. Clarkson and her son, Kevin, have recently been dislocated from their home because of a house fire, and as a result, have temporarily relocated to the home of Mrs. Clarkson's sister in a neighboring town. Upon learning of this relocation, the high school principal of Traditional School System has informed Mrs. Clarkson that her son is no longer eligible to attend school in the district, and must transfer to the school district that services the community in which Mrs. Clarkson's sister lives, the Novel School System. Mrs. Clarkson has consulted with the state Department of Disabilities because she alleges that while other students in similar situations have been permitted to be educated in Traditional School System on a temporary basis, the principal is refusing to allow her son to attend because he "doesn't like him."

The Department of Disabilities has referred Mrs. Clarkson to the Traditional School System social worker, Ms. Campbell, to assist her with her complaint. Upon contacting the principal, Ms. Campbell finds that the principal is unwilling to allow Mrs. Clarkson's son to return to the district. Ms. Campbell explains that state law requires that homeless students must be educated in the district in which they last had permanent residence, even if they are living elsewhere as a result of being homeless. She also informs the principal that the Clarksons are living with Mrs. Clarkson's sister on a temporary basis until permanent housing can be found for them within the Traditional School System's service area. Despite this information, the principal refuses to allow Mrs. Clarkson's son back into the district. Ms. Campbell, the school social worker, is unsure what she should do in light of the principal's response.

Discussion Questions

1. Whose problem is this?
2. What are the barriers to implementation of a process intervention?
3. How should implementation support be sought?
4. How can a reward system be set up to encourage the principal to follow state law?

SUMMARY

In this chapter, OSC was introduced, including the history of and rationale for use of the model. The issues of organizational development and organizational change were discussed, including the stages of organizational readiness, implementation support, and diffusion. Two general models of OSC were presented, ODC and IAC. The processes of ODC were reviewed, including problem definition, assessment, and diagnosis, development of implementation standards, and measurement and evaluation of implementation standards. Regarding IAC, several issues were discussed, such as the individual versus team approach, training in consultation and data-based interventions, leadership and team membership, recordkeeping, permission to intervene, diagnostic interventions, process interventions, technostructural interventions, individual interventions, and program evaluation and accountability. Finally, the evidence supporting the effectiveness of OSC methods was presented.

CHAPTER 7

Instructional Consultation

OVERVIEW

Rosenfield (1995), the pioneer of instructional consultation (IC), describes the process as a merging of instructional psychology in the discipline of school psychology with the process of collaborative consultation from the field of special education. In comparison to the previous chapters, in which consultation practices have been presented that have equal utility for both educational and mental health support personnel, this chapter discusses IC, which is particularly appropriate for educational specialists consulting regarding students' academic problems. Moreover, because educational professionals are often called upon to engage in consultation regarding students' educational progress and problems, IC is an excellent fit because of its focus upon evidence-based practices (EBPs). Although IC has a specific focus on academic concerns, with consideration of appropriate academic progress, consultants can also use IC to address issues of classroom management (Rosenfield, 2002). The information presented in this chapter has been largely taken from Rosenfield's (1984, 1987, 1992, 1995, 2003) and Gravois's and Rosenfield's (2002, 2006) various writings on this topic, and readers are encouraged to consult the original works for greater detail.

There is much evidence that instructional quality and time spent in learning both powerfully influence students' learning outcomes (Walberg, 1985). These factors appear to be particularly important in preschool and early elementary school, and also for children demonstrating low academic achievement. Unfortunately, teachers often fail to use high-quality instructional strategies, ensure that children are actively working on academic tasks, or encourage mastery learning through their teaching behaviors (Rosenfield, 1995). Further, there is research documenting that teachers tend not be as current with the professional source literature as would be desirable, consequently failing to use the recent EBP described in scholarly journals and other such sources, preferring more practical approaches (Rosenfield, 1995). Thus, there appears to be a need for educational specialists and support personnel to use IC to assist teachers in improving their pedagogical practices.

Underlying Assumptions of IC

While "within-child" attributions have been historically made for students' academic difficulties, in which problems that children are experiencing in their educational achievement are believed to be due to characteristics of the child, there is increased emphasis in the discipline of education in examining more easily altered variables, such as quality of instruction. Within the fields of school psychology and special education, a strong movement toward prereferral interventions in the form of high-quality instruction and EBPs has occurred, with a view toward reducing the number of students being classified as disabled and found eligible for special education services. Such prereferral interventions have also been designed in order to help diminish the disproportionate referral and placement of students of diverse backgrounds into special education (Gravois & Rosenfield, 2006; Rosenfield, 1995). Focus on the instructional system, including the task (what is to be learned), the learner (his or her readiness to undertake the learning task), and the treatment (the instructional and management strategies), instead of on the concept of a malfunctioning learner, allows consultants to avoid making within-child attributions for learning difficulties (Rosenfield, 1984).

Children's difficulties in learning can be conceptualized as an instructional mismatch, and consultation may be used by educational specialists to work with teachers, analyze the mismatch, and facilitate a synchronized interaction of the task, the learner, and the treatment (Rosenfield, 1995). Through the consultative process, the relationship between the teacher and the consultant is of utmost importance in encouraging the change process (Rosenfield, 1995). Thus, the underlying assumptions of IC are: (1) all children can learn, (2) the appropriate place for intervention is the interaction between teachers and students in the classroom, and (3) it is productive for teachers to consult with each other and other educational support personnel in a collegial, problem-solving relationship (Rosenfield, 1992; Wizda, 2004).

Communication in IC

One major assumption of IC is that a language-systems approach should be used to establish a foundation for the process of consultation (Rosenfield, 2000). This systems approach categorizes consultation as a linguistic event in which the consultant and consultee co-construct new meanings of instruction and student progress through dialogue. In participating in the co-construction with the consultee, the consultant manages the process of the consultative conversation, develops the space for it, and encourages its continuation. Rosenfield (2000) asserts that prospective consultants, when learning to fulfill these responsibilities, should be cognizant of such communication tendencies as audience tuning, shared reality, and correspondence bias, topics that have been researched in social psychology (Higgins, 1999).

Audience tuning refers to people modifying their messages to accommodate their perceptions about what someone else wants to hear. Shared reality is the phenomenon in which a person generates beliefs about a message's objectivity (for example, the more a teacher talks about a problem with a consultant who evidences active listening responses, the greater the likelihood that the teacher will see the problem as objectively real). Correspondence bias is the tendency to view the person instead of the situation as the source of behavior (e.g., seeing the student as the source of the problem instead of the systemic variables as maintaining the problem; Rosenfield, 2002).

Process of IC

Rosenfield (1995, 2002) describes IC as a problem-solving process that is similar in its underlying structure to other forms of consultation that have been detailed in the psychological literature. It may encompass all four levels of consultation described by Meyers, Parsons, and Martin (1979): (1) providing direct service to the client by assembling data about the student through assessment, interviewing, or observation; (2) providing indirect service to the client through the consultee (the level most often used with IC, in which the consultee is responsible for most of the data gathering and intervention implementation; (3) providing service to the consultee when the primary goal is to change the consultee's behavior in order to encourage subsequent change in the student clients; and (4) providing service to the system in order to effect change in the instructional system in the school, hopefully leading to improved organizational functioning (Rosenfield, 1995).

Knotek, Rosenfield, Gravois, and Babinski (2002) found that IC works as a socially constructivistic endeavor due to features associated with consultee-centered consultation (Caplan & Caplan, 1993; Caplan, Caplan, & Erchul, 1995), including effective alliance building, orderly reflection, and the generation of alternative hypotheses. Moreover, IC has stages, much like other models of consultation, including entry, problem identification, intervention design, intervention implementation, and finally, intervention evaluation (Gravois, Rosenfield, & Gickling, 1999; Rosenfield, 2002).

Step One: Entry and Contracting

Instructional consultation is most successful when a collaborative relationship has been established between the consultant and the teacher to facilitate the solution of instructional issues or problems. In this relationship the teacher must: (1) understand and accept his or her role as consultee, (2) be prepared for the consultation process, (3) have a general sense of the purpose of consultation, and (4) recognize how consultation may differ from other experiences with educational or mental health support personnel (Rosenfield, 1995). Gillies (2000) talks about the steps for educational professionals to embed consultation in practice, including focusing on the knowledge of and commitment to consultation in recruiting new teachers, providing continuing professional development in consultation, developing scripts to assist consultative practitioners in working through difficult issues, allocating one day each year for peer observation of consultation in practice, and organizing annual administrative meetings to review and plan new work in relation to consultation.

One of the first challenges in establishing the consultative relationship is to encourage the teacher to move away from a medical model/ within-child attribution for problems the student is experiencing to a collaborative, classroom-centered, problem-solving approach to learning problems. This may be a difficult cognitive shift, since adopting the latter approach involves focusing upon one's own role in either causing or remedying the problem. Knotek et al. (2002) describe the use of social constructivism in the process of IC stating,

> "Vygotsky's tenets of the social construction of knowledge are aligned with the goal and process of consultee-centered consultation. Likewise, these tenets can be restated in terms of the process of IC and the development of team members' own understanding as instructional consultants. Development within the social

context of the consultation relationship occurs as the interpersonal process supports the redefinition of the consultation dilemma and the consultee acquires a new conception of the consultation problem" (p. 305).

In acquiring a new view of the problem, consultees develop an understanding of the instructional problem through rational communication initiated to promote greater problem-solving skills and the internalization of these enhanced skills.

An impediment that educators may face when changing their attributions about the source of an instructional problem is their perceptions regarding the ability of educational support personnel to help remedy instructional mismatches between children and the curriculum. Rosenfield (1995) explains that teachers may not consider professionals such as school psychologists as able to solve instructional problems because of teachers' perceptions of school psychologists' lack of training in this area. To remedy this bias, the teacher must be willing to commit to being a part of a problem-solving relationship to determine whether the child's learning problem or the instructional question can be answered (Rosenfield, 1995).

Step Two: Problem Identification and Analysis
The Referral Process
In IC, the stage of problem identification is an extremely important one that typically begins with the teacher's referral of the child in an initial referral interview or series of interviews. The consultant should begin by explaining the nature of the working relationship in the consultative process and then focusing on eliciting the information necessary to assist in problem identification (Rosenfield, 1995).

In the initial interview, the consultant's language should be carefully chosen, based upon specific behavioral cues by the consultee in order to obtain concrete information about the behavior. The use of such language can be helpful in encouraging the teacher's optimism in his or her ability to solve a problem in the classroom. Additionally, good communication skills are essential, particularly to avoid misunderstandings that result when two individuals do not engage in clarification in order to fully understand what the other is saying. At the end of the interview, the educational professional and the teacher should have: (1) identified the problem, (2) determined what additional information needs to be gathered in order to illuminate the disparity between the desired performance of the student and the child's current functioning, (3) clarified problem frequency, duration, intensity, and antecedents, and (4) gathered data on the instructional strategies currently utilized by the teacher and the classroom tasks with which the child is experiencing difficulty (Rosenfield, 1995).

Observations

In the problem identification and analysis stage, data can be gathered through structured observations. In conducting observations, unexpected factors can sometimes be discovered, and teachers may recognize previously unknown information about their behavior or teaching styles in the classroom (Rosenfield, 1995). For a more thorough explanation of conducting structured observations, the reader is encouraged to review the information presented on observations in chapter 3.

Curriculum-Based Assessment and Curriculum-Based Measurement

A contribution from the disciplines of special education and school psychology, curriculum-based assessment (CBA), a process in which information is gathered about the child's instructional level using probes developed from the classroom curriculum in various subject areas, can provide valuable information. Curriculum-based assessment is used to answer five questions, including (1) what does the student know? (2) what can the student do? (3) how does the student think? (4) how does the student approach what he or she is unsure of? and (5) what should the teacher do (Gickling & Rosenfield, 1995)? Curriculum-based measurement (CBM), a specific type of CBA, emphasizes the relationship between measurement and instruction. In using CBM, teachers repeatedly measure students' performance while completing curricular materials using standardized measurement procedures (Wesson, 1991).

Both CBA and CBM use frequent and repeated measures, include short-duration testing, involve product responses, such as reading aloud and writing spelling words, and can be used for the assessment and evaluation stages of consultation (Shinn, Rosenfield, & Knutson, 1989). However, CBA and CBM take different approaches to diagnosis: CBA data is used for problem identification by determining a mismatch between skill and curriculum or instruction, while CBM allows for problem identification by examining the discrepancy between student achievement and the achievement of typical peers (Deno, 1989). In CBM there is an assumption that the problem is identified on the basis of a comparison to peers and resides within the child. In this case the curriculum is used to what degree the difficulty exists (Burns, MacQuarrie, & Campbell,

1999). In CBA, the instructional approach is directly connected to the problem, has links to instructional planning, and supports the interdependent nature of problem identification and intervention suggested by Gutkin and Curtis (1999; Burns, 2004). Both CBA and CBM data are reliable and valid in comparison to traditional achievement test data, information gathered from program placement, and teachers' appraisals of competence (Deno, 1985; Wesson, 1991). Often the teacher is unsure of the accuracy of his or her subjective impressions regarding such information, since he or she may be more confident in describing only whether or not the information has or has not been presented to the child (Rosenfield, 1995).

In comparison to the information that can be obtained through norm-referenced, standardized measures, CBA yields data that can be used for curriculum-intervention decisions, including the frustration and instructional levels in the curriculum for the youngster, and the effectiveness of various instructional strategies (Rosenfield, 1995; Zigmond & Miller, 1986). Another important function of CBA is error analysis, in which the type of performance error made by the child can often be identified through analyzing his or her performance on the curriculum materials or through discussing with the child about how the task was approached (Myers, 1985; Rosenfield, 1995). Rosenfield (1995) explains, "Usually there is a logic to the child's error pattern that either reflects a consistent but incorrect underlying error in strategy or one that reflects a deficiency in the instruction itself" (p. 311). Knowledge of such errors is necessary in planning effective interventions.

Burns (2004) explains that data examining the effectiveness of CBA within a consultative model are limited. However, research done by Kovaleski, Gickling, Morrow, and Swank (1999) demonstrated that the use of CBA by consultants for problem identification and intervention design resulted in increases in students' task completion, task comprehension, and time on task. Burns (2004) asserts that this, in conjunction with other studies completed by Gickling and Rosenfield (1995) and Bickel, Zigmond, McCall, and McNelis (1999), is suggestive that CBA can be effectively used in consultation.

However, CBM, which can be used for both formative and summative evaluations, has been associated with significantly improved achievement for students in special education (Fuchs, Deno, & Mirkin, 1984; Wesson, 1991). Fuchs and Fuchs (1986) conducted a meta-analysis of systematic formative evaluation and found statistical and practical increases in student achievement after the use of CBM. In particular, graphing students' achievement data seemed to produce more advantageous results in comparison to recording data in a tabular format. This finding seems to stem from teachers more accurately and frequently analyzing the graphed data and consequently providing more direct feedback to children (Wesson, 1991).

In a study to determine the effects of goal-setting and progress-monitoring strategies (teacher developed or CBM) and follow-up consultation formats (university consultant or group follow-up consultation) upon gains in words read correctly per minute, first, the researcher found that the CBM groups made more progress than the students in the teacher-developed goals groups. Second, the treatment group that received CBM goal- and progress-monitoring procedures and group follow-up consultation significantly exceeded the other groups on one reading passage and on the total for the Passage Reading Test (words read correctly per minute; Wesson, 1991).

However, when consultation methods are examined (discounting the effects of CBM), neither format (the university consultant nor group follow-up consultation) appeared to be superior on the number of words read correctly per minute by students. Teachers meeting in groups without CBM goals and measurement systems indicated that they did not understand the purpose of their meetings, and did not know what to converse about. The CBM consultation groups, however, discussed students' progress on graphs and made specific comments about the progress of their targeted students. The researcher concludes that while neither consultation group outperformed the other, educational administrators may favor group consultation because it appears to be more cost-effective. Clearly, the most meaningful variable appears to be the use of CBM with consultation in order to produce the most desirable outcomes (Wesson, 1991).

Step Three: Design of Interventions
In order to suggest appropriate interventions, consultants must be knowledgeable about instruction quality, particularly because teachers tend to be less likely to consult the relevant literature than would be desirable, often assigning tasks that are not matched to children's instructional levels (Rosenfield, 1995). There is also evidence suggesting that teachers have difficulty identifying and modeling skills that must be learned in small steps, using suitable and specific examples, and assessing students' mastery of the material. Consequently, consultants must be able to design and evaluate quality intervention sequences, assisting teachers

in fostering academic engaged time, which is the time actually spent learning, and mastery learning through their teaching practices. Collaboration with the teacher should address the student's work setting, using consequences based upon the learner's performance, the curricular materials, and the instructional procedures (Haring & Gentry, 1976). Further, ongoing evaluation is a critical aspect of quality instruction because not every evidence-based intervention will be effective with every child (Rosenfield, 1995).

Just as the process expertise of school-based mental health and educational specialists is important for the success of IC, so is their content knowledge related to empirically supported instructional and intervention techniques (Hart, Berninger, & Abbott, 1997). Interventions that can be implemented as a part of quality instruction should be part of evidence-based practice (EPD), including teaching methods and techniques that have been empirically proven to be efficacious in the source literature. An extremely brief discussion follows regarding use of IC in facilitating CBA/CBM and EBPs in the areas of reading/written language and mathematics.

Reading and Written Language Problems and Instructional Consultation

Reading problems are common among school children, with 25% of U.S. students suffering from mild to severe reading problems (Gunning, 1998). In the last 2 decades, researchers have found that phonological awareness, the ability to segment spoken words into component sounds, facilitates the word recognition process, and increases as word recognition skill improves (Berninger, Thalberg, DeBruyn, & Smith, 1987; Wagner, Torgesen, & Rashotte, 1994). Effective readers have knowledge and ability in oral and receptive language, phonemic awareness, sight word recognition, word analysis (phonics, structural analysis, context clue use), passage fluency, listening and reading vocabulary, and text comprehension (Margolis, 2004).

Further, phonological awareness training alongside of phonics instruction appears to be more effective than phonological awareness training alone (Williams, 1980). Recent evidence is suggestive of the coupling of orthographic awareness training (directing children's attention to the letter elements and patterns in words) with phonological awareness training and phonics instruction as a means for encouraging improvement in word recognition skills. Thus, word recognition instruction that combines phonological awareness training, accompanied by orthographic awareness training, and phonics to form letter-phoneme connections, seems to be helpful in increasing students' word recognition (Hart et al., 1997).

In a study comparing three different treatments with children with mild to moderate reading disabilities (the use of IC along with CBM, CBM alone, and a control group of no CBM), Fuchs, Fuchs, Hamlett, and Ferguson (1992) found that while both CBM groups outperformed their control-group peers on reading outcome measures of fluency and comprehension, teachers who received IC assisting them in implementing the CBM procedures planned more diverse lessons, with children in the IC-CBM group also performing better on a written language outcome measure requiring written recall of information.

Additionally, in another investigation using multilevel hierarchical linear modeling to compare growth curves for elementary school children receiving instruction aimed at a single orthographic–phonological connection or instruction aimed at multiple orthographic–phonological connections, rate of growth on the phonics probes was significantly faster for the group receiving the multiple-connections instruction. The authors of this study suggest that multiple strategies (phonics, word families, whole-word strategies) should be recommended by consultants in the IC process to help children improve their word recognition skills (Hart et al., 1997). Further, IC consultants can encourage teachers to follow a sequence of direct, systematic instruction, in which modeling precedes guided practice. Educators should review each strategy often, give students feedback on the task, provide coaching in how to use the strategy, promote self-monitoring and evaluation, and instruct children to self-reinforce when they correctly use the strategy (Margolis, 2004).

Mathematics Problems and Instructional Consultation
In another study, investigators evaluated the differential effects of self-monitoring and consultation upon teachers' use of CBM to monitor students' math computation achievement. One group of teachers received university-based consultation, while the other group engaged in self-monitoring techniques in order to increase the fidelity of CBM techniques used to track the progress of students with mild disabilities in math computation. Both groups responded comparably in their implementation of CBM, although neither group responded to students' academic progress as vigorously and frequently as expected, with teachers appearing unwilling or unable to make instructional changes (Allinder & BeckBest, 1995). Thus, when proposing that teachers adopt new instructional techniques in the IC process, consultants must be cognizant that

making changes is difficult and that change occurs slowly. Teachers need to be reinforced frequently in their implementation of new instructional techniques, particularly because the natural consequences—students' increased achievement—may not occur as rapidly and with as great an amplitude as would be optimally reinforcing.

Step Four: Intervention Implementation

Since instructional interventions are typically implemented or directed by the classroom teacher, in this step the role of the consultant is to help the teacher modify and manage classroom instructional procedures. Rosenfield (1995) describes this process stating, "The instructional decisions that need to be implemented for vulnerable children are often at variance with the 'normal' way of doing things in many schools and must be integrated into the daily activities of the teacher" (p. 311). Teachers may evidence resistance due to being concerned with the dual responsibilities of working through the curriculum at a prescribed pace and adjusting the curriculum so that the child can achieve mastery at a slower pace. It seems counterintuitive to teachers that children make more progress through material that is at their instructional level, even though research is supportive of this finding. Consultants can reinforce this with teachers, and also ensure that there is treatment fidelity and validity with the interventions being implemented (Rosenfield, 1995).

Step Five: Intervention Evaluation

In the final stage of the process, the consultant and consultee must first determine the success of the intervention, which can be accomplished through the use of CBA/CBM as described previously. Further, the consultant can confer with the consultee regarding any changes made in the consultee's functioning. Research supports the finding that the IC process results in positive changes in consultees' skills. In a qualitative study examining IC's support of consultees' problem-solving skills and their perception of pertinent work problems, Knotek et al. (2003) indicated that participation in IC was associated with notable and recurring factors of consultee change, including a shift in focus of concern from larger, undefined issues to achievable, positive goals. Additionally, teachers who participated in IC developed a novel understanding of the student population that could help the teacher to be successful in working with students in regular education classes. Finally, participation in IC encouraged the effective use of data in developing instruction for those students evidencing academic problems. After the goals of IC have been achieved, the consultant and consultee terminate their relationship in regard to the particular problem or client, and provide written documentation regarding the course and outcome of IC. In this step, the consultant should provide clear communication about the process and end of the consultation process to enable future work with that student or others (Rosenfield, 1995).

Instructional Consultation Teams

Along with her colleagues, Rosenfield developed a specific support-team model called the Instructional Consultation Team (ICT; Rosenfield & Gravois, 1996) to facilitate the process of delivering IC to school systems. These teams were created in response to requests by school systems to assist them in constructing alternative service-delivery programs, because of such problems as the over-referral of children of diverse backgrounds to special education, or to develop an alternative to the special education classification and placement process (Rosenfield, 1995).

Instructional Consultation Teams represent an early intervention system in which the primary focus is on resolving student learning and behavioral concerns within general education settings through support offered to teachers. The ICT model is configured based on the concept of an interdisciplinary school-based support team in which IC or collaborative problem solving is combined with an educational delivery system and an evaluation design. Figure 7.1 illustrates the three components of ICT. A change facilitator, an essential component of the ICT, who is trained and experienced in ICT components and the process of school change, develops the team and coaches them in consultation skills. The members of the ICT work to develop an adeptly functioning multidisciplinary team through focusing on the skill development of individual team members (Gravois, Knotek, & Babinski, 2002). In Table 7.1, various training methods and the associated level of impact upon participants' development of knowledge and skills are represented.

In the ICT, members use consultation-based service delivery by requiring each member to develop and apply consultation skills. Individual team members work as case-manager consultants to a teacher who has requested assistance from the ICT (see Table 7.2). The structure of this service delivery model thus moves focus away from group or team problem solving to the dyadic relationship between a team member and the teacher, which is a consultant–consultee relationship. The central goal of the ICT design is to reduce the emphasis upon traditional group problem solving, and instead use the team as a context for developing individual

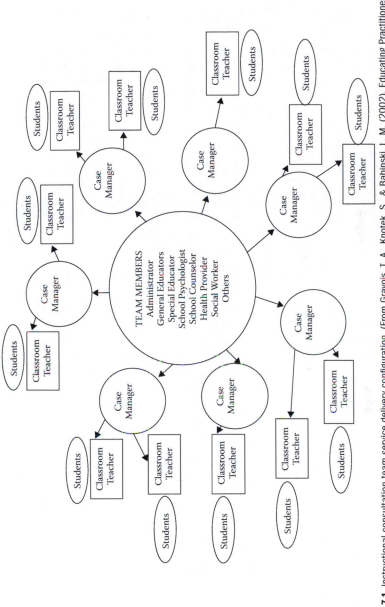

Figure 7.1 Instructional consultation team service delivery configuration. (From Gravois, T. A., Knotek, S., & Babinski, L. M. (2002). Educating Practitioners as Consultants: Development and Implementation of the Instructional Consultation Team Consortium, *Journal of Educational and Psychological Consultation*, 13, p. 117.

Table 7.1 Training Methods and Impact upon Participants

TRAINING METHOD	LEVEL OF IMPACT	EVIDENCE OF IMPACT
Didactic presentation of theory and concepts	Awareness	Participant can articulate general concepts and identify problem
Modeling and demonstration (i.e., live, video, etc.)	Conceptual understanding	Participant can articulate concepts clearly and describe appropriate actions required
Practice in simulated situations with feedback (i.e., role play, written exercises, etc.)	Skill acquisition	Participant can begin to use skills in structured or simulated situations
Coaching and supervision during application	Application of skills	Participant can use skills flexibly in actual situations

Source: (From Educating Practitioners as Consultants: Development and Implementation of the Instructional Consultation Team Consortium, by T. A. Gravois, S. Knotek, & L. M. Babinski, 2002, *Journal of Educational and Psychological Consultation*, 13, p. 115.)

team members' skills as independent instructional consultants. Weekly team meetings are held in order to encourage problem solving, case discussion, and support for teachers and students, and to initiate and maintain individual members' development of effective consultation skills. Additionally, the ICT helps to confront the existing culture of school organizations and to apply consultation services to such settings. Although advocated in numerous research studies, consultation still is not as widely adopted as would be optimal, with investigators suggesting that an increased use of consultation requires a change in organizational assumptions and policies, as described by Zins, Elias, Greenberg, and Pruett (2000; Gravois et al., 2002). When prospective consultees are busy trying to solve students' academic and behavioral problems through traditional service delivery methods, they have less time to devote to learning the new skills associated with consultation, even if such a process eventually works to diminish the size of future caseloads.

Research is ongoing in documenting the efficacy of these teams, and Fudell, Gravois, and Rosenfield (1994) have developed a level-of-implementation measure for ICT to ensure the model is in place prior to outcome evaluation, since the model must be utilized as it was intended in order to ensure treatment integrity and, ultimately, accurate assessment of intervention effectiveness (Rosenfield, 1995). Similarly, Bartels and Mortenson (2005) have used performance feedback and checklists to

Table 7.2 Three Components of Instructional Consultation

PROCESS VARIABLES	DELIVERY VARIABLES
Collaborative Consultation Process: Stage based problem solving utilizing nonhierarchical relationships among diverse professionals	Structure by which the Collaborative Consultation Process is delivered and maintained within a school
· Problem solving stages and interactions between Case Manager and Referring Teacher.	· Representative team membership which meets regularly
· Effective Communication between Case Manager and Teacher.	· Clearly articulated referral process
· Stages of Problem Solving:	· Referring teachers become part of the problem solving process
Contracting	· Active administration support and participation
Problem Identification	· Use of case management
Collaborative Intervention Development	· Documentation of referrals and student progress
Responsibilities Delineated	
Monitoring Plan for Interventions Specified	
Data Collected, Organized, and Graphed	
· Accurate Analysis Procedures using CBA and Observation Based Assessments.	

EVALUATION DESIGN
· Evaluation of Training
· Evaluation of Implementation
· Evaluation of Outcomes

Source: (From The Practice of Instructional Consultation," by S. Rosenfield, 1995, *Journal of Educational and Psychological Consultation*, 6, p. 322.)

improve the degree to which school teams adhered to the IC model, finding improvements in systematic problem solving following the presentation of feedback and checklists measured in a repeated measures design. In evaluations of the efficacy of ICT, research has found that in 85% of the cases handled by the team, goals are met, the number of students referred for multidisciplinary evaluations and placed in special education programs is decreased, and teachers who participate in the process tend to evidence high satisfaction regarding their experiences (Gravois & Rosenfield, 2002; Knotek, Rosenfield, Gravois, & Babinski, 2003).

Response to Intervention and IC

In the next section, a brief overview of response to intervention (RTI) will be presented, along with how it can be used with an IC model. Knotek (2005) has provided an excellent review of the use of RTI in collaborative consultation, which will comprise much of the information subsequently presented. As discussed in chapter 6, RTI is a multitiered, problem-solving paradigm based upon children's responses to evidence-based interventions (EBIs). The intensity of such interventions are matched to the severity of children's academic or behavioral problems, and depending upon his or her responsiveness to the evidence-based strategies, a student may move through increasingly intensive interventions in the tiered system of RTI (Gresham, 2004; Knotek, 2005).

Although numerous versions of RTI exist, an important element in such models is the dual-discrepancy decision (DD) framework, which is used to assess and intervene with students demonstrating high-incidence, mild-to-moderate problems at school. In the DD framework, decisions are made in response to students' levels of performance, before and after an EBI has been utilized (Gresham, 2002). The rationale behind this framework is that if a student is performing poorly in his or her critical academic skills and also demonstrates inadequate learning when exposed to effective instructional practices, then he or she may be described as having a learning disability (Knotek, 2005; Kovaleski, 2003).

The RTI process represents three or four levels of increasingly intensive interventions utilized with a progressively smaller group of children in a school system. Regardless of the level, a problem-solving process of defining the need, developing a plan, implementing the plan, and evaluating the student's response to the intervention(s) is facilitated through consultation. In following an RTI model, IC may be used in assisting educators in using data-based decision making to inform intervention, and in acquiring the skills necessary to design and implement EBIs (Knotek, 2005).

Knotek (2005) describes a process of awareness, conceptual understanding, skill acquisition, and application of skills as being facilitated through instructional consultation in response to intervention models (IC/RTI). Consultants can first work to increase awareness of RTI in professionals from different disciplines, who frequently have various levels of experience and prior knowledge of the multitiered problem-solving process. Second, consultants can use IC to introduce and develop a conceptual understanding of RTI within consultees, including an emphasis on assessment for intervention and targeted delivery of effective instruction in order to meet students' academic and behavioral needs. In this step, consultants can work with educators to help them develop alternative ways and means of addressing students' problems instead of relying upon the traditional test-and-place into special education model. Third, since RTI often requires new skill development for those designing and implementing EBIs, consultants can work with educators to help them identify ways to gain and practice necessary skills. Finally, in order to promote application of skills, consultants can arrange for practice of the RTI model with appropriate feedback and discussion (Knotek, 2005).

In using the IC process to assist educators in learning and adopting the RTI model, consultants provide a problem-solving framework that facilitates consultees' ability to identify important information and operationalize aspects of students' functioning so that appropriate EBIs can be implemented. Consultants can also assist consultees in monitoring the fidelity of interventions, thereby supporting their integrity. Moreover, the IC/RTI model helps to institutionalize RTI in school systems because of its inclusion of the implementation of an embedded teaming structure (Knotek, 2005). Because those who may be in particular need of the benefits of IC are those of limited English proficiency and English language learners, in the next section, multicultural issues in IC will be discussed.

Multicultural Issues in IC

Those who may particularly benefit from the IC process are minority students of limited English proficiency (LEP) and English language learners (ELL; Lopez, 2000). Such LEP/ELL students frequently receive bilingual education, multicultural education, and English-as-a-second-language program educational services (Macias, 1998), and IC has been suggested as a means to support efforts of school personnel implementing such services (Lynch & Hanson, 1998). In providing IC services to LEP/ELL students and their families, consultants and consultees engage in collaborative relationships to determine how cultural and language issues influence the learning of LEP/ELL students (Lopez, 2000). Assessment of LEP/ELL students in an IC context requires knowledge of second language acquisition, bilingualism, and language proficiency (Rhodes, Ochoa, & Ortiz, 2005). However, one of the major obstacles in working with LEP/ELL students and their families are language differences that create communication barriers. Thus, educators often rely upon the services of school interpreters to eliminate such barriers (Lopez, 1995; Ochoa, Gonzalez, Galarza, & Guillemard, 1996).

In her qualitative investigation of the use of interpreters in IC, Lopez (2000) concludes that such services can be a facilitation of the process as well as a barrier. In this study, it was found that interpreters who were familiar with the setting of the school and with clients' cultural background assisted consultants and consultees in assessing how the students' school experiences in their native countries and current school differed and shaped the clients' approach to academic tasks and events, including portfolio assessments and classroom discussions (Rosenfield, 1987). The insights of the interpreters also helped lead to interventions designed to assist students in acquiring the skills necessary to complete the projects that were expected in their academic programs. Thus, interpreters internal to the school setting may be helpful in establishing a bridge connecting the school culture and the cultural background of the students. Further, internal interpreters established better rapport with clients than did external interpreters, suggesting that schools may wish to consider training internal interpreters in the consultation process. However, consultees in this study also noted that a lot of information was lost due to being unable to communicate directly with students and their parents. For example, clients who were not familiar with the interpreter felt uncomfortable communicating personal and confidential information. Other concerns stemmed from the fact that some interpreters either distorted messages or failed to translate everything said during the students' and parents' interviews (Lopez, 2000).

Thus, Lopez (2000) identified several implications based on this research for the IC process, including: (1) Interpreters who are not competent to work an IC context can hinder the development of rapport with consultation clients; (2) important problem-identification data may be distorted or omitted when working through interpreters; and (3) the costs and benefits of using interpreters must be analyzed during consultation so that consultants and consultees can determine whether the quality of services offered to LEP/ELL students is seriously compromised by the use of interpreters. Thus, Lopez (2000) recommends, "When locating interpreters, hire interpreters who have training in providing translation services. If trained interpreters are not available, hire bilingual school personnel and provide them with training on how to translate during consultation activities. Consultants also should hire interpreters who have high levels of language proficiency in all languages used for translation services and who are familiar with the clients' cultural backgrounds" (p. 386). In later research, Lopez (2006) concluded that while IC can be helpful in assisting LEP/ELL students, consultants must address second language acquisition issues in order for the IC process to be maximally effective.

In another study, researchers examined the impact of ICTs on the disproportionate rates of referral and placement of minority students in comparison to majority students in special education. Two years after implementation, there were significant decreases in the risk of minority students in ICT project schools being referred for and placed in special education in comparison to nonproject schools, with the odds of minority students being referred and placed in special education being decreased by almost half in the ICT schools. These findings echo those of prior research documenting that the implementation of the ICT model has consistently resulted in a reduction of total referrals and placements of students in special education (Gravois & Rosenfield, 2002, 2006; Levinsohn, 2000). The researchers emphasize the importance of quality instruction in helping to bridge the recognized achievement gap between minority and nonminority students (Gravois & Rosenfield, 2006).

Obstacles to Implementation

One of the primary impediments to the use of IC is that educational professionals may view special education as a desirable alternative to serving children with learning problems in the regular education classroom, thereby shifting ownership of the problem to someone else, who may be perceived as having more effective skills in dealing with such issues. Further, since students with academic problems often evidence behavioral difficulties in the classroom, the responsibility for dealing with behavior management and classroom disruption is transferred to someone else. Another issue is that of staff mobility; because true change tends to take 3 to 5 years to accomplish, staff who are trained in consultation and collaboration may leave the profession or take another position in another location, thus impeding the smooth process of change within the school (Hall & Hord, 2001; Wizda, 2004).

Other sources of resistance include school psychologists who are reluctant to tackle students' academic concerns (National Research Center on English Learning and Achievement, 1998). Wizda (2004) explains that the literature regarding change is helpful in explaining such resistance. Change is a slow process because systems are unable to change until the individuals within them have changed. When teachers or psychologists have to learn, comprehend, practice, and become proficient in a new service delivery model while maintaining all of the responsibilities of their current roles, such demands may seem overwhelming, and may deter individuals from attempting to adopt a new set of skills.

Wizda (2004) suggests that change should not be rushed, and that individuals should be allowed to grieve in relinquishing their former skills, which may be comfortable and familiar, if not effective. Further, a period of time should be allowed in which individuals can adopt new practices immediately or take a minimal or a moderate amount of time in adjusting to adopting the new skills (Hall & Hord, 2001). Such practices will result in educational staff demonstrating a range of skill levels at any one point in time (Wizda, 2004), consequently allowing some individuals to model the process of IC, while others are afforded time to learn and demonstrate the skills at their own pace.

CASES IN INSTRUCTIONAL CONSULTATION
IC/Child Example 1

Mike is a third grade student at Progressive Elementary School, and has a history of academic problems, primarily in the subjects of reading, language, and social studies. He was retained in first grade due to "reasons of immaturity and poor behavior that interfered with his ability to make good progress in reading." He has been referred to the student assistance team because he is hiding under the desk during reading or is making frequent trips to the pencil sharpener, the bathroom, or the nurse's office. In addition, he refuses to complete any writing activities.

At this point in time, despite Mike's difficulties, his teacher has continued using the basal reading series in his instruction, although she has placed him in the lowest reading group, with just a few students, so he can receive more of her time and assistance. In order to increase his time-on-task during reading activities, his teacher has used a cost-response system, whereby he can subtract one homework problem or question for every 10 minutes he stays in his seat and works appropriately during reading activities. However, Mike has been unable to earn any of these benefits because he does not work for 10 minutes consistently during reading. Further, he seems to be falling farther behind, earning "Ds" and "Fs" in reading class.

Mike's teacher cannot understand his poor progress because she feels he is verbally adept, and he evidences good understanding during oral activities. When questioned about his reading comprehension, she explains, "Mike has good reading comprehension. When I read passages to him, he clearly understands what is happening in the story. My only guess is that he is being lazy during reading activities."

Discussion Questions

1. Why is this a case example in which the presenting problem can be addressed through IC?
2. What should be the first goal of the consultant?

3. How should the teacher be approached in the consultative relationship?
4. How can RTI be used with Mike?

IC/Child Example 2

Paige is a fifth grade student at Innovation Middle School, and is described as a sweet, lovely girl. She has good attention, works hard at school, and always has her homework completed, with frequently 90% or greater accuracy in her take-home assignments. While she is earning "As" and "Bs" in reading and language, she seems to be having less success in math. Her teacher notices that Paige still counts on her fingers or makes lines on the page to add or subtract sums. Paige does not demonstrate automaticity in her math facts, using a multiplication table that has been provided for her to solve multiplication problems.

Paige's teacher notices that she does best when given several examples, and then consistently practices the same kind of problem (e.g., division) in her workbook. When she is given worksheets or assignments in which there are multiple kinds of problems (e.g., addition, subtraction, word problems, multiplication, division), she makes frequent errors and is likely to only correctly solve 25% or fewer of the problems.

Paige's standardized test scores range from the 50th national percentile rank or above in all areas with the exception of math, in which her scores during the last 3 years have been in the 18th, 17th, and the 22nd national percentile rank, respectively. Her parents have requested a conference, explaining that Paige has been having difficulty getting to sleep and seems worried about going to school.

Discussion Questions

1. What is the role of IC in this case study?
2. How can information from CBM assist the consultant and consultee in better understanding the problem?
3. Who is the consultee in this scenario?
4. How should the effectiveness of the interventions be measured?

IC/Child Example 3

Noah is a student who is spending his second year in kindergarten. According to his school records, Noah had no preschool experiences before attending kindergarten for the first time during the previous school year. Noah's prior kindergarten teacher described Noah as a pleasant yet quiet boy, who generally did not participate in class. When the teacher or the classroom aide worked with him individually, however, Noah was eager to participate and worked hard to please the adult with whom he was working. Despite almost a whole school year of one-on-one individual instruction, Noah completed his first year of kindergarten recognizing only five lower case letters, two capital letters, and no letter sounds. Because of his lack of progress during his first year of kindergarten, and also because Noah was "immature" and had no prior schooling, it was suggested that Noah spend another year in kindergarten.

After one marking period in his second year of kindergarten, Noah can still only recognize the same lower case and capital letters he knew upon completing his first year of schooling. His teacher has been working with him individually for approximately ½ hour in the morning and 45 minutes in the afternoon using materials from the regular education curriculum in an attempt to increase his letter and sound recognition skills. While Noah's classmates are learning about five letters and letter sounds each month, Noah continues to be "stuck" in the development of his prereading skills. When questioned about Noah's behaviors at school, his teacher states that he feels that Noah is paying attention during instruction and is motivated to perform well. Noah seems to enjoy being praised and also basks in the attention of the teacher or the classroom aide. However, Noah's lack of progress is very worrisome, particularly because this is his second year of kindergarten. Stymied by Noah's lack of progress, his teacher brings his case to the student services committee to elicit help in working with Noah more effectively.

Discussion Questions

1. What would the role of RTI be in this case example?
2. What is an appropriate amount of time to ascertain the effectiveness of an intervention?
3. Is there a curriculum mismatch between the information being presented and the child's instructional level?
4. What behaviors demonstrated by Noah should be measured as a part of the consultative process?

IC/Family Example 1

Ms. Whitley, an émigré from Brazil, is a busy single mother with five children, ranging in age from 16 to 5, all of whom are enrolled in the local school system. Ms. Whitley has two jobs that she maintains in order to provide for her family; during the day she is a legal secretary for a prestigious law firm, and in the evenings she works as an office manager for a small hardware store in town. Ms. Whitley relies on her older children, a 16-year-old young lady, and a 15-year-old young man to supervise the younger children, who are 12 years of age, 9 years of age, and 7 years of age, respectively. Historically, all of the children have been average students, earning "Bs" and "Cs," until recently. The 9-year-old, Sam, has been having a lot of difficulty maintaining passing grades in his fourth grade class.

Sam's teacher, Mr. Ramirez, explains that he is earning "Ds" and "Fs" on his tests and "Fs" on all of his homework assignments, which, when he submits them for grades, are always incomplete and mostly incorrect. Mr. Ramirez feels that Sam is simply not getting enough practice in reinforcing the skills learned in class, and that if he would simply complete his homework, he would do much better.

However, Ms. Whitley is not home during the evenings to provide guidance and supervision when Sam is working on his homework because she is working at her second job. She asks her older children to oversee Sam's homework completion, but they protest, saying that Sam doesn't know what he is supposed to do, they don't know how to do what Sam is supposed to do, and they have their own homework to complete.

Sam is in danger of failing the fourth grade, and Ms. Whitley is very worried because she does not know how to help him while holding down her second job. She is also concerned that if she is completely forthright about her time commitments and financial situation, Mr. Ramirez and the school will feel that she is unfit and uncaring as a parent.

Discussion Questions

1. What are the multicultural issues in IC that must be considered?
2. Is this example appropriate for IC, or would another consultative theory be more appropriate?
3. Who is the client in this scenario?
4. Who could serve as a consultant in this case study?

IC/Family Example 2

Jamal is an articulate, bright youngster who recently completed a preschool program in the community. His parents, Mr. and Mrs. Wilson, believing Jamal possesses a mentally gifted intellect, decided to have

Jamal tested by a school psychologist to determine whether he would satisfy the state eligibility requirements to be diagnosed as a mentally gifted learner. The school psychologist, Mr. Truscore, indicated in his evaluation report that Jamal had a full scale IQ of 124, with characteristics that are frequently associated with gifted learners, including an intense interest in studying certain topics, a large vocabulary, and the ability to solve math problems with great speed.

The Wilsons' presented this report to the school district, whose gifted education identification team reviewed the evaluation and concluded that while the information in the report was suggestive of Jamal's giftedness, they would like to suggest a reevaluation late in the next school year, when Jamal would be 5, with possible stronger evidence supporting the hypothesis of a gifted intellect. In the intervening time, the team suggests to the Wilsons that they enroll Jamal in one of the district's kindergarten programs, and let him continue to grow and mature.

Before enrolling their son in kindergarten, Mr. and Mrs. Wilson decide to observe the class where Jamal would be enrolled for the following school year. While they like the teacher, and feel that the classroom has a cheery, inviting atmosphere, they are very concerned that all of the information reviewed that day consisted of concepts Jamal already knows very well. Based upon this experience, they decide that Jamal should go on directly to the first grade.

The next week, during kindergarten registration, Mr. and Mrs. Wilson complete forms requesting that Jamal start first grade during the following school year. When questioned by the building principal, they explain that since the school district is unwilling to recognize their son's giftedness, they have no other recourse to make sure he is suitably challenged and interested at school.

Discussion Questions

1. Why would the issue of communication be important to consider in this case study?
2. Why can IC be used in this case study?
3. Who are the consultee and the client in this scenario?
4. What kinds of interventions could be considered for this case?

IC/Family Example 3
The Brownes, a wealthy and successful family, have sent their youngest child, John, to public school after completing the elementary grades in

a private school. The Browne children, of which John is the fifth in the birth hierarchy, have performed very well in school and have gone on to attend prestigious, competitive colleges and universities. When enrolling John in the public school, Mr. and Mrs. Browne confessed that the private school that John had been attending was "too competitive," and that they believed John would fare better in the public school system.

John begins the seventh grade as an industrious, studious, and quiet student, and his teachers marvel at his accurate, neat class work and homework. However, they do note that John seems anxious, rarely speaking in class, appearing flushed, and socializing minimally with his classmates. At the first parent–teacher conference of the school year, John's parents report that John typically spends 4 to 6 hours each night completing his homework, often correcting and re-correcting answers that already appear to be satisfactory. John's teachers are stunned because they expect that homework completion should take approximately 30 to 45 minutes each night, at the most. They inform John's parents that they will discuss his progress at the next student services meeting, and see if they can figure out how to solve this problem.

As promised, John's teachers raise the issue of John's homework completion behaviors at the student services meeting the following week. The team appears confused, and several members are unsure if it is appropriate to suggest interventions, since the problem appears to be one that is experienced only at home. These members point to John's grades as evidence of his school progress, and wonder if there really is a problem at all.

Discussion Questions

1. Is this case appropriate for IC?
2. Is adequate school progress sufficient to determine whether or not a problem exists?
3. Who is the consultee in this scenario?
4. Why is it important to work with John's family in this case?

IC/Educator Example 1

Mr. Puzzled is a fifth-year high school math teacher at Know-It-All High School. Previously, Mr. Puzzled taught calculus to students at a private, elite high school, where he was a lauded, respected teacher. However, he decided to take a position at the public school in order to obtain a better benefits and retirement package.

Since being employed at the school, Mr. Puzzled has met with mixed success in his teaching. While his calculus students seem to do well, his success in teaching students in his algebra I and geometry classes has been less notable. Mr. Puzzled has been asked to conference with the head of the math department, Ms. Sharp, who has concerns about the number of mid-year student failures in his courses, as well as numerous parent complaints about their children's performance in their math classes. Mr. Puzzled is truly mystified regarding the reasons for the failure of his students, and invites Ms. Sharp into his class to observe his teaching practices.

While in his class, Ms. Sharp notices that the students seem to genuinely like Mr. Puzzled, and feels that he has good rapport with them. Mr. Puzzled begins the class by writing a challenge problem on the whiteboard, and collects the previous night's homework assignment, which he puts aside to grade during his preparatory period. As instruction commences, Ms. Sharp becomes aware that Mr. Puzzled gives students the homework for the day's instruction the night before he teaches the lesson. Mr. Puzzled continues his lesson, explaining the concepts of the homework of the previous night, and finishes the class period by assigning the class the next homework assignment, filled with problems the students have not yet learned how to solve.

Discussion Questions

1. Who is the client in this case study?
2. How can the use of observations be helpful in planning interventions?
3. How will success be measured?
4. What other consultative approaches might also be effective in addressing this problem?

IC/Educator Example 2

Ms. Salty is a junior-high-school French teacher, and has been teaching for 20 years. She teaches college-preparatory French for eighth and ninth grade students, and truly loves speaking the language. However, Ms. Salty is not a beloved teacher, and has a reputation for being sarcastic and impatient with her students.

Over the years, the junior high school has had two kindly, yet hands-off-style administrators. Although Ms. Salty had a reputation for being "difficult," these administrators believed that the teacher knew best, and cloughed off concerns regarding her teaching style. They reasoned that her students completed her class being very prepared for high school French, and thus, she must be doing her job.

However, these administrators have retired, and a new assistant principal and new principal have taken the helm of the junior high school. When doing some investigation about uneven class sizes, they come to learn that enrollment in Ms. Salty's classes has drastically diminished during the last 5 years, with the German, Spanish, and Latin class sizes overflowing.

When the assistant principal does a routine evaluation of Ms. Salty's fifth-period French class, she notices that the behavior demonstrated in Ms. Salty's class is unruly, with students text messaging, talking to each other, and disobeying Ms. Salty's requests to complete a classroom assignment. A small group of students rudely talk back to Ms. Salty when she speaks to them, eventually stalking out of class despite having no hall pass. Further, a few students sit slumped deep in their seats in the back row, looking worried and trying not to engage Ms. Salty's attention. The assistant principal leaves the class at the end of the period, enters the principal's office, and says, "We have a problem."

Discussion Questions

1. What is the problem, and how can it be defined?
2. What should be done if the consultee is resistant to the consultative process?
3. Who might be an appropriate consultant in this case study?
4. What other obstacles to IC might there be?

IC/Educator Example 3

Mr. Young has been working in the Progressively Smaller School District for the past 25 years as a physical education and health teacher. Due to an increasingly smaller student population, the district has been downsizing as teachers have retired by not hiring new personnel to fill the vacated positions. Despite such methods, however, the upper administration in the school system finds it necessary to relocate one physical education teacher to a position teaching English to middle school students. Since Mr. Young has the least seniority in the physical education department, he must take the English teacher position if he wishes to stay employed by the school system. Although Mr. Young would like to retire, he realizes that he needs to stay in his job for another 5 years in order to receive his full pension.

Since Mr. Young is motivated to perform well at whatever job in which he is employed, he meets with the assistant principal of the middle school in early July, explaining that he believes that he needs some training in order to perform adequately in his new role. Specifically, Mr. Young feels that he needs to receive training in evidence-based interventions because he understands, through his professional readings, that such are the preferred interventions to use when students are having difficulty in succeeding in the classroom. Mr. Young understands that in an English class it is important that students can read fluently, and guesses that he will have some children and adolescents who have difficulty in reading.

Although pleased and surprised by Mr. Young's motivation and initiative, the principal has no money in the budget to provide special training for Mr. Young. Consequently, she contacts the student services team to see if they can plan some training activities on EBIs during the pre-school-year in-service sessions. Additionally, she would like the team to set up an ICT to support teachers in the use of an RTI model for the next school year.

Discussion Questions

1. What can be done in the short amount of time before school begins?
2. What resources should the student services team consult?
3. What is the most expeditious way to set up an ICT?
4. How long will it take a district to institutionalize an RTI model?

IC/Systems Example 1

The Cutting Edge School District is a school system that services students from various ethnic, cultural, and socioeconomic groups, including the most affluent and least affluent communities in the county. In the past, the school's curriculum coordinator, a kindly yet non-research-friendly gentleman, has selected the reading series for the district based on cost and representation of diverse backgrounds in the curriculum.

After the retirement of this gentleman, the district hired a new curriculum director, Ms. Savvy, who, among other tasks, oversees the standardized testing of the student body, as well as the selection of a new curriculum every few years. Upon reviewing the reading achievement scores of the students in the school system, Ms. Savvy is concerned that the bottom quartile of these students continues to make only minimal gains from year to year in their reading skills.

Ms. Savvy continues to gather research about this problem, conducting a number of observations in both regular and special education classrooms in the district. Through her time spent in inclusive and pull-out educational programs in which reading is taught, Ms. Savvy discovers that there is no true curriculum. The teachers appear to be picking and choosing lessons and activities from the general reading curriculum, and providing additional drill to students in an attempt to improve their reading skills.

Although Ms. Savvy recalls from her study of the source literature that curriculum-based assessment strategies have been used to identify whether students are reading at independent, instructional, or frustration levels in other school systems, teachers in the Cutting Edge School District have not adopted this practice, and have no idea regarding students' grade level reading achievement, aside from the standardized achievement test data that are gathered at the end of the school year. Ms. Savvy feels that the school district could do better for its struggling readers, and wonders what is to be done.

Discussion Questions

1. Why is the issue of instructional mismatch relevant in this case?
2. What criteria should be used to determine whether a curriculum meets the criteria for evidence based practices?
3. Who is the consultee in this case?
4. Who is the client in this case?

IC/Systems Example 2

Desiree is an African-American second grade student enrolled in the Everyman School System. Adopted by Caucasian parents, Desiree and her younger sister Calinda, who is also African-American, all live in a rural, largely Caucasian community. After completing the first grade, demonstrating satisfactory progress, Desiree moved on to the second grade at the local elementary school. After the first marking period of her second grade year, Desiree's teacher reported to the student services team that Desiree was performing very poorly in all of her academic classes, and suggested that Desiree should be evaluated by the school psychologist in order to determine her eligibility for special education.

Because the school psychologist had a relatively light caseload at that time, Desiree was evaluated during the second marking period of the school year. The school psychologist, along with the other multidisciplinary team members, found that Desiree's cognitive functioning and academic achievement skills all fell within the average range. Desiree's visual and auditory perceptual skills appeared to fall within normal limits, and the only elevation in a behavioral rating scale completed by Desiree's parents was a negative attitude toward school. While conducting an observation of Desiree in the classroom, the school psychologist noted that there was a "bad vibe" between Desiree and her teacher, which she concluded was the probable source of the problem.

Based upon the evaluation results, the issue was referred to the student services team, since Desiree has approximately ½ of the year remaining in the second grade. Although not explicitly stated in the evaluation report, it is obvious that the school psychologist and other multidisciplinary team members see the problem as a personality mismatch between Desiree and her teacher. The team feels unsure of how to proceed in remedying this problem, particularly because Desiree's teacher is part of the student services team.

Discussion Questions

1. How can this case be viewed as a problem appropriate for IC?
2. Who is the client in this scenario?
3. How can observations be used to improve the teacher's and Desiree's classroom experiences?
4. How will it be determined if the interventions are successful?

IC/Systems Example 3

In Expeditious School District, a medium-sized suburban school system, students with mild to moderate academic and behavioral disabilities are included in the regular education setting. For these students, adaptation and accommodation services are provided by itinerant special education support teachers who collaborate with regular education teachers to meet the needs of these children and adolescents.

Children and adolescents with moderate to severe academic and behavioral disabilities receive their instruction in pull-out special education classrooms, but they are integrated into regular education classrooms for some of the school day. The pull-out classrooms are essentially designed for students with learning and mild intellectual disabilities, and an evidence-based academic curriculum is used to build skills, along with repetition and fold-in drills.

However, in each of these classes, approximately 15% to 20% of the student population consists of students with moderate to severe emotional and behavioral disabilities, who tend to exhibit behavior that interferes with their learning. The administrators in the Expeditious School District rationalize that because these students do have academic problems, their inclusion with students with learning and intellectual disabilities is appropriate.

However, some of the parents of students with emotional and behavioral disorders are concerned that the instruction in these classrooms is not sufficiently differentiated from the curriculum used with the students with learning and intellectual disabilities. Specifically, there is no curriculum involving social skills, anger management, anxiety diminishment, functional life skills, and so forth, designed to improve the emotional and behavioral skills of students with these kinds of disabilities. The parents of these youngsters do not so much object to grouping the children with learning and behavioral/emotional problems together, but do feel that the lack of programming for their children's emotional and behavioral needs is problematic.

Discussion Questions

1. Why can this be considered an IC case rather than an OSC case?
2. What kinds of interventions would be appropriate?
3. How should observations be used in the data collection process?
4. Should issues of diversity be explored in this case?

SUMMARY

In this chapter, information was presented regarding the use of IC in school systems. First, IC was defined, followed by information supporting the importance of increasing quality instruction in schools. The underlying assumptions of IC were then reviewed, along with the communication patterns and the process of IC. The stages of IC, including entry and contracting, problem identification and analysis (including the use of CBM/CBA), intervention implementation, termination, and development of a written record were also presented. Information regarding ICT, the role of the consultee in IC, IC/RTI, and multicultural issues relating to IC were reviewed. Finally, obstacles to the implementation of IC were explored. In the final chapter of this book information regarding the efficacy of each consultative method will be reviewed.

CHAPTER 8

Effectiveness of Consultation

There is a detailed literature base regarding the theoretical assumptions of various models of consultative services that can be used in schools. Additionally, there is research that has been published addressing the implementation process in school systems for the different consultative approaches. Based upon numerous studies, the theory, concept, and practice of consultation seems to be largely understood by school-based personnel, along with the recognition of the need for consultative services in school systems (Bramlett & Murphy, 1998; Cummings et al., 2004; Farrell, 2006; Gilman & Gabriel, 2004; Meyers, Meyers, & Grogg, 2004; Sheridan, Welch, & Orme, 1996; Zins & Erchul, 2002). However, some aspects of consultation are not as well understood; areas that still need to be investigated are the number, type, and style of teaching experiences, both in academic and field settings, that result in the development of a good consultant.

In chapter 1, recommendations for teaching consultation were reviewed. However, as Alpert and Taufique note in their 2002 article, the quality of these learning experiences are largely left to chance. Further, to date there has been limited movement in defining the essential coursework and competencies to be demonstrated by students, what an appropriate field-based experience would include, and the important characteristics of a supervisor. It seems that while college and university instructors in human-service professions agree that they will teach consultation, the identification and measurement of what constitutes effective teaching in this area has not yet occurred.

Evaluating the outcomes of consultation processes upon consultees and clients also remains elusive. The nature of indirect services necessitates inference regarding which interactions resulted in change. While much of psychological research suffers from evaluating data based on inference, information about a process in which a consultant influences a consultee to carry out an intervention that has the potential to affect the functioning of a client increases the distance between intervention and outcome. It is unclear if the strength of the change can travel far enough to be measured accurately. Further, even if the change in behavior of the client can be measured, the clinical significance also needs to be interpreted clearly. To date, the characteristics associated with some consultative theories more easily lend themselves to being measured, while others suggest stronger clinical importance.

In applied settings such as school systems, matching the problem, as defined by the consultee, to the appropriate consultative model is a goal of many service delivery providers. In order to accomplish this, consultants need to learn multiple consultative models, and also need to be familiar with the outcome data regarding the effectiveness of those models. In this final chapter, the efficacy studies of the consultative models presented in this book are summarized so that readers may easily make comparisons.

Mental Health Consultation

There is limited research examining the outcomes of mental health consultative (MHC) processes. Of the studies available, most do not focus on MHC. Researchers conducting a meta-analysis of the use of MHC found that this approach had a positive effect on both consultees and clients (Medway & Updyke, 1985). However, others have argued that the studies examined were not pure examples of MHC (Gutkin & Curtis, 1990). Sheridan et al. (1996) examined efficacy studies published after the Medway and Updyke (1985) investigation, and again found positive effects of MHC. However, Sheridan et al. (1996) were also unable to document that the consultation provided in these later studies were indeed purely MHC. At present, there is little supporting empirical evidence for the effectiveness of MHC (Brown, Pryzwansky & Schulte, 2006; Gutkin & Curtis, 1999).

Supporters of MHC argue that measurement of the changes in interpersonal variables proves to be just as difficult for the consultation models as for the counseling models. That is, interpersonal issues are subjective and are difficult to measure without inference. For the empiricist, the reality of behaviors inferred to be the result of the consultants' influence is problematic. Exhortations to implement studies using randomized clinical trials to increase clarity in the measurement and interpretation of findings are countered by the inapplicability of such findings to practice. These researchers highlight the importance of interpersonal and social context, concluding that the objective comparison of sanitized samples hinders accurate interpretations applicable to diverse groups (Henning-Stout & Meyers, 2000). Others argue that it is the quality of the consultant–consultee relationship that should be measured, rather than the indirect effects. For example, a quality interpersonal relationship with a consultant is often reported to improve teacher functioning (Bostic & Rauch, 1999).

Complicating the search for empirical support is the need to make modifications to MHC. Researchers who consider the role of culture and diversity, as they relate to the consultation experience, found that MHC and other consultative models required substantial modification when being used with diverse groups (Behring, Cabello, Kushida & Murguia, 2000).

Behavioral Consultation (BC)

Empirical evidence for behavioral consultation (BC) is primarily presented in single-case study designs. Through this design, researchers have concluded that BC is effective in promoting positive behavior changes (Brown et al., 2001; Guli, 2005; Kratochwill & Van Someren, 1995; Medway, 1979, 1982; Sheridan et al., 1996; Wilkinson, 2005; Zins & Erchul, 2002). In a review of 18 parent consultation studies, in which academic (homework completion), social and emotional (social skills), and behavioral (aggression) concerns were targeted, Guli (2005) found that the conjoint behavioral consultation (CBC) model was the more effective in producing positive changes in the school setting than other forms of BC. Effect sizes for the parent consultation studies ranged from moderate to large, suggesting that the use of parental cooperation, which is emphasized in the CBC model, may improve outcomes when used in BC.

Although the use of BC may result in clinically significant treatment outcomes, there are several methodological issues to consider. As previously mentioned, intervention effectiveness is usually determined using case study designs in which one or two participants are studied. Using a small sample size limits the generalizability of the research findings to other groups. Such small samples limit the ability to replicate findings, decrease the certitude of treatment integrity, and offer more opportunity to muddle identifiable procedures (Guli, 2005; Wilkinson, 2005). Suggestions to improve the rigor of BC effectiveness studies include using between-subjects research designs; multiple baselines in single participant research; the reporting of effect sizes, reliability, and validity data in each study; and study replication (Guli, 2005).

In addition to single-subject research designs, there are barriers to the implementation of effective BC strategies. Examples include lack of consultant training, difficulty identifying the target behavior(s), and lack of consultee training, among other factors (Kratochwill & Van Someren, 2005). Overall, while researchers suggest that BC is a useful indirect mode of service delivery, replicating studies that use more diverse populations and problems are needed in order to clarify its effectiveness.

Social Cognitive Theory Consultation

There is limited empirical research documenting the efficacy of social cognitive theory consultation (SCTC). In the case of SCTC, the interventions used have received more research support (Bandura, 1977b, 1978, 1982b) than the model (Brown & Schulte, 1987). Thus, it is unknown if the effectiveness observed in outcomes is specifically related to the consultation process (Kratochwill & Van Someren, 2005). For example, SCTC emphasizes the importance of the consultant and consultee relationship. When a good relationship is established, researchers have shown that teachers have positive perceptions of the consultation process regardless of the effectiveness of the intervention (Athanasiou, Geil, Hazel, & Copeland, 2002). Moreover, because the SCTC process is collaborative in nature, a poor consultant–consultee relationship may negatively affect treatment outcomes.

Other factors that may be related to SCTC effectiveness include the role of motivation and self-efficacy beliefs instilled in the consultee during the consultative process. The consultant's role in SCTC is to enhance the consultee's motivation in establishing behavioral standards for both the consultee and the client. This may occur through direct instruction, feedback, and modeling (Bandura, 1977a, 1982b). The success of SCTC relies upon the ability of the consultant to teach the consultee new skills that ultimately increase the consultee's motivation and self-efficacy beliefs, which in turn contribute to positive consultation outcomes (Brown & Schulte, 1987). This circuitous route has potential for many missteps, potentially negating the effectiveness of the process.

Adlerian Consultation

There is limited empirical support for Adlerian consultation (AC). As noted in the review of MHC, most consultation research does not examine approaches where inferences about the cause of behaviors are employed. Further, the individual focus of AC does not lend itself to control sample comparisons. Of the limited research available, there are some case studies that conclude this type of consultation is successful with teachers (Mortola & Carlson, 2003; Schneider, 1983; White & Mullis, 1998) and parents (Kottman & Ashby, 1999). Researchers examining the use of AC have often focused on teacher encouragement. When teachers provide encouragement to students, there is also an improvement in student on-task behaviors (Hillman & Shields, 1975; Rathvon, 1990). Despite its lack of substantial empirical support, however, Dinkmeyer (2006) maintains that Adler's individual psychology is "exceptionally suited" as a consultative model. Barriers to providing AC include the limited ability to measure outcomes in an age where evidence-based decisions drive school setting conclusions. Also, university training programs have a limited focus in teaching Adlerian concepts.

Organizational and Systems Consultation

Organizational and systems consultation (OSC), including organizational development consultation (ODC) and intervention assistance consultation (IAC), has not been adequately studied (Forman, 1995). While many organizational factors related to consultation have been explored in the literature, school organizational variables, such as authority, decision making, reward dissemination, and communication structures of school systems have not been adequately investigated. Thus, in the last decade, theorists have attempted to operationally define OSC in school systems, and researchers have begun to conduct outcome studies regarding the effectiveness of these approaches.

Gottfredson (1993) described the use of the ODC method in a 3-year program designed to improve student behavior in middle schools (Gottfredson, Gottfredson, & Hybl, 1993). In this program, the program development evaluation method was used to address the causes of misbehavior. The program focused on (1) clarification of school rules, (2) increased consistency in rule enforcement, (3) improved classroom management and organization, (4) increased communication with parents regarding student behavior, and (5) reinforcement of appropriate behavior. Consultants worked with teachers and administrators to identify concrete performance standards for each program component and to monitor the implementation of new strategies, with frequent feedback used to foster implementation. Gottfredson et al. (1993) reported that schools with the most effective improvement teams ensured strong treatment fidelity, with corresponding significant increases in appropriate student conduct. Thus, there is some support for the ODC model (Gottfredson et al., 1993).

Although many school systems have adopted IAC, there is limited data about the short- and long-term effectiveness of this approach (Zins & Illback, 1995). Numerous researchers (Illback & Zins, 1995; Zins et al., 1988; Zins & Illback, 1995; Zins & Ponti, 1990) have identified a need for establishing the effectiveness of OSC. Specifically, measuring the effects of organizational factors upon the behavior of consultants, consultees, and clients is needed before strong conclusions can be made about OSC effectiveness.

Instructional Consultation

Instructional consultation (IC) is a process born from the merging of instructional psychology in the discipline of school psychology with the process of collaborative consultation from the field of special education (Rosenfield, 1995a). To date, there is limited research on IC effectiveness; however, there is a concerted effort to conduct studies measuring its associated outcomes. For example, Fudell, Gravois, and Rosenfield (1994) developed a level-of-implementation measure for instructional consultation teams to ensure that the model has been implemented correctly prior to outcome evaluation. This step is used to ensure treatment integrity to facilitate an accurate assessment of intervention effectiveness (Rosenfield, 1995).

Similarly, Bartels and Mortenson (2005) have used performance feedback and checklists to improve and describe the degree to which school teams adhered to the IC model. In research evaluating the efficacy of instructional consultation teams, researchers have found that 85% of the cases handled by the team met goals. Specifically, the number of students referred for multidisciplinary evaluations and placed in special education programs decreased, and teachers participating in the IC process rated high levels of satisfaction regarding their experiences (Gravois & Rosenfield, 2002; Knotek, Rosenfield, Gravois, & Babinski, 2003). Thus, the efficacy of IC as documented in these studies, appears promising.

CONCLUSIONS

Given the continued need for consultative services, the emphasis upon the use of evidence in decision making and the reality that many human processes cannot be observed, students are encouraged to consider multiple factors when choosing a consultative model. The theoretical frame of each consultative model, the feasibility of implementation, and the empirical evidence supporting the approach should all be considered when selecting a consultative model to help solve a problem. In Table 8.1,

Table 8.1 Selecting a Consultation Model

CASE DESCRIPTION	UNIQUE SETTING CONSIDERATIONS	MODEL(S) CONSIDERED APPROPRIATE & RATIONALE	PROS & CONS FOR IMPLEMENTATION	EMPIRICAL SUPPORT OR CLINICAL UTILITY	MATCH WITH THE PROBLEM (YES/NO/ POSSIBLE)
(Defined by consultee)	Child	Mental health			
	Parent	Behavioral			
	Teacher	Social cognitive			
	Classroom	Adlerian			
	School	Organizational/Systems			
(Defined by consultant)* if appropriate	District	Instructional			
	State standards				
	Federal mandates				

an organizational chart is provided to assist individuals in making decisions regarding the match between the various consultative approaches and particular cases. Finally, once becoming practitioners, students of consultation are encouraged to contribute to the research base needed to inform school personnel about appropriate and efficacious practices. When using consultation in school settings, consider evaluating the processes used to make decisions regarding a consultative model, the outcome of the consultation, and the fidelity of the process. It is only through research regarding the practice of consultation that meaningful conclusions and recommendations develop.

REFERENCES

Achinstein, B., & Barrett, A. (2004). (Re)Framing classroom contexts: How new teachers and mentors view diverse learners and challenges of practice. *Teachers College Record, 106,* 716–746.

Adelman, H. S., & Taylor, L. (2007). Systemic change for school improvement. *Journal of Educational and Psychological Consultation, 17,* 55–77.

Adler, A. (1957). *The education of children.* London: George Allen & Unwin Ltd.

Adler, A. (1992). *Understanding human nature* (C. Brett, Trans.). Oxford: Oneworld Publications. (Original work published 1927)

Agresta, J. (2004). Professional role perceptions of school social workers, psychologists, and counselors. *Children and Schools, 26,* 151–163.

Akin-Little, K. A., Little, S. G., & Delligatti, N. (2004). A preventative model of school consultation: Incorporating perspectives from positive psychology. *Psychology in the Schools, 4,* 155–162.

Alderman G. L. & Gimpel, G. A. (1996). The interaction between type of behavior problem and type of consultant: Teachers' preference for professional assistance. *Journal of Educational and Psychological Consultation, 7,* 305–313.

Allen, S. J., & Graden, J. L. (1995). Best practices in collaborative problem-solving for intervention design. In A. Thomas & J. Grimes (Eds.), *Best practices in school psychology III* (pp. 667–678). Washington, DC: National Association of School Psychologists.

Allinder, R. M., & BeckBest, M. A. (1995). Differential effects of two approaches to supporting teachers' use of curriculum-based measurement. *School Psychology Review, 24,* 287–298.

Alpert, J. (1976). Conceptual basis of mental health consultation in schools. *Professional Psychology, 7,* 619–626.

Alpert, J. L., & Taufique, S. R. (2002). Consultation training: 26 years and three questions. *Journal of Educational and Psychological Consultation, 13,* 13–33.

American Academy of Child and Adolescent Psychiatry (AACAP), Official Action. (2005). Practice parameters for psychiatric consultation to schools. *Journal of the American Academy of Child and Adolescent Psychiatry, 44,* 1068–1083.

American Psychological Association (2002). Rules and procedures: October 1, 2001 [Ethics Committee Rules and Procedures]. *American Psychologist, 57,* 626–645.

Ansbacher, H. L. & Ansbacher, R. R. (1956). *The individual psychology of Alfred Adler: A systematic presentation in selections from his writings.* Oxford, England: Basic.

Anton-LaHart, J., & Rosenfield, S. (2004). A survey of preservice consultation training in school psychology programs. *Journal of Educational and Psychological Consultation, 15,* 41–62.

Arra, C. T., & Bahr, M. W. (2005). Teachers' and students' preferences for mathematics interventions: Implications for teacher acceptability in consultation. *Journal of Educational and Psychological Consultation, 16,* 157–174.

Arrendondo, P., Toporek, R., Brown, S. P., Jones, J., Locke, D., Sanchez, J., & Stadler, H. (1996). Operationalization of multicultural counseling competencies. *Journal of Multicultural Counseling and Development, 24,* 42–78.

Astor, R. A., Pitner, R. O., & Duncan, B. B. (1996). Ecological approaches to mental health consultation with teachers on issues related to youth and school violence. *Journal of Negro Education, 65,* 336–355.

Athanasiou, M. S., Geil, M., Hazel, C. E., & Copeland, E. P. (2002). A look inside school-based consultation: A qualitative study of the beliefs and practices of school psychologists and teachers. *School Psychology Quarterly, 17,* 258–298.

Auster, E. R., Feeney-Kettler, K. A., & Kratochwill, T. R. (2006). Conjoint behavioral consultation: Application to the school-based treatment of anxiety disorders. *Education and Treatment of Children, 29,* 243–256.

Bacon, E. H., & Dougherty, A. M. (1992). Consultation and coordination services for prekindergarten children. *Elementary School Guidance and Counseling, 27,* 24–32.

Baker, H. L. (1965). Psychological services: From the school staff's point of view. *Journal of School Psychology, 3,* 36–42.

Bandura, A. (1971). Psychotherapy based on modeling principles. In A. E. Bergin & S. L. Garfield (Eds.), *Handbook of psychotherapy and behavioral change: An empirical analysis* (pp. 653–708). New York: Wiley.

Bandura, A. (1976). Self-reinforcement: Theoretical and methodological considerations. *Behaviorism, 4,* 135–155.

Bandura, A. (1977a). Self-efficacy: Toward a unifying theory of behavioral change. *Psychological Review, 84,* 191–215.

Bandura, A. (1977b). *Social learning theory.* Oxford, England: Prentice Hall.

Bandura, A. (1978). The self system in reciprocal determinism. *American Psychologist, 33,* 344–358.

Bandura, A. (1982a). The assessment and predictive generality of self-precepts of efficacy. *Journal of Behavior Therapy and Experimental Psychiatry, 13,* 195–199.

Bandura, A. (1982b). Self-efficacy mechanism in human agency. *American Psychologist, 37,* 122–147.

Bartels, S. M., & Mortenson, B. P. (2005). Enhancing adherence to a problem-solving model for middle-school pre-referral teams: A performance feedback and checklist approach. *Journal of Applied School Psychology, 22,* 109–123.

Beer, M. (1980). *Organizational change and development: A systems view*. Santa Monica, CA: Goodyear.

Behring, S. T., Cabello, B., Kushida, D., & Murguia, A. (2000). Cultural modifications to current school-based consultation approaches reported by culturally diverse beginning consultants. *School Psychology Review, 29*, 354–367.

Benard, B. (2004). *Resiliency: What we have learned*. San Francisco: West Ed.

Bergan, J. R. (1977). *Training in consultation Mental health, behavioral, and organizational perspectives*. Springfield, IL: Charles C Thomas.

Bergan, J. R., & Kratochwill, T. R. (1990). *Behavioral consultation and therapy*. New York: Plenum.

Bergan, J. R., & Schnapps, A. (1983). A model for instructional consultation. In J. Alpert & J. Meyers (Eds.), *Training in Consultation* (pp. 104–119).

Bergan, J. R., & Tombari, M. L. (1976). Consultant skill and efficiency and the implementation and outcomes of consultation. *Journal of School Psychology, 14*, 3–14.

Berninger, V. W., Thalberg, S., DeBruyn, I., & Smith, I. (1987). Preventing reading disabilities by assessing and remediating phonemic skills. *School Psychology Review, 16*, 554–565.

Bickel, W. E., Zigmond, N., McCall, R., & McNelis, R. H. (1999). *Final report: Instructional support team best practices in Pennsylvania*. Pittsburgh, PA: University of Pittsburgh.

Bostic, J. Q., & Rauch, P. K. (1999). The 3 R's of school consultation. *Journal of the American Academy of Child and Adolescent Psychiatry, 38*, 339–341.

Bramlett, R. K., & Murphy, J. J. (1998). School psychology perspectives on consultation: Key contributions to the field. *Journal of Educational and Psychological Consultation, 9*, 29–55.

Bramlett, R. K., Murphy, J. J., Johnson, J., Wallingsford, L., & Hall, J. D. (2002). Contemporary practices in school psychology: A national survey of roles and referral problems. *Psychology in the Schools, 39*, 327–335.

Brofenbrenner, U. (1979). *The ecology of human development*. Cambridge, MA: Harvard University Press.

Brown, D., Pryzwansky, W. B., & Schulte, A. C. (2001). *Psychological consultation: Introduction to theory and practice* (5th ed.). Needham Heights, MA: Allyn & Bacon.

Brown, D., Pryzwansky, W. B., & Schulte, A. C. (2006). *Psychological consultation: Introduction to theory and practice* (6th ed.). Needham Heights, MA: Allyn & Bacon.

Brown, D., & Schulte, A. (1987). A social learning model of consultation. *Professional Psychology: Research and Practice, 18*, 283–287.

Brown, M. B., Holcombe, D. C., Bolen, L. M., & Thomson, W. S. (2006). Role function and job satisfaction of school psychologists practicing in an expanded role model. *Psychological Reports, 98*, 486–496.

Burns, M. K., Dean V. J., & Klar, S. (2004). Using curriculum-based assessment in the responsiveness to intervention diagnostic model for learning disabilities. *Assessment for Effective Intervention, 2a*, 47–56.

Burns, M. K., MacQuarrie, L. L., & Campbell, D. T. (1999). The difference between instructional assessment (curriculum-based assessment) and curriculum-based measurement: A focus on purpose and result. *Communiqué, 27,* 18–19.

Busse, R. T., Kratochwill, T. R., & Elliott, S. N. (1999). Influences of verbal interactions during behavioral consultations on treatment outcomes. *Journal of School Psychology, 37,* 117–143.

Caplan, G. (1963). Types of mental health consultation. *American Journal of Orthopsychiatry, 33,* 470–481.

Caplan, G. (1970). *The theory and practice of mental health consultation.* New York: Basic Books.

Caplan, G. (1974). *Support systems and community health.* New York: Behavioural Publications.

Caplan, G. (1995). Types of mental health consultation. *Journal of Educational and Psychological Consultation, 6,* 7–21.

Caplan, G., & Caplan, R. B. (1993). *Mental health consultation and collaboration.* San Francisco: Jossey-Bass.

Caplan, G., Caplan, R. B., & Erchul, W. P. (1994). Caplanian mental health consultation: Historical background and current status. *Consulting Psychology Journal: Practice and Research, 46,* 2–12.

Caplan, G., Caplan, R. B., & Erchul, W. P. (1995). A contemporary view of mental health consultation: Comments on types of mental health by Gerald Caplan 1963. *Journal of Educational and Psychological Consultation, 6,* 23–30.

Colton, D. L., & Sheridan, S. M. (1998). Conjoint behavioral consultation and social skills training: Enhancing the play behaviors of boys with attention deficit hyperactivity disorder. *Journal of Educational and Psychological Consultation, 9,* 3–28.

Conoley, J. C., & Conoley, C. W. (1991). Collaboration for child adjustment: Issues for school and clinic-based child psychologists. *Journal of Consulting and Clinical Psychology, 59,* 821–829.

Cramer, K., & Rosenfield, S. (2003). Clinical supervision of consultation. *The Clinical Supervisor, 22,* 111–124.

Croake, J. W., & Myers, K. M. (1985). Adlerian methods in the pediatric setting: A response to Sperry and Meyer. *Individual Psychology: Journal of Adlerian Theory, Research, and Practice. 41,* 514–517.

Cummings, J. A., Harrison, P. L., Dawson, M. M., Short, R. J., Gorin, S., & Palomares, R. S. (2004). The 2002 conference on the future of school psychology: Implications for consultation, intervention, and prevention services. *Journal of Educational and Psychological Consultation, 15,* 239–256.

Curtis, M. J., Hunley, S. A., Walker, K. J., & Baker, A. C. (1999). Demographic characteristics and professional practices in school psychology. *School Psychology Review, 28,* 104–116.

Davis, K. M. (2003). Teaching a course in school-based consultation. *Counselor Education and Supervision, 42,* 275–285.

Davis, J. M., & Hartsough, C. S. (1992). Assessing psychosocial environment in mental health consultation groups. *Psychology in the Schools, 29,* 224–229.

Deno, S. L. (1985). Curriculum-based measurement: The emerging alternative. *Exceptional Children, 52,* 219–232.

Deno, s. L. (1989). Curriculum-based measurement and special education services: A fundamental and direct relationship. In M. R. Shina (Ed.), *Curriculum-based measurement: Assessing special needs children,* (pp. 1–17). NY: Guilford.

Deno, S. L. (1995). School psychologist as problem solver. In A. Thomas & J. Grimes, (Eds.), *Best Practices in School Psychology III* (pp. 471–484). Washington, DC: National Association of School Psychologists.

Derr, C. B. (1976). "OD" won't work in schools. *Brooklyn Education and Urban Society, 8,* 227–241.

Dinkmeyer, D., Jr. & Carlson, J. (2006). School consultation using individual psychology. *Journal of Individual Psychology, 62,* 180–187.

Dinkmeyer, D., Jr., & Carlson, J. (2006). *Consultation: Creating school-based interventions* (3rd ed.). New York: Routledge.

Dinkmeyer, D., Jr., & Carlson, J. (2006). School consultation using individual psychology. *Journal of Ind. Psych., 62,* 180–187.

Dinkmeyer, D., Jr., Carlson, J., & Dinkmeyer, D., Sr. (1994). *Consultation: School mental health professionals as consultants.* Muncie, IN: Accelerated Development.

Doll, B., Haack, K., Kosse, S., Osterloh, M., Siemers, E., & Pray, B. (2005). The dilemma of pragmatics: Why schools do not use quality team consultation practice. *Journal of Educational and Psychological Consultation, 16,* 127–155.

Dougherty, A. M. (2004). *Psychological consultation and collaboration in schools and community settings* (3rd ed.). Belmont, CA: Wadsworth.

Dougherty, A. M., Tack, F. E., Fullam, C. B., & Hammer, L. M. (1996). Disengagement: A neglected aspect of the consultation process. *Journal of Educational and Psychological Consultation, 7,* 259–274.

Dreikurs, R. R. (1953). *Fundamentals of Adlerian psychology.* Chicago: Alfred Alder Institute.

Dreikurs, R. R. (1968). *Psychology in the classroom* (2nd ed.). New York: Harper & Row.

Dreikurs, R. R., & Cassel, P. (1971). *Discipline without tears.* New York: Harper & Row.

Drisko, J. W. (1993). Special education teacher consultation: A student-focused, skill-defining approach. *Social Work in Education, 15,* 19–28.

Dwyer, K., Osher, D., & Warger, C. (1998). *Early warning, timely response: A guide to safe schools.* Washington, DC: U.S. Department of Education.

Egan, G. (1994). The skilled helper: A problem management approach to helping (5th ed.). Belmont, CA: Thomson/Brooks/Cole.

Elliot, S. N. (1988). Acceptability of behavioral treatments: Review of variables that influence treatment selection. *Professional Psychology: Research and Practice, 19,* 68–80.

Erchul, W. P., & Chewning, T. G. (1990). Behavioral consultation from a request-centered relational communication perspective. *School Psychology Quarterly, 5,* 1–20.

Erchul, W. P., Raven, B. H., & Wilson, K. E. (2004). The relationship between gender of consultant and social power perceptions within school consultation. *School Psychology Review, 33,* 582–590.

Fairweather, G. W., Sanders, D. H., & Tornatzky, L. G. (1974). *Creating change in mental health organizations.* New York: Pergamon.

Farouk, S. (2004). Group work in schools: A process consultation approach. *Educational Psychology in Practice, 20,* 207–220.

Farrell, P. (2006). Developing inclusive practices among educational psychologists: Problems and possibilities. *European Journal of Psychology of Education, 21,* 293–304.

Flinders, D. J. (2005). The failings of NCLB. *Curriculum and Teaching Dialogue, 7,* 1–9.

Forman, S. G. (1995). Organizational factors and consultation outcome. *Journal of Educational and Psychological Consultation, 6,* 191–195.

French, W. L., & Bell, C. H. (1978). *Organization development: Behavioral science interventions for organization improvement* (2nd ed.). Englewood Cliffs, NJ: Prentice Hall.

French, J. R. P., & Raven, B. H. (1959). The bases of social power. In D. Cartwright (Ed.), *Studies in social power* (pp. 150–167). Ann Arbor, MI: Institute for Social Research.

Friedlander, F., & Brown, L. D. (1974). Organization development. *Annual Review of Psychology, 25,* 313–341.

Fuchs, D., & Fuchs, L. S. (1994). Inclusive schools movement and the radicalization of special education reform. *Exceptional Children, 60,* 294–309.

Fuchs, L., Deno, S., & Mirkin, P. K. (1984). The effects of frequent curriculum-based measurement and evaluation on pedagogy, student achievement, and student awareness of learning. *American Educational Research Journal, 21,* 449–460.

Fuchs, L., & Fuchs, D. (1986). Effects of systematic formative evaluation: A meta-analysis. *Exceptional Children, 53,* 199–208.

Fuchs, L. S., Fuchs, D., Hamlett, C. L., & Ferguson, C. (1992). Effects of expert system consultation within curriculum-based measurement, using a reading maze task. *Exceptional Children, 58,* 436–450.

Fudell, R., Gravois, T. A., & Rosenfield, S. (1994). *Level of Implementation Scale for instructional consultation teams.* Unpublished manuscript.

Fullan, M. (1982). *The meaning of educational change.* New York: Teachers College Press.

Fullan, M., Miles, M. B., & Taylor, G. (1980). Organization development in schools: The state of the art. *Review of Educational Research, 50,* 121–183.

Fuqua, D. R., & Newman, J. L. (2006). Moral and ethical issues in human systems. *Consulting Psychology Journal: Practice and Research, 58,* 206–215.

Gallessich, J. (1982). *The profession and practice of consultation.* San Francisco: Jossey-Bass.

Galloway, J., & Sheridan, S. M. (1994). Implementing scientific practices through case studies: Examples using home-school interventions and consultation. *Journal of School Psychology, 32,* 385–413.

Gazda, G. M. (1973). *Human relations development: A manual for educators.* Boston: Allyn & Bacon.

Gickling, E., & Rosenfield, S. (1995). Best practices in curriculum-based measurement. In A. Thomas & J. Grimes (Eds.), *Best practice in school psychology III* (pp. 587–595). Washington, DC: National Association of School Psychologists.

Gillies, E. (2000). Developing consultation partnerships. *Educational Psychology in Practice, 16,* 31–37.

Gilman, R., & Gabriel, S. (2004). Perceptions of school psychological services by education professionals: Results from a multi-state survey pilot study. *School Psychology Review, 33,* 271–286.

Gilmore, G., & Chandy, J. (1973). Teachers' perception of school psychological services. *Journal of School Psychology, 11,* 139–147.

Glasser, W. (1998). *The quality school: Managing students without coercion.* New York: HarperCollins.

Goldstein, L. D. (1978). *Consulting with human service systems.* Reading, MA: Addison-Wesley.

Gonzalez, J. E., Nelson, J. R., Gutkin, T. B., & Shwery, C. S. (2004). Teacher resistance to school-based consultation with school psychologists: A survey of teacher perceptions. *Journal of Emotional and Behavioral Disorders, 12,* 30–37.

Gortmaker, V., Warnes, E. D., & Sheridan, S. M. (2004). Conjoint behavioral consultation: Involving parents and teachers in the treatment of a child with selective mutism. *Proven Practice, 5,* 66–72.

Gottfredson, D. C. (1984). A theory-ridden approach to program evaluation: A method for stimulating researcher-implementer collaboration. *American Psychologist, 39,* 1101–1112.

Gottfredson, D. C. (1993). Strategies for improving treatment integrity in organizational consultation. *Journal of Educational and Psychological Consultation, 4,* 275–279.

Gottfredson, D. C., Gottfredson, G. D., & Hybl, L. G. (1993). Managing adolescent behavior: A multiyear, multischool study. *American Educational Research Journal, 30,* 179–215.

Gottfredson, G. D., Rickert, D. E., Gottfredson D. C., & Advani, N. (1984). Standards for program development evaluation plans. *Psychological Documents, 14,* 32.

Graczyk, P. A., Domitrovich, C. E., Small, M., & Zins, J. E. (2006). Serving all children: An implementation model framework. *School Psychology Review, 35,* 266–274.

Graden, J. L. (2004). Arguments for change to consultation, prevention, and intervention: Will school psychology ever achieve this promise? *Journal of Educational and Psychological Consultation, 15,* 345–359.

Gravois, T. A., Knotek, S., & Babinski, L. M. (2002). Educating practitioners as consultants: Development and implementation of the Instructional Consultation Team consortium. *Journal of Educational and Psychological Consultation, 13,* 113–132.

Gravois, T. A., & Rosenfield, S. A. (2002). A multi-dimensional framework for evaluation of instructional consultation teams. *Journal of Applied School Psychology, 19,* 5–29.

Gravois, T. A., & Rosenfield, S. A. (2006). Impact of instructional consultation teams on the disproportionate referral and placement of minority students in special education. *Remedial and Special Education, 27,* 42–52.

Gravois, T., Rosenfield, S., & Gickling, E. (1999). *Instructional consultation teams: Training manual*. College Park: University of Maryland, Instructional Consultation Lab.

Greenberg, M. T., Weissberg, R. P., O'Brien, M. U., Zins, J. E., Fredericks, L., Resnik, H., & Elias, M. J. (2003). Enhancing school-based prevention and youth development through coordinated social, emotional, and academic learning. *American Psychologist, 58*, 466–474.

Gresham, F. M. (2002). Responsiveness-to-intervention: An alternative approach to the identification of learning disabilities. In R. Bradley, L. Danielson, & D. P. Hallahan (Eds.), *Identification of learning disabilities: Research to practice* (pp. 467–519). Mahwah, NJ: Lawrence Erlbaum.

Gresham, F. M. (2004). Current status and future directions of school-based behavioral interventions. *School Psychology Review, 33*, 326–343.

Guli, L. A. (2005). Evidence-based parent consultation with school-related outcomes. *School Psychology Quarterly, 20*, 455–472.

Gunning, T. G. (1998). *Assessing and correcting reading and writing difficulties*. Boston: Allyn & Bacon.

Gutkin, T. B. (1986). Consultees' perceptions of variables relating to the outcomes of school-based consultation interactions. *School Psychology Review, 15*, 375–382.

Gutkin, T. B. (1993). Cognitive modeling: A means for achieving prevention in school-based consultation. *Journal of Educational and Psychological Consultation, 4*, 179–183.

Gutkin, T. B. (2002). Training school-based consultants: Some thoughts on grains of sand and building anthills. *Journal of Educational and Psychological Consultation, 13*, 133–146.

Gutkin, T. B., & Bossard, M. D. (1984). The impact of consultant, consultee, and organizational variables on teacher attitudes toward consultation services. *Journal of School Psychology, 22*, 251–258.

Gutkin, T. B., & Curtis, M. J. (1982). School-based consultation: Theory and techniques. In C. R. Reynolds & T. B. Gutkin (Eds.), *The handbook of school psychology* (pp. 796–828). New York: Wiley.

Gutkin, T. B., & Curtis, M. J. (1990). School-based consultation: Theory, techniques, and research. In T. B. Gutkin & C. R. Reynolds (Eds.), *The handbook of school psychology* (2nd ed., pp. 577–611). New York: Wiley.

Gutkin, T. B., & Curtis, M. J. (1999). School-based consultation theory and practice: The art and science of indirect service delivery. In C. R. Reynolds & T. B. Gutkin (Eds.), *The handbook of school psychology* (3rd ed., pp. 598–637). New York: Wiley.

Gutkin, T. B., & Hickman, J. A. (1990). The relationship of consultant, consultee, and organizational characteristics to consultee resistance to school-based consultation: An empirical analysis. *Journal of Educational and Psychological Consultation, 1*, 111–122.

Hale, J. (1998). *The performance consultants' fieldbook*. San Francisco: Pfeiffer.

Hall, G. E., & Hord, S. M. (2001). *Implementing change: Patterns, principles, and potholes*. Boston: Allyn & Bacon.

Halpin, A. W. (1966). *Theory and research in administration*. New York: Macmillan.

Hanko, G. (2002). Making psychodynamic insights accessible to teachers as an integral part of their professional task: The potential of collaborative consultation approaches in school-based professional development. *Psychodynamic Practice, 8,* 375–389.

Hargreaves, A. (1995). *Changing teachers, changing times: Teachers' work and culture in a postmodern age.* New York: Teachers College Press.

Haring, N., & Gentry, N. D. (1976). Direct and individualized instructional procedures. In N. Haring & R. Schiefelbusch (Eds.), *Teaching special children* (pp. 72–111). New York: McGraw-Hill.

Harris, K. C., & Zetlin, A. G. (1993). Exploring the collaborative ethic in an urban school: A case study. *Journal of Educational and Psychological Consultation, 4,* 305–317.

Hart, T. M., Berninger, V. M., & Abbott, R. D. (1997). Comparison of teaching single or multiple orthographic-phonological connections for word recognition and spelling: Implications for instructional consultation. *School Psychology Review, 26,* 279–297.

Havelock, R. G., & Zlotolow, S. (1995). *The change agent's guide* (2nd ed.). Englewood Cliffs, NJ: Educational Technology Publications.

Hazel, C. E. (2007). Timeless and timely advice: A commentary on "Consultation to facilitate planned organizational change in schools," an article by Joseph E. Zins and Robert J. Illback. *Journal of Educational and Psychological Consultation, 17,* 125–132.

Henning-Stout, M., & Meyers, J. (2000). Consultation and human diversity: First things first. *School Psychology Review, 29,* 419–425.

Hersey, P., & Blanchard, K. H. (1982). *Management of organizational behavior: Utilizing human resources* (4th Ed.). Englewood Cliffs, NJ: Prentice Hall.

Higgins, E. T. (1999). "Saying is believing" effects: When sharing reality about something biases knowledge and evaluations. In L. L. Thompson, J. M. Levine, & D. M. Messick (Eds.), *Shared cognition in organizations: The management of knowledge.* (pp. 33–48). Mahwah, NJ: Lawrence Erlbaum Associates, Inc.

Hillman, B. W., & Shields, F. L. (1975). The encouragement process in guidance: Its effects on school achievement and attending behavior. *The School Counselor, 22,* 166–173.

Hojnoski, R. L. (2007). Promising directions in school-based systems level consultation: A commentary on "Has consultation achieved its primary prevention potential?" an article by Joseph E. Zins. *Journal of Educational and Psychological Consultation, 17,* 157–163.

Horton, D. (2005). Consultation with military children and schools: A proposed model. *Consulting Psychology Journal: Practice and Research, 57,* 259–265.

Hughes, J. N. (1994). Back to basics: Does consultation work? *Journal of Educational and Psychological Consultation, 5,* 77–84.

Hughes, J. N., & DeForest, P. A. (1993). Consultant directiveness and support as predictors of consultation outcomes. *Journal of School Psychology, 31,* 355–373.

Idol, L., Paolucci-Whitcomb, P., & Nevin, A. (1994). *Collaborative consultation* (2nd ed.). Austin, TX: PRO-ED.

Illback, R. J., & Zins, J. E. (1995). Organizational interventions in educational settings. *Journal of Educational and Psychological Consultation, 6,* 217–236.

Individuals with Disabilities Education Improvement Act (2004). Public Law 108-446 (20 U.S.C. 1400 et seq.).

Ingraham, C. L. (2000). Consultation through a multicultural lens: Multicultural and cross-cultural consultation in schools. *School Psychology Review, 29,* 320–343.

Ingraham, C. L. (2004). Multicultural consultee-centered consultation: Supporting consultees in the development of cultural competence. In N. M. Lambert, I. Hylander, & J. H. Sandoval (Eds.), *Consultee-centered consultation: Improving the quality of professional services in schools and community organizations* (pp. 135–148). Mahwah, NJ: Erlbaum.

Jacobsen, P. (2005). The Cleo Eulau center resiliency consultation program: Development, practice, challenges and efficacy of a relationship-based consultation model for challenged schools. *Smith College Studies in Social Work, 75,* 7–23.

Jeltova, I., & Fish, M. C. (2005). Creating school environments responsive to gay, lesbian, bisexual, and transgender families: Traditional and systemic approaches for consultation. *Journal of Educational and Psychological Consultation, 16,* 17–33.

Jones, K. M., & Lungaro, C. J. (2000). Teacher acceptability of functional assessment-derived treatments. *Journal of Educational and Psychological Consultation, 11,* 323–332.

Juras, J. L., Mackin, J. R., Curtis, S. E., & Foster-Fishman, P. G. (1997). Key concepts in community psychology: Implications for consultating in educational and human service settings. *Journal of Educational and Psychological Consultation, 8,* 111–133.

Kalafat, J., Illback, R. J., & Sanders, D., Jr. (2007). The relationship between implementation fidelity and educational outcomes in a school-based family support program: Development of a model for evaluating multidimensional full-service programs. *Evaluation and Program Planning, 30,* 136–148.

Kaslow, N. J., Pate, W. E., & Thorn, B. (2005). Academic and internship directors' perspectives on practicum experiences: Implications. *Professional Psychology: Research and Practice, 36,* 307–317.

Katz, D., & Kahn, R. L. (1978). *The social psychology of organizations.* (2nd ed.). New York: Wiley.

Keller, H. R. (1981). Behavioral consultation. In J. C. Conoley (Ed.), *Consultation in schools: Theory, research, procedures* (pp. 59–90). NY: Academic Press.

Kelley, M. F. (2004). Reconciling the philosophy and promise of itinerant consultation with the realities of practice. *Journal of Educational and Psychological Consultation, 15,* 183–190.

Kelly, J. G. (1993). Gerald Caplan's paradigm: Bridging psychotherapy and public health practice. In W. P. Erchul (Ed.), *Consultation in community, school and organizational practice: Gerald Caplan's contributions to professional psychology* (pp. 75–85). Philadelphia, PA: Taylor & Francis.

Kerr, M. M. (2001). High school consultation. *Child and Adolescent Psychiatric Clinics of North America, 10,* 105–115.

Kerwin, C. (1995). Consultation models revisited: A practitioner's perspective. *Journal of Educational and Psychological Consultation, 6,* 373–383.

Keyser, V., & Barling, J. (1981). Determinants of children's self-efficacy beliefs in an academic environment. *Cognitive Therapy and Research, 5,* 29–40.

Kiresuk, T. J., & Sherman, R. E. (1968). Goal attainment scaling: A general method for evaluating comprehensive community mental health programs. *Community Mental Health Programs, 4,* 443–453.

Klein, M. D., & Harris, K. C. (2004). Considerations in the personnel preparation of itinerant early childhood special education consultants. *Journal of Educational and Psychological Consultation, 15,* 151–165.

Knoff, H. M. (2000). Organizational development and strategic planning for the millennium: A blueprint toward effective school discipline, safety, and crisis prevention. *Psychology in the Schools, 37,* 17–32.

Knotek, S. E. (2003). Making sense of jargon during consultation: Understanding consultees' social language to effect change in student study teams. *Journal of Educational and Psychological Consultation, 14,* 181–207.

Knotek, S. E. (2005). Sustaining RTI through consultee-centered consultation. *California School Psychologist, 10,* 93–104.

Knotek, S. E. (2006). Administrative crisis consultation after 9/11: A university's systems response. *Consulting Psychology Journal: Practice and Research, 58,* 162–173.

Knotek, Rosenfield, Gravois, & Babinski (2002). The process of fostering consultee development during instructional consultation. *Journal of Educational and Psychological Consultation, 14,* 303–328.

Koopman, D. K. (2007). Secondary-level teachers' perceptions of the utilization of school psychological services. *Dissertation Abstracts International: Section A: Humanities and Social Sciences, 67* (8-A), 2881 (UMI No. AA13232334).

Koslowsky, M., Schwarzwald, J., & Ashuri, S. (2001). On the relationship between subordinates' compliance to power sources and organizational attitudes. *Applied Psychology: An International Review, 50,* 455–476.

Kottman, T., & Ashby, J. (1999). Using Adlerian personality priorities to custom-design consultation with parents of play therapy clients. *International Journal of Play Therapy, 8,* 77–92.

Kovaleski, J. F. (2003). *The three tier model of identifying learning disabilities: Critical program features and system issues.* Paper presented at the National Research Center on Learning Disabilities Responsiveness-to-Intervention Symposium, Kansas City, MO.

Kovaleski, J. F., Gickling, E. E., Morrow, H., & Swank, P. (1999). High versus low implementation of instructional support teams: A case for maintaining program fidelity. *Remedial and Special Education, 20,* 170–183.

Kratochwill, T. R., & Bergan, J. R. (1990). *Behavioral consultation in applied settings: An individual guide.* New York: Springer.

Kratochwill, T. R., & Van Someren, K. R. (1995). Barriers to treatment success in behavioral consultation: Current limitations and future directions. *Journal of Educational and Psychological Consultation, 6,* 125–143.

Kress, J. S., Norris, J. A., Schoenholz, D. A., Elias, M. J., & Seigle, P. (2004). Bringing together educational standards and social and emotional learning: Making the case for educators. *American Journal of Education, 111,* 68–89.

Kuhnert, K. W., & Lahey, M. A. (1993). Approaches to organizational needs assessment. In R. T. Golembiewski (Ed.), *Handbook of organizational consultation* (pp. 467–474). New York: Marcel Dekker.

Kurpius, D. J., & Fuqua, D. R. (1993). Fundamental issues in defining consultation. *Journal of Counseling and Development, 71, 598–600.*

Kurpius, D. J., Fuqua, D. R., & Rozecki, T. (1993). The consulting process: A multidimensional approach. *Journal of Counseling and Development, 71,* 601–606.

Kurpius, D. J., & Lewis, J. E. (1988). Introduction to consultation: An intervention for advocacy and outreach. In D. J. Kurpius & D. Brown (Eds.), *Handbook of consultation: An intervention for advocacy and outreach* (pp. 1–4). Alexandria, VA: American Counseling Association.

Kurpius, D. J., & Rozecki, T. (1992). Outreach, advocacy, and consultation: A framework for prevention and intervention. *Elementary School Guidance and Counseling, 26,* 176–189.

Larney, R. (2003). School based consultation in the United Kingdom: Principles, practice and effectiveness. *School Psychology International, 24,* 5–19.

LaRoche, M. J., & Shriberg, D. (2004). High stakes exams and Latino students: Toward a culturally sensitive education for Latino children in the United States. *Journal of Educational and Psychological Consultation, 15,* 205–223.

Levinsohn, M. (2000). *Evaluating instructional consultation teams for student reading achievement and special education outcomes.* Unpublished doctoral dissertation, University of Maryland, College Park.

Levinson, H. (2002). Assessing organizations. In R. L. Lowman (Ed.), The California School of Organizational Studies: *Handbook of organizational consulting psychology: A comprehensive guide to theory, skills, and techniques.* (pp. 315–343). San Francisco: Jossey-Bass.

Lewin, K. (1951). *Field theory in social science.* NY: Harper & Row.

Lin, M., Kelly, K. R., & Nelson, R. C. (1996). A comparative analysis of the interpersonal process in school-based counseling and consultation. *Journal of Counseling Psychology, 43,* 389–393.

Lippitt, G. L., Langseth, P., & Mossop, J. (1985). *Implementing organizational change.* San Francisco: Jossey-Bass.

Loe, S. A., & Miranda, A. H. (2005). An examination of ethnic incongruence in school-based psychological services and diversity-training experiences among school psychologists. *Psychology in the Schools, 42,* 419–432.

Lopez, E. C. (2000). Conducting Instructional Consultation through Interpreters. *School Psychology Review, 29,* 378–388.

Lopez, E. C. (1995, August). *Survey of school psychologists: Training and practice uses in the use of interpreters.* Poster session presented at the American Psychological Association Conference, New York.

Lopez, E. C. (2006). Targeting English language learners, tasks, and treatments in instructional consultation. *Journal of Applied School Psychology, 22,* 59–79.

Lowman, R. L. (1993). *Counseling and psychotherapy of work dysfunctions.* Washington, DC: American Psychological Association.

Lowman, R. L. (2005). Importance of diagnosis in organizational assessment: Harry Levinson's contributions. *Psychologist-Manager Journal, 8,* 17–28.

Luthens, F., & Kreitner, R. (1975). *Organizational behavior modification.* Glenview, IL: Scott Foresman.

Lynch, E. W., & Hanson, M. J. (1998). *Developing cross-cultural competence: A guide for working with children and their families* (2nd ed.). Baltimore: Paul H. Brookes.

Macias, R. F. (1998). *Summary report of the survey of the states' limited English proficient students and available educational programs and services 1995–1996.* Washington, DC: U.S. Department of Education, Office of Grants and Contracts Services.

Margolis, H. (2004). Struggling readers: What consultants need to know. *Journal of Educational and Psychological Consultation. 15,* 191–204.

Martens, B. K., & Witt, J. C. (1988). Expanding the scope of behavioral consultation: A systems approach to classroom behavior change. *Professional School Psychology, 3,* 271–281.

McDougal, J. L., Clonan, S. M., & Martens, B. K. (2000). Using organizational change procedures to promote the acceptability of prereferral intervention services: The school-based intervention team project. *School Psychology Quarterly, 15,* 149–171.

Medway, F. J. (1979). How effective is school consultation? A review of recent research. *Journal of School Psychology, 17,* 275–282.

Medway, F. J. (1982). School consultation research: Past trends and future directions. *Professional Psychology, 13,* 422–430.

Medway, F. J., & Updyke, J. F. (1985). Meta-analysis of consultation outcome studies. *American Journal of Community Psychology, 13,* 489–505.

Meichenbaum, D., & Turk, D. (1987). *Facilitating treatment adherence: A practitioner's guide book.* New York: Plenum.

Meyers, J. (1973). A consultation model for school psychological services. *Journal of School Psychology, 11,* 5–15.

Meyers, J. (1985, August). *Diagnoses diagnosed: 1985.* Paper presented at the annual meeting of the American Psychological Association, Los Angeles, California.

Meyers, J. (1995). A consultation model for school psychology services: Twenty years later. *Journal of Educational and Psychological Consultation, 6,* 73–81.

Meyers, J. (2002). A 30-year perspective on best practices for consultation training. *Journal of Educational and Psychological Consultation, 13,* 35–54.

Meyers, J., Brent, D., Faherty, E., & Modafferi, C. (1993). Caplan's contributions to the practice of psychology in schools. In W. P. Erchul (Ed.), *Consultation in community, school and organizational practice: Gerald Caplan's contributions to professional psychology* (pp. 99–122). Philadelphia, PA: Taylor & Francis.

Meyers, J., Friendman, M. P., & Gaughan, E. J., Jr. (1975). The effects of consultee-centered consultation on teacher behavior. *Psychology in the Schools, 12,* 288–295.

Meyers, J., Meyers, A. B., & Grogg, K. (2004). Prevention through consultation: A model to guide future developments in the field of school psychology. *Journal of Educational and Psychological Consultation, 15,* 257–276.

Meyers, J., & Nastasi, B. K., (1999). Primary prevention in school settings. In C. R. Reynolds & T. B. Gutkin (Eds.), *The handbook of school psychology* (3rd ed., pp. 764–799). New York: Wiley.

Meyers, J., Parsons, R. D., & Martin, R. (1979). *Mental health consultation in the schools: A comprehensive guide for psychologists, social workers, psychiatrists, counselors, educators and other human service professionals.* San Francisco: Jossey-Bass.

Mischel, W. (1973). Toward a cognitive social learning reconceptualization of personality. *Psychological Review, 80,* 252–283.

Mischly, M. (1973). Teacher preference for consultation methods and its relation to selected background personality and organization variables. *Dissertation Abstracts International, 34,* 2312B.

Mortola, P., & Carlson, J. (2003). Collecting an anecdote: The role of narrative in school consultation. *The Family Journal: Counseling and Therapy for Couples and Families, 11,* 7–12.

Nastasi, B. K. (2004). Meeting the challenges of the future: Integrating public health and public education for mental health promotion. *Journal of Educational and Psychological Consultation, 15,* 295–312.

Nastasi, B. K. (2006). Multicultural issues in school psychology practice: Introduction. *Journal of Applied School Psychology, 22,* 1–11.

National Center on English Learning and Achievement (1998, Fall). Effective early literacy teachers bring low achievers' scores way up. *English Update.*

O'Brien, L., & Miller, A. (2005). Challenging behaviour: Analysing teacher language in a school-based consultation within the discursive action model. *Educational and Child Psychology, 22,* 62–73.

Ochoa, S. H., Gonzalez, D., Galarza, A., & Guillemard, L. (1996). The training and use of interpreters in bilingual psycho-educational assessment: An alternative in need of study. *Diagnostique, 21,* 19–22.

Ochoa, S. H., & Rhodes, R. L. (2005). Assisting parents of bilingual students to achieve equity in public schools. *Journal of Educational and Psychological Consultation, 16,* 75–94.

O'Neill, D. K. (2001). Enabling constructivist teaching through telementoring. In L. J. Kruger, (Ed.), *Computers in the delivery of special education and related services: Developing collaborative and individualized learning environments* (pp. 33–58). New York: Haworth.

Peterson, D. W. (1968). *The clinical study of social behavior.* East Norwalk, CT: Appleton-Century-Crofts.

Phillips, B. N. (1990). *School psychology at a turning point: Ensuring a bright future for the profession.* San Francisco: Jossey-Bass.

Piersel, W. C. (1985). Behavioral consultation: An approach to problem solving in educational settings. In J. R. Bergan (Ed.), *School psychology in contemporary society.* Columbus, OH: Merill.

Protulipac, S. W. (2004). A descriptive analysis of the relationship between years of experience and the frequency and style of consultation employed by school counselors with teachers, administrators, parents, and counselors in community agencies. *Dissertation Abstracts International Section A: Humanities and Social Sciences, 64,* 4373.

Pryzwansky, W. B. (1974). A reconsideration of the consultation model for delivery of school-based psychological services. *American Journal of Orthopsychiatry, 44,* 579–583.

Rappaport, J. (1981). In praise of paradox: A social policy of empowerment over prevention. *American Journal of Community Psychology, 9,* 1–25.

Rathvon, N. W. (1990). Effects of encouragement on off-task behavior and academy productivity. *Elementary School Guidance and Counseling, 24,* 189–199.

Raven, B. H. (1993). The bases of power: Origins and recent developments. *Journal of Social Issues, 49,* 227–251.

Reimers, T. M., Wacker, D. P., & Koeppl, G. (1987). Acceptability of behavioral interventions: A review of the literature. *School Psychology Review, 16,* 212–227.

Reschly, D. J., & Wilson, M. S. (1995). School psychology practitioners and faculty: 1986 to 1991–92 trends in demographics, roles, satisfaction, and system reform. *School Psychology Review, 24,* 62–80.

Reschly, D. J., & Wilson, M. S. (1997). Characteristics of school psychology graduate education: Implications for the entry level discussion and doctoral-level specialty definitions. *School Psychology Review, 26,* 74–92.

Reynolds, C. R., Gutkin, T. B., Elliot, S. N., & Witt, J. C. (1984). *School psychology: Essentials of theory and practice.* New York: John Wiley & Sons.

Rhodes, R. L., Ochoa, S. H., & Ortiz, S. O. (2005). *Assessing culturally and linguistically diverse students: A practical guide.* New York: The Guilford Press.

Richardson, T. Q., & Molinaro, K. J. (1996). White counselor self-awareness: A prerequisite for developing multicultural competence. *Journal of Counseling and Development, 74,* 238–242.

Riley-Tillman, T. C., & Chafouleas, S. M. (2003). Using interventions that exist in the natural environment to increase treatment integrity and social influence in consultation. *Journal of Educational and Psychological Consultation, 14,* 139–156.

Rogers, M. R. (2000). Examining the cultural context of consultation. *School Psychology Review, 29,* 414–418.

Rosenfield, S. (1984, August). *Instructional consultation.* Paper presented at the annual meeting of the American Psychological Association. Toronto, Canada.

Rosenfield, S. A. (1987). *Instructional consultation.* Hillsdale, NJ: Lawrence Erlbaum Associates.

Rosenfield, S. A. (1992). Developing school based consultation teams: A design for organizational change. *School Psychology Quarterly, 7,* 27–46.

Rosenfield, S. A. (1995). The practice of instructional consultation. *Journal of Educational and Psychological Consultation, 6,* 317–327.

Rosenfield, S. (2000). School based collaboration and teaming. Encyclopedia of Psychology vol. 7 (pp. 164–167). Washington, DC: American Psychological Association. Oxford University Press.

Rosenfield, S. A. (2002). Developing instructional consultants: From novice to competent expert. *Journal of Educational and Psychological Consultation, 13,* 97–111.

Rosenfield, S. A. (2004). Consultation as dialogue: The right words at the right time. In N. M. Lambert, I. Hylander, & J. Sandoval (Eds.), *Consultee-centered consultation: Improving the quality of professional services in schools and community organizations* (pp. 337–347). Mahwah, NJ: Lawrence Erlbaum Associates.

Rosenfield, S., & Gravois, T. A. (1996). *Instructional consultation teams: Collaborating for change.* New York: Guilford.

Rosenthal, T. L., & Bandura, A. (1978). Psychological modeling: Theory and practice. In S. L. Garfield & A. E. Bergin (Eds.), *Handbook of psychotherapy and behavior change: An empirical analysis* (2nd ed., pp. 621–658). New York: Wiley.

Rouwette, E. A. J. A., & Vennix, J. A. M. (2006). System dynamics and organizational interventions. *Systems Research and Behavioral Science, 23,* 451–466.

Russell, M. L. (1978). Behavioral consultation. *Personnel and Guidance Journal, 56,* 346–350.

Sadker, M., & Sadker, D. (1982). *Year 3: Final report promoting effectiveness in classroom instruction.* Washington, DC: National Institute of Education.

Sandoval, J., & Davis, J. M. (1984). A school-based mental health consultation curriculum. *Journal of School Psychology, 22,* 31–42.

Schmidt, J. J., & Osborne, W. L. (1981). Counseling and consulting: Separate processes or the same? *Personnel and Guidance Journal,* 168–171.

Schmuck, R. A. (1995). Process consultation and organization development today. *Journal of Educational and Psychological Consultation, 6,* 207–215.

Schneider, M. F. (1998). An Adlerian model for fostering competence: Reduction of children with emotional disorders. *Individual Psychology, 39,* 378–395.

Scholten, T., Pettifor, J., Norrie, B., & Cole, E. (1993). Ethical issues in school psychological consultation: Can every expert consult? *Canadian Journal of School Psychology, 9,* 100–109.

Schwarzer, R., & Jerusalem, M. (1995). Generalized Self-Efficacy scale. In J. Weinman, S. Wright, & M. Johnston, *Measures in health psychology: A user's portfolio. Causal and control beliefs* (pp. 35–37). Windsor, UK: NFER-NELSON.

Sheridan, S. M., & Colton, D. L. (1994). Conjoint behavioral consultation: A review and case study. *Journal of Educational and Psychological Consultation, 5,* 117–139.

Sheridan, S. M., & Henning-Stout, M. (1994). Consulting with teachers about girls and boys. *Journal of Educational and Psychological Consultation, 5,* 93–113.

Sheridan, S. M., & Kratochwill, T. R. (1992). Behavioral parent-teacher consultation: Conceptual and research considerations. *Journal of School Psychology, 30,* 211–228.

Sheridan, S. M., Kratochwill, T. R., & Elliot, S. N. (1990). Behavioral consultation with parents and teachers: Delivering treatment for socially withdrawn children at home and school. *School Psychology Review, 19,* 33–52.

Sheridan, S. M., Welch, M., & Orme, S. F. (1996). Is consultation effective? A review of outcome research. *Remedial and Special Education, 17,* 341–354.

Shinn, M. R., Rosenfield, S., & Knutson, N. (1989). Curriculum-based assessment: A comparison of models. *Social Psychology Review, 18,* 299–316.

Shullman, S. L. (2002). Reflections of a consulting counseling psychologist: Implicatins of the principles for education and training at the doctoral and post-doctoral level in consulting psychology for the practice of counseling psychology. *Journal of Counseling Psychology: Practice & Research, 54, 242–251.*

Slesser, R.A., Fine, M. J., & Tracy, D. B. (1990). Teacher reactions to two approaches to school-based psychological consultation. *Journal of Educational and Psychological Consultation, 1,* 243–258.

Snow, K. (2007). To ensure inclusion, freedom and respect for all we must use person first language. Retrieved June 2, 2007. Disability is Natural at http://ftp.disabilityisnatural.com/documents/PFL.pdf

Srebalus, D. J., & Brown, D. (2001). *Becoming a skilled helper.* Boston: Allyn & Bacon.

Stein, H. T., & Edwards, M. E. (1998). Alfred Adler: Classical theory and practice (pp. 64–93). In P. Marcus & A. Rosenberg (Eds.). *Psychoanalytic versions of the human condition: Philosophies of life and their impact on practice.* New York: New York University Press.

Stenger, M. K., Tollefson, N., & Fine, M. J. (1992). Variables that distinguish elementary teachers who participate in school-based consultation from those who do not. *School Psychology Quarterly, 7,* 271–284.

Stinnett, T. A., Havey, J. M., & Oehler-Stinnett, J. (1994). Current test usage by practicing school psychologists: A national survey. *Journal of Psychoeducational Assessment, 12,* 331–350.

Sugai, G., Horner, R. H., Dunlap, G., Hieneman, M., Lewis, T. K., Nelson, C. M., Scott, T., Liaupsin, C., Sailor, W., Turnbull, A. P., Turnbull, H. R., III, Wickham, D., Wilcox, B., & Ruef, M. (2000). Applying positive behavior support and functional behavioral assessment in schools. *Journal of Positive Behavior Interventions, 2,* 131–143.

Tanner-Jones, L. A. (1997). Teacher preference for consultation models: A study of presenting problems and cognitive style. *Dissertation Abstracts International Section A: Humanities and Social Sciences, 58,* 2090.

Tharp, R. G., & Wetzel, R. J. (1969). modification in the natural environment. NY: Academic Press.

Tindal, G., Parker, R., & Hasbrouck, J. E. (1992). The construct validity of stages and activities in the consultation process. *Journal of Educational and Psychological Consultation, 3,* 99–118.

Truscott, S. D., Richardson, R. D., Cohen, C., Frank, A., & Palmeri, D. (2003). Does rational persuasion influence potential consultees? *Psychology in the Schools, 40,* 627–640.

Wagner, R., Torgesen, J., & Rashotte, C. (1994). The development of reading-related phonological processing abilities: New evidence of bidirectional causality from a latent variable longitudinal study. *Developmental Psychology, 30,* 73–87.

Walberg, H. J. (1985). Instructional theories and research evidence. In M. C. Wang & H. J. Walberg (Eds.), *Adapting instruction to individual differences* (pp. 3–23). Berkeley, CA: McCutchan Publishing Company.

Wasburn-Moses, L. (2006). Obstacles to program effectiveness in secondary special education. *Preventing School Failure, 50,* 21–30.

Watkins, C. (2000). Introduction to the articles on consultation. *Educational Psychology in Practice, 16,* 5–8.

Watson, J. (1930). *Behaviorism*. New York: Norton.

Welch, M., Sheridan, S. M., Fuhriman, A., Hart, A. W., Connell, M. L., & Stoddart, T. (1992). Preparing professionals for educational partnerships: An interdisciplinary approach. *Journal of Educational and Psychological Consultation, 3,* 1–23.

Wesson, C. L. (1991). Curriculum-based measurement and two models of follow-up consultation. *Exceptional Children, 57,* 246–256.

West, J. F., & Idol, L. (1993). The counselor as consultant in the collaborative school. *Journal of Counseling and Development, 71,* 678–683.

White, J., & Mullis, F. (1998). A systems approach to school counselor consultation. *Education, 119,* 242–252.

Wilkinson, L. A. (2005). Bridging the research-to-practice gap in school-based consultation: An example using case studies. *Journal of Educational and Psychological Consultation, 16,* 175–200.

Wilson, C. P., Gutkin, T. B., Hagen, K. M., & Oats, R. G. (1998). General education teachers knowledge and self-reported use of classroom interventions for working with difficult-to-teach students: Implications for consultation, pre-referral intervention and inclusive services. *School Psychology Quarterly, 13,* 45–62.

Winzer, M. A. (2000). The inclusion movement: Review and reflections on reform in special education. In M. A. Winzer & K. Mazurek (Eds.), *Special education in the 21st century: Issues of inclusion and reform* (pp. 5–26). Washington, DC: Gallaudet University.

Witt, J. C. (1986). Teachers' resistance to the use of school-based interventions. *Journal of School Psychology, 24,* 37–44.

Witt, J. C., Elliott, S. N., & Martens, B. K. (1984). Acceptability of behavioral interventions used in classrooms: The influence of amount of teacher time, severity of behavior problem, and type of intervention. *Behavioral Disorders, 9,* 95–104.

Wizda, L. (2004). An instructional consultant looks to the future. *Journal of Educational and Psychological Consultation, 15,* 277–294.

Ysseldyke, J. E., Christenson, S., Algozzine, B., & Thurlow, M. L. (1983). *Classroom teachers' attributions for students exhibiting different behaviors* (Report No. BBB17903). Minneapolis, MN: Minneapolis Institute for Research on Learning Disabilities.

Zigmond, N., & Miller, S. (1986). Assessment for instructional planning. *Exceptional Children, 52,* 501–509.

Zins, J. E. (1989). Building applied experiences into a consultation training program. *Consultation, 8,* 191–201.

Zins, J. E., Curtis, M. J., Graden, J., & Ponti, C. R. (1988). *Helping students succeed in the regular classroom: A guide for developing intervention assistance programs*. San Francisco: Jossey-Bass.

Zins, J. E., & Elias, M. J. (2006). Social and emotional learning: Promoting the development of all students. In G. G. Bear, K. M., Minke, & A. Thomas (Eds.), *Children's needs III: Development, prevention, and intervention* (pp. 1–13). Bethesda, MD: National Association of School Psychologists.

Zins, J. E., & Erchul, W. P. (2002). Best practices in school consultation. In A. Thomas & J. Grimes (Eds.), *Best practices in school psychology Vol. 1* (4th ed., pp. 625–643). Bethesda, MD: National Association of School Psychologists.

Zins, J. E., & Forman, S. G. (Eds.). (1988). Primary prevention: From theory to practice [Special issue]. *School Psychology Review, 17,* 539–541.

Zins, J. E., & Illback, R. J. (2007). Consulting to facilitate planned organizational change in schools. *Journal of Educational and Psychological Consultation, 17,* 109–117.

Zins, J. E., & Ponti, C. R. (1996). Strategies to facilitate the implementation, organization, and operation of system-wide consultation programs. *Journal of Educational and Psychological Consultation, 1,* 205–218.

Zins, J. E., & Wagner, D. I. (1987). Children and health promotion. In A. Thomas & J. Grimes (Eds.), *Children's needs: Psychological perspectives* (pp. 258–267). Washington, DC: National Association of School Psychologists.

INDEX

A

AC. See Adlerian consultation
acceptance, conveying, 126
achievement motivation, 98
act, actor, differentiation, 126–127
actual self goal, fictional final self
    goal, distinguished, 125
adaptive development, delays in, 52
Adderall, use of, 53
ADHD. See Attention deficit
    hyperactivity disorder
adjudicated youth, 141–142
adjustment disorder, 89–90
Adler, Alfred, 123
Adlerian consultation, 123–144
  acceptance, 126
  act, actor, separation of, 126–127
  actual self goal, fictional final self
    goal, distinguished, 125
  adjudicated youth, 141–142
  Adler, Alfred, 123
  aggressive behavior, 141–143
  alcohol abuse history, of parent,
    139–140
  alcohol use, 125, 134–135
  analysis of results, 129–130
  Ansbacher, Heinz, 123
  anxiety, as means to explain
    failures, 124
  assumptions of, 126–127
  attention, as child's goal in
    behavior, 124–125
  attitudes, power of choice in
    controlling, 123
  behaviors, power of choice in
    controlling, 123

belongingness, 123
birth order, importance of, 125
bullying, prevention program for,
    142–143
cases in, 133–143
celiac disease, 138
communicating about problems,
    126
confirmation of inadequacy, as
    child's goal in behavior,
    124–125
conscious goals, significance of,
    125–126
conscious ignoring, concept of,
    126
courage, development of, 124
crisis consultation, 133
current functioning
    focus on *vs.* prior behavior, 127
    as more important than past,
    126
defiant behavior, 133–134
depression, as means to explain
    failures, 124
developmental consultation, 131
Diagnostic Student Interview, 129
diet, special, request for, 138
disruptive classroom behaviors,
    133–134
Dreikurs, Rudolf, 123
drug use, 125, 134–137
  of parent, 139–140
early experiences, in development
    of personality, 124
educator examples, 138–140
effectiveness of, 133

discourse, with consultee-centered consultation, 14
disengagement process, 79
    characteristics of, 79
    psychological underpinnings, 79
dislocation from home, eligibility for district school, 174–175
disruptive classroom behaviors, 133–134
diversity, recognition of, 151
divisions of consultation, differentiation, 41
dogmatic personality, 85
Downs syndrome, 97
Dreikurs, Rudolf, 123
drug use, 125, 134–137
    by parent, 139–140

E

early experiences, in development of personality, 124
eating disruptions, 121
ecological-developmental perspective, 146
ecosystem of client, 107
educational specialists, 177
effective relationship, establishing, 65–67
effectiveness of consultation, 209–216
effort, valuing over outcomes, 126
electors, 64
ELL. See English language learners
embedded behaviors, 123
emitters, 64
emotional abuse, 116–117
emotional disturbance, 46–47
emotional underpinnings, disengagement process, 79
emotions, difficulty experiencing, expressing, 121
empathy, 37–38, 103, 124, 127
encopresis, 93–94
encouragement, 126–127
    praise, differences between, 128
English language learners, 193–195

enmeshed relationships, 37
environment, influence of, 40, 62, 105, 107
epileptic disorder, 173–174
equal collaboration, 127
equifinality, 76
equity for families in school system, 150
establishing objectives, 81
ethical considerations, 18–20
ethnic background, 84–85
    mismatching in, 85
ethnic biases, understanding of, 85
ethnic sensitivity, 85
excessive time on homework, 200–201
excitement, as adolescents' goal in behavior, 125
expectations regarding performance, informal interviews, 106
exploitation by peers, 136
exposure to practice opportunity situations, 103
expressive language disorder, 53, 89–90
external forces, behavioral change and, 101
eye contact, 66

F

fading, 82
family, client's relationship with, 107
family environment, children supported in, 124
FAS. See Fetal alcohol syndrome
fear of making incorrect choices, 138–139
fear of students, by teachers, 141–142
feedback, importance of, 103, 160
feigning, 140–141
fetal alcohol syndrome, 139–140
fictional final self goal, actual self goal, distinguished, 125
fidelity, APA ethical code, 19
field-based supervision, in teaching consultation, 28–29

systems examples, 172–174
team
    approach of, *vs.* individual
        approach, 155–156
    budget, 152
    building of, 159
    continuing education, 153
    facilitators, 152
    membership of, 156–157
technology of work, satisfaction,
    interrelationship, 160
technostructural interventions,
    160–161
tenure, 160
timelines, psycho-educational
    evaluations, difficulty
    meeting, 172–173
tongue movement, difficulty with,
    170–171 (See also Apraxia)
training in consultation, 156
organizational change
    readiness for, 146
    stages of, 148
organizational design, 160
OSC. See Organizational and system
    consultation
outcomes, consultation processes,
    evaluation of, 209–216

P
pain, 45–46
palate movement, difficulty with,
    170–171
pampered children, mental health
    problems, 124
pants wetting, 93–94
parameters of behavior, 62
parent absence from home, 198–199
parent assisting student with
    homework, 88–89
parent refusal of special education,
    97
partnership between consultant,
    consultee, 35–36
passive manner, 83
pay scales, 160

pedagogical practices, 177–178
peer acceptance, as adolescents' goal
    in behavior, 125
peer socialization, 121–122
perception of positive behaviors, 107
perfection, need for, 37
performance enactments, 109–110
personal aide use, 165–166
personal coercion, 7
personal development, delays in, 52
personal reward, 7
personality choices, 125
personality mismatch, student,
    teacher, 206
philosophical assumptions, 102
phonological awareness training, 185
physical abuse, 116–117, 120
    mental health problems with, 124
physical outbursts, 49–51, 53, 90–91,
    95–96
PII. See Problem identification
    interview
PIIDS. See Problem identification
    interview data sheet
placenta previa, 49–51
plan implementation, 81
    evaluation, 79–80
policy guidelines, state, federal
    regulations, 160
positive expert, 5, 7
positive outcomes of consultation
    process, alerting consultee
    to, 103
positive referent, 7
positive regard, 13
positive reinforcement, 107
posttraumatic stress disorder,
    116–117
posture, 66
power, as child's goal in behavior,
    124–125
power struggle with parents,
    teachers, adolescents and,
    125
praise, encouragement, differences
    between, 128
predatory behavior, 53

preschool experiences, lack of, 197
preventative nature of, 59
preventatively addressing issues, 33
previous intervention plans, 63
privacy, 19
problem analysis, 79–80
problem identification, 79–81
problem identification interview,
        68–74
problem identification interview data
        sheet, 75
process consultation, 159
productivity, satisfaction,
        interrelationship, 160
professional distance, loss of, 37
professional source literature,
        familiarity with, 178
program centered administrative, 41
promotion, 160
pronunciation, difficulty with,
        170–171. See also Apraxia
prototype implementation, 147
psycho-educational evaluation
        timelines, difficulty meeting,
        172–173
psychostimulant medications,
        90–91, 94. See also specific
        medication
pull-out classrooms, instruction in,
        206–207
punishment, logical consequences,
        differences between, 132

Q
questions during client assessment,
        106
questions during consultee
        assessment, 105

R
rages, 53
readiness for change, 149
reading problems, 96, 117–118,
        169–170, 185–186
reciprocal determinants, human
        behavior, 102

reciprocal determinism, 67, 102, 104
reciprocal interactions, 104
reciprocity, social, emotional, lack of.
        See Asperger's disorder
recognition for effort, 160
reflection on consultation process, 41
regressive behaviors, 138–139
regulating emotions, difficulty with,
        92–93
reinforcement contingencies, fading,
        82
relationship with consultee, 38
relocation, eligible to attend district
        school, 174–175
removing wheat from diet, request
        for, 137–138
reporting medical difficulties, parent
        history of, 49
request for unneeded evaluation,
        91–92
resistance, sources of, 195
resources in classroom, 107
respect for rights of others, APA
        ethical code, 19
responsibilities, formal contracts, 40
responsibility, APA ethical code, 19
restrictive education program, request
        for, 94–95
retribution, behaviors of, 53
revenge
        behaviors of, 53
        as child's goal in behavior,
        124–125
reward systems, 160
Ritalin, use of, 50, 90–91
role-playing, 110
roles, formal contracts, 40

S
sarcasm, teacher's, 202–203
satisfaction, technology of work,
        interrelationship, 160
schizophrenia, 47–48
scholarly journals, familiarity with,
        178
school consultation, defined, 5